A Search for
ADVENTURE
Leads to Alaska

WOLF HEBEL

Publication Consultants — *Since 1978*

PO Box 221974 Anchorage, Alaska 99522-1974
books@publicationconsultants.com—www.publicationconsultants.com

ISBN 978-1-59433-332-3
eISBN 978-1-59433-333-0
Library of Congress Catalog Card Number: 2013935506

Manufactured in the United States of America.

Dedication

To my children
Daniela, Diana and Logan, and their children

Acknowledgement

My appreciation is given to Publications Consultants for their work in the publication of my manuscript in English.

My sincere thanks to my belated friend and journalism teacher, Charles Keim; it is he who encouraged me to write about my adventurous life and is responsible for my writing style. To my daughter Diana goes my thanks for her patience while introducing me to the world of the computer and for her help in the electronic production of my manuscript.

Siglinde Fischer and Walter Steinberg (mail@waltersteinberg.de) have my thanks for editing my manuscript in German and for finding and negotiating with my publisher.

The publisher Neumann-Neudamm I thank especially for the hard work of cleaning and restoration of some of my old slides for use in the book.

Foreword

Imagine a world close to nature—no electricity, no phone, no running water, and no computers to entertain you. For entertainment, people take walks, use their imagination, and actually speak to their friends face to face. People read books and write letters by candlelight or by the light of an oil lamp. This is the world I grew up in for the majority of my childhood. I did not think of myself as different from anyone else in the world. To me this was normal, just like your childhood was most likely normal to you. Now that I have grown and can see the greater scope of the world around me, I feel fortunate to have lived like this and to have had the experiences that come with that style of life.

I fondly remember when I was three years old and my parents and I made the boat trip from Fairbanks to Ruby. I remember stopping along the way and looking in old abandoned cabins, seeing the old sheds that stand on stilts, called caches, or just watching wildlife along the way and counting the numbers of bears or moose we would see in one day. I enjoyed a visit to Kokrines, where I first met Frank and Josephine, an old couple who were the last to live there in the little town. Next to the old village site was, or is, a crystal clear creek that bubbles out and into the Yukon River. I was only three, but I remember building boats and sending them down the creek into the silty water of the Yukon. I created villages along the sides of that creek and sent barges, loaded with imaginary supplies, back and forth between them. Perhaps my daydreams, at that age anyhow, were not as adventurous as my father's, but they did take on a similar manner in their expression.

Another experience I remember, and I enjoy telling the story of, is a time when I was nine years old and my brother was age two. My parents took us on a camping or fishing trip on the Nowitna River. The tent was pitched and my mom was either cooking or otherwise poking around at the campfire. My dad was taking a walk along the beach looking for whatever thing of interest he might find, be it an agate or even a bit of fossil. It was a nice, calm, beautiful day to be out on the river.

My mother, always afraid of bears, was looking across the river checking out every little spot of brown she might see. This was usual for her and I knew she had to be looking at a waterlogged bit of stump lying in the water.

"Is that a bear?" she asks me.

"No… that's a log" I reply.

We argue back and forth on this point for a little while, when suddenly my brother who was behind me and next to my mom says, excitedly, "big puppy! big puppy!"

We turn around and just past our tent and not more than 20 feet away is, to me, a very large black bear standing on its hind legs. My mom, in her fear, reaches by the tent to retrieve a rifle, and using the rifle to gesture, she starts hollering, "Shoo! Go away!"

I remember asking her what she was doing. She said she had hoped the bear would see the gun, know what it is, and get scared off some how.

I don't know if my dad noticed something was off, or heard us, or maybe just happened to look back in the direction of camp, but he dropped whatever he was looking at or carrying at the time and ran full speed, straight toward the bear, cussing every obscenity he could think of while waving his arms around. The bear just looked at him like, "This guy must be nuts!" But soon, the bear must have decided that it did not want to tangle with a crazy man and turned and ran off into the forest.

I had taken these little side adventures and stories for granted while growing up. Now I feel fortunate to have lived them.

The time that I lived without all the amenities of modern life and, for the most part, a life dependent on subsistence, was only a short moment in time compared to my father's adventures. A take-it-or-leave-it kind of guy with a short fuse and great sense of humor, Wolf had the privilege of living a life we can only dream about. His childhood included worries associated with being a child during WWII, the teenage years associated with growing up and finding a career path he could live with, and later, his nature and adventure filled daydreams that took him to California, Mexico, and finally Alaska. While some of the adventures of these earlier days are still possible, the constant changes of time prevent a complete re-creation of these events to ever occur quite like this again.

Diana Hebel

Contents

Chapter 1
Memories and Dreams for the Future

Thinking back to the years of 1957-1958, I seemed to have few, if any, problems. My health was as good as the health of any average twenty-three-year old. I was securely employed in my trade as a glassblower, lived in the upstairs apartment of my parent's house, and last but not least, I had a beautiful wife. We were not rich by any stretch of imagination, but we were as well off as just about any of our friends and acquaintances. Our future was neatly laid out before us, but in spite of it all, I was restless and had the feeling that my life was running toward a dead end. *There had to be more to life than accumulating possessions, raising children, and growing old.* What I needed was something that was not yet determined, something like an adventure, with some degree of danger or uncertainty in it.

Even though I was born in Berlin, the capital of Germany at that time, on August 8, 1935, I always loved nature, animals, and stories about explorations of wild places.

It doesn't even seem that long ago since I visited the zoo and the aquarium in Berlin with my parents, or spent the weekends at one of my grandmothers in the wooded outskirts of the city. On those hikes through these woods, we often picked mushrooms, and my father might catch a lizard or two for our terrarium.

Another thing that firmly sticks to my mind from that time of my life is the aroma of the tobacco store, which my father patronized. There, I always was fascinated by the display of the collector's cigarette pictures, which displayed African animals and landscapes from the one-time German colonies. It probably stands to reason that all these things of my early past had a part in my ever growing love for the wild and my longing for adventure, without even being aware that my life already was an adventure of sorts at the time.

Germany was at war with the world, and the sound of sirens and bombs became part of our lives. At first, we used to go to the basement of our apartment housing, but later, we just played games after the sirens woke us and waited for the all clear signal. My father used to say, "The one that hits us, we won't hear anyway!"

Eventually, my father was able to arrange for my mother, my younger brother and sister, and me to travel to Prussia in order to get away from the bombing attacks. It was shortly after my seventh birthday when we traveled by train to the town of Goldap in East Prussia. In a little village at Lake Goldap, we moved into a small farmhouse with the elderly couple who owned the place. My father, after being excused from military service because of stomach ulcers, was employed by the city of Berlin and therefore had to stay behind.

Living on a small farm with an increased exposure to animals and nature was something I greeted with great enthusiasm. It also helped me get over the absence of my father. The clearest memories I have of Lake Goldap was the day when my new, mostly older friends took me out on the lake in a rowboat, from where they speared burbots. The picture of the bottom dwelling fish in that clear lake water stuck forever with me as a symbol for unspoiled nature.

In the shallower part of the lake, where we went often to bathe, I also caught my own first fish with a small, homemade net, even if it only was a finger-long sucker. Proudly, I made my mother promise me that she would cook the fish for me, but since she already had dinner planned for that day, she put the little sucker out on the porch to keep it cool, where the farmer's cat promptly ate it, just what my mother most likely had hoped for.

The bad part was that all my fun in nature and my ignorance about the war did not last very long. In less than a year after our arrival, a military camp was established near our village and the news that the Russian army was advancing toward us spread fast. Then, one sunny morning, we—including our luggage, as well as other refugees and their belongings—were loaded onto oxcarts and transported to the train station in the town of Goldap.

I do not remember exactly how many days and nights we spent in trains and train stations on our way to the Sudetenland in Czechoslovakia. What I do remember clearly is that somewhere along the way, we came under machinegun fire from low-flying airplanes.

When the train came to a halt, everybody jumped off and headed for the surrounding fields. Only my mother was left standing at the door, holding my sister in her arm and my brother by his hand. Without the elevated platform of a train station, my mother was not able to get down. Well, the planes were gone and even if they should return, their pilots, too, would know that the people had deserted the train to take cover outside. After I mentioned that to my mother, she smiled at me in agreement and we returned to our seats. Later on, at the next station, the dead and wounded were taken off the train, and I got to see dead people for the first time in my young life. Our family was lucky enough to have remained unharmed due to some empty train coaches on a neighboring track.

We, too, had to get off this train and wait at this station for a connecting train. Sometime farther on down the track, we had to change trains at least one more time, in what I always thought was the town of Dresden. But since the actual bombing of Dresden happened sometime later, I can't be sure. In any case, the arriving trains at that station, in which we were supposed to continue our journey, were so overloaded that people were even hanging on the outside of the trains. Luck seemed to be on our side once more, when one of the arriving trains had two empty, but locked coaches. A Hitler Youth lifted me through the window of one of the locked coaches, in order to open the door from the inside. Finally, our family and some others could continue the journey.

As this train left the station, we could see the big flares in the night sky, which we called Tannenbaeume, referring to lit-up Christmas trees. These flares were used by Allied planes to illuminate their intended bombing targets, and on that night, the train station we just had left must have been on their list, for it was bombed almost out of existence.

I often wondered about what happened to that Hitler Youth and what would have happened to us, had he not been there to lift me through that window.

A day or two later or so, our journey ended once more in a small village. All refugees had to spend the first couple of days in the big dance hall of the guesthouse in that village until we could be distributed to different available accommodations. Our family was eventually housed in a very small, deserted or evacuated farmhouse, which had a narrow courtyard with a small stall and shed facing the house. What was even more exciting about our new home was that this small village was totally surrounded by old fruit orchards. The wasp and hornet nests in the hollow trunks of the older trees were of little concern to us kids. What was important was to know at what time each of the trees would carry ripe fruits and which kind of apple, pear, or plum were the sweetest. We ate fruit till we had blisters on our tongues and lips.

But for me, there were a lot of other lasting impressions to take away from there. For instance, the day I found a sparrow's nest in a tipped-over vase in our attic, or discovered the muskrats at a nearby duckweed-covered pond; when I found that the hedges along the roadsides harbored big, fat, green caterpillars, or when I caught a hedgehog and brought it home with me. An especially proud day for me was when I was allowed to tag along with the farmers of the village on a hunt for hares. A less pleasurable experience was my acquaintance with a free-running billy goat, which harbored a strong dislike toward me and from which I often had to flee by slipping through a small opening for the chickens in the gate to our courtyard.

On a frosty morning in early fall, I wandered aimlessly to the outskirts of the village and then followed a wagon track into a field. The whole field was covered by hoar frost, except a big circle, from which a farmer obviously had removed piled-up straw. Listlessly kicking around in the straw rests, I scared up a field mouse. My boredom was gone and the hunt was on for more mice. Probably due to the effect of the cold, the mice were fairly easy to catch and I discovered quite a few of them. I had no intention of killing those animals; instead, I set my captured critters in a straw-padded, frozen wagon rut, where I covered them with more straw to keep them warm. In a short time, I must have rescued close to a dozen mice from freezing to death and I kept on searching intensely for more.

By the time I noticed the approaching farmer with horse and wagon coming my way, it was too late for me to do anything but watch the wagon wheels flatten my whole collection of mice. I don't recall the details of my emotions at that moment, but it might be safe to assume that this particular farmer was not my favorite person of the day.

My father, in the meantime, had been transferred from Berlin to the town of Braunschweig. And while I felt sorry for a bunch of field mice, he was arranging for us to join him in what was to be our new hometown in the future.

By this time, as with most people in our country, there were no more questions in my father's mind about the outcome of the war or that it was going to end soon. Therefore, he thought it best that our family should be at last together.

With our relocation to the outskirts of Braunschweig, we soon were once more exposed to the bombs, but our family again was spared from personal tragedy till the end of the war in 1945.

At that year, I was to be ten years old and gave little thought to the future of my country.

My main interest, besides scrounging for food for our family, was still wild-life and nature. Living next to cow pastures, fields, and a small river called the Schunter was just what the doctor had ordered.

During those hard years right after the war, I developed certain survival skills, such as catching fish by hand. That little trick did not only put food on our plates, but also on the plates of some of our neighbors, and I sometimes stayed home from school to play provider for our family, and others, by catching fish.

By the time our lives had returned closer to normal again, my parents leased some land in our area and we built our first house from whatever materials we were able to secure from bombed out places or even from the dump. But the greatest significance of living on our own property was for me that we now had a garden that allowed me to keep pets. Even if the type of pets I brought home, such as a *kreutzotter* (which is a small viper and our only poisonous snake in Germany), was not exactly to my parents' liking.

Close to the end of my school years, I had many dreams for my future, ranging from animal trainer to forester, but because of my limited schooling and the limited finances of my parents, all these goals were out of my reach. At that time, there were not too many openings for an apprenticeship in any trade outside of car mechanic or related fields, in which I had little or no interest. These realities, however, did not keep me from dreaming about a more adventurous future.

In front of our property was a ditch the waters of which flowed through the cattle meadows and into the nearby river; the same ditch was an inspiration for one of my biggest adventure fantasies.

I needed no more than an old, oval herring tin to let my imagination run away with me. Two short sticks as pilots for my tin-can boat and the wilderness river trip of my dreams was on the way; the grass and the reeds along the ditch were now thick jungle groves. Schools of minnows turned to game fish and flying insects became birds. Frogs substituted as alligators and the occasional water shrew would be a bear.

Sometimes we made camp, portaged around obstacles, or were delayed by a mishap.

The adventure would end about a mile or so away from where we had started, where the ditch joined the river, and my imaginary adventurers took an imaginary plane ride back home.

At that time, I had no idea that something along that line actually lay in my future. But for now, my basic schooling came to an end and my dreams had to give way to reality. Following normal procedure, I would now have to enter some kind of an apprenticeship to enable me to make a living in the years ahead, but what should that be?

As already mentioned, for anything I would be interested in, I needed higher schooling, which my parents could not afford. Times were hard in many ways and work was hard to get, especially at my education level. Available apprenticeships as a mechanic were of no consideration to me and to work for an inland shipping company, I was looked upon as physically unsuited, not that my enthusiasm for such work would have been any greater.

Then, my father came home one night with the news that he might have found an opening for me at the Technical High School of Braunschweig as a glassblowing apprentice for laboratory supplies. Without other alternatives, I had to admit that glassblower at least sounded somewhat artistic.

Three and a half years later, I received my journeyman certificate as a glassblower. At the technical high school, I also met my lifetime friend, Herbert Dannenbaum. What brought us close was our mutual interest in the American Indians and the outdoors. Herbert also introduced me to a judo club, which in turn contributed a lot to my self-confidence. There even had been a moment during that time when I wanted to run off with a traveling circus, but my father intercepted and said, "First, you learn a trade and then you can do what you want."

Well, Father was right, but I still looked at my profession only as a temporary solution and instead of searching for steady employment as a glassblower after receiving my certificate, I joined the German Border Patrol.

While I appreciated the experience, it took me only about seventeen months to decide that military life was not my cup of tea either.

Somehow, however, I had to make a living till something better came along. Soon, I found myself working as a glassblower for neon signs in Wolfenbuettel, a town near Braunschweig. At home, I helped my parents build a new house and then I moved into the upstairs apartment. At my workplace, I had met my future wife, Inge, and eventually got married.

Chapter 2
Emigration

Married or not, my general idea on what my future should be had not changed. My career as a glassblower would always take second place to my interest in wildlife, nature, and adventure. I continued my activities at the judo club and, once a week, it was boy's night out with my closest friends. Some weekends we traveled either with or without our women to our special place near Harz Mountains or to some other nature hideout, where we emulated the life of the American Indian. This was something we had done since I had met my friend, Herbert. Books about Indians were something most Germans of my generation had grown up with; we only took it a little more seriously than most, which gave us a chance to escape from what we considered an everyday boring existence, while it brought us closer to nature at the same time.

When I visited Herbert one day, he already had visitors, but from Canada. It was a couple he had known in earlier years, before they immigrated to that country. After being introduced to the visiting couple, Gerhard and

Anita Laschkowsky, I partook eagerly in the conversation with them and my interest in Canada grew constantly.

In the Harz Mountains

After meeting those people, I had kept in contact with Gerhard and Anita by mail and the idea of immigrating to Canada soon became my obsession.

To my surprise, my wife Inge was not too hard to persuade to consider the idea. My parents were not surprised at all about my plans; they most likely had expected something like that from me sooner or later. And then again, they might just have relied on the fact that getting our visas and being admitted into Canada was not a sure thing.

My wife's parents and some of our friends, however, expressed their concerns, especially about our financial situation. From that aspect, their concerns were probably not totally unfounded. My boss, Kurt Hunze, at the neon sign firm, where I was employed, even promised to pay our way back if things should not work out for us, and he assured me that I would be reinstated anytime. But after we had received our visas and our departure date was set, everybody seemed to accept the facts and stopped trying to change our minds.

"How do your finances look?" asked my friend, Wolfgang Wegener, as we sat in a *gasthaus* over a glass of wine.

"I'll make it, one way or another," I answered in a more self-assured tone than I actually was. Wolfgang dropped the subject and ordered another drink for us, but as we met once more a few days later, for what was supposed to be our final good-bye, my friend pushed a thick envelope across the table toward me and said, "That will help!"

I didn't have to look inside the envelope to know its contents, as I pushed it back, saying, "No way!"

"Shut up!" my buddy replied, as he pushed the envelope my way again.

"I cannot guarantee that you ever will see that money again!" I argued, but Wolfgang just lifted his glass for a toast and said, "If I don't see that money again, I'll let you shovel a few rounds of coal for me in hell instead!"

Far less humorous were the final good-byes from our parents, but it had gone better than we had expected. After hugs, good wishes, and the usual promises to write regularly, we finally boarded the Greek ocean liner, Arkadia, at the port of Bremerhafen.

On board the Arkadia

Before we knew how to feel about it, we found ourselves on a trip halfway around the world. The luxury on the ship was far greater than we had expected and, for the next ten days, I at least felt more like a rich person on a vacation, rather than one of a bunch of poor emigrants, which most of us were. My wife, on the other hand, had been a little quiet after the first couple of days and seemed to suffer from depression. When I inquired about it, Inge announced that she would not accompany me to dinner that day, because she didn't feel too great.

"What's the matter?" I tried to tease her. "Are you seasick?"

Inge let out a dry chuckle and replied, "No, but I'm pregnant!"

For the next minute or two, the silence in our cabin was deafening; the only thing to be heard was the motor noises of the ship.

I was at a loss for words. A baby was certainly not what we needed at that time, but there was little we could change about that situation now, and I knew that Inge was observing me closely for my reaction to her announcement.

"That's how it goes, but the world won't end because of it," I finally managed to stammer. If my wife was satisfied with my answer, only she knew, but the subject of her condition did not come up anymore during our conversations in the immediate future.

In Montreal, Canada, the luxury life on the ocean liner came to an end for us. There were only a few more formalities to be taken care of at customs before we continued our journey across Canada by train. For two days and a night, we sat, ate, and slept on the hard, wooden benches on the train while crossing the full breadth of the North American continent to Vancouver, British Columbia. We had no acquaintances or other people we could converse with during our train ride and no meals were served to us. If there was a dining car on that train, we didn't know about it, nor did we think to inquire about it. Whenever the train stopped somewhere at some train station, I tried to buy whatever snacks I could find, and hurried back to the train and to my wife. As long as we had daylight, I only slept for short intervals along the way, because I didn't want to miss any of the wilderness landscape. Totally fascinated, I found myself constantly on the lookout for wildlife, but to my disappointment, outside of some waterfowl, some beavers, or evidence thereof, I did not get to see anything worth mentioning.

At our arrival in Vancouver, we were greeted by our acquaintances, Gerhard and Anita Laschkowsky, and enjoyed their hospitality for about a week or ten days, while we were introduced to our new hometown and searched for an affordable apartment.

It soon became apparent to us that work was not any easier to find in Canada than at home in Germany.

In 1961, the town of Vancouver, B.C. was only a fraction of the size of what it might be now and full time employment opportunities were rare to nonexistent, especially for a glassblower. I had to be content with part-time jobs, such as cutting or splitting firewood, digging ditches, painting old houses, or even doing some house sitting for some already established emigrant on vacation. One of my more lucrative employments was a lonely night shift job in a plating factory.

Vancouver B.C.

While our lives might have been an adventure of sort, it certainly was not the adventure I had been searching for, but rather a constant struggle to bring in enough money to pay the next rent and buy the cheapest food items we could find in the nearest stores. These facts plus the suggestion of a friend of our acquaintances had led us to apply for immigration visas to the United States. Big mistake! In order to be allowed into the USA, we now needed five-hundred dollars per person of our family, or a signed statement that would assure my employment in the United States.

Then, on February 22, 1962, our daughter, Daniela, came into the world. I was still in negotiation with the official at the emigration office, who claimed to be unable to give me a visitor visa, because I had applied for an immigration visa. But since I would be unable to save up $1,500 under the existing conditions, I needed a statement of employment. In order to secure that statement, I needed the visitor visa to go and find a potential employer in the USA.

My English at that time was far from perfect and the immigration officer not speaking any German contributed to a very comical go around between us. Almost every other day, like clockwork, I would show up at his immigration office to continue our "catch twenty-two" situation.

In time, I harbored the suspicion that the immigration officer was quite amused about my persistence and actually was only testing my resiliency.

"You're driving me crazy!" he said finally and put some papers in front of me to sign.

A short time later, the officer handed me my visitor visa with the instruction to find a job and return as soon as possible. Then, with a final good luck wish, he escorted me out of his office.

The following morning, after saying good-bye to my wife and child, I sat in a bus toward Portland, Oregon. That was how far my traveling money lasted, but since my goal was Long Beach, California, where my new German acquaintance lived at the time, I had to hitch-hike from there on. Having no real conception about the distance from Portland, Oregon, to Long Beach California, and with only a few cars stopping to give me a ride, I soon reached a point when I asked myself, "What in the hell are you doing?"

I had left my wife and newborn behind in a different country, more or less to take care of themselves, while I was heading south toward a still uncertain future. As I walked along the highway through the Oregon countryside, under an exceptional sunny sky, the song of a meadowlark reminded me of similar places back in Germany and I became quite uncertain about my whole undertaking. I had to assure myself that my family would be all right after all; turning around at this point would have done nothing but wasted all my efforts. So I hitched on. Some of the rides I got were more pleasant and the people were friendly and encouraging, while others made me feel uneasy with their never ending questions or because of their general strange behavior.

It was early in the morning when I surprised my future friend, Karl Engelke, by ringing his doorbell before his alarm clock had gone off, and I had the feeling that Karl was not exactly euphoric about my appearance. But Karl was at least in part responsible for my desperate action, since he had encouraged me to take such a step by describing the work situation in the United States considerably more favorable than that in Canada.

Well, my friend certainly did his best to accommodate me, and soon he even found employment for me. Karl's English naturally was a lot better than mine and, therefore, it was he who did the negotiating with my prospective employers. I understood enough to follow the general drift of the conversation, but as for the details, I would have to trust my friend. When next Karl told me, after the successful interview, that my employer would like me to start right away, I was in no position to argue that point.

"But I have no working permit yet!" I said.

"We'll fix that!" was Karl's short reply, and off we went to the emigration office. A couple of hours later, I was a legal emigrant of the United States of America, with a work permit. But I also was told at that time that my family could follow me from Canada within about six weeks. At least that was the way I understood it at the time and everything seemed to go smooth. I took a hotel room in Anaheim, California, which was close enough to my workplace. That same day, I wrote a letter to my wife about the situation.

My employment was not exactly as a glassblower, but rather as a general worker with a souvenir manufacturer for the Knott's Berry Farm in Buena Park, California. Outside of enclosing pennies into small glass bottles, my job had little to do with glassblowing. The pay wasn't the greatest either, but for now at least it was a steady income, and a foot in the door. My boss belonged to a group of businessmen who were working on the now well-known Movie Land Wax Museum in Buena Park. In order to fill the need for cheap labor at that place, I soon was sent to work as a carpenter's and decorator's helper to this construction site, which created an unexpected, new problem for me.

I had no transportation of my own, and, on my wages, I could not afford to rent a hotel room in this fancy neighborhood to be near enough to my workplace. There was no bus line between my hotel in Anaheim and Buena Park, and nobody cared how I got to and from work back home. To heighten my despair, an immigration officer showed up one morning and wanted to arrest me as an illegal worker. Some helpful coworkers wanted to usher me out the back door to avoid my arrest, but since I had no bad conscience, I decided to face the music.

Armand Lapiere, a French Canadian whom I had befriended, came to my assistance and promised the officer that we would be at his office the following morning, and thereby saved me from having to spend that night in jail.

"I'm so sorry!" the officer greeted us the next day at his office. In the meantime, the man had found my papers and I was assured that everything was in order. However, during this incident, I also learned that my family would only be able to follow me to the States after six months time, instead of in six weeks as I had thought. Whoever was to blame for that little mis-understanding didn't really matter anymore at this point, it was too late and too risky for me to return to Canada, even though I knew that my wife would be very unhappy about the news.

By the time we left the emigration office, our workday had already been a loss for both of us and my friend suggested we could look for a better job for me instead. Only hours later, I had a real job as a glassblower with Greiner Glassblowing in East Los Angeles. To get even for the noncaring attitude of my first boss in California, I just called the office to have them send my last meager check to my new address, but never went back there or talked to him again.

With a new job and renewed confidence, I had moved into a hotel in Alhambra, from where I was able to reach my workplace by bus. The increase in my wages at my new job was not that great in the beginning, but eventually it afforded me to buy a used bicycle, so I would be independent of public transportation.

By the time my family was supposed to arrive in California, I had rented a small house in South Pasadena. Then I made another big mistake. As if the long separation between me and my family wasn't enough to overcome, I also had taken advantage of a friend's offer to drive to the Los Angeles Airport in order to get my family. That my friend happened to be a woman who had been living in the same hotel as I might not have mattered to me, but it certainly irritated my wife—especially since my friend had been fashionably late, and Inge's plane arrived somewhat early. To say the least, our reunion got off on a very rocky start, which, in time, contributed to our eventual separation.

Chapter 3
Starting a new Life

In the meantime, my brother, Peter, had also immigrated to Canada and now wanted to move to the US as well. Even though the emigration laws had undergone a slight change since my arrival, it was still possible. While Peter was allowed to stay and live with us, we had to feed him, since he was not allowed to work for the first six months, by which time he would receive his green card.

My brother Peter with Snake

Well, there always was room for one more in our home and soon, there would be even more room than I had thought. As already indicated, my wife and I were in the process of separating. Shortly after our daughter Daniela's first birthday, Inge's mother came from Germany for a short visit and took our daughter back to the old country with her, to give us time to sort out our differences. Without Daniela, it became even easier to go our separate ways and our separation was soon followed by a divorce. A short time later, Inge, too, returned to Germany, at least for a while.

A new chapter in my life had started. In some ways, my brother's company helped me to readjust to the bachelor life, and since he had the same love for nature and wildlife as I, we often spent many weekends at the nearby San Gabriel Mountains, where we caught and photograph snakes and lizards.

During one of these expeditions, I had captured several snakes, while Peter had to be content with lizards. When it got late and we had decided to return home, I suddenly heard my brother calling out from behind me, "Is it poisonous?"

I turned and saw Peter in a bend-over position, ready to grab what most likely would be a snake. Since according to some local people, whom we had met here, not even benign snake should have been in this area, I saw no reason to spoil my brother's chance to catch whatever it was he had found. Since I already had disproved the absence of snakes in the area, I should have known better, but instead I called out to my brother, "Go ahead and grab that sucker!"

After Peter straightened up again, holding a snake by the neck, I hardly wanted to believe my eyes. I walked over to him and took the animal from him, before I told him that he had caught a rattlesnake.

"Bull!" was Peter's disbelieving reply.

"And what do you think this is?" I asked, motioning toward the rattle at the animal's tail.

A second incident involving a snake occurred on an outing with my new friend, Horst Stumpf. Horst, also an emigrant from Germany, had married an American woman over there during the occupation period and they had settled in California. I had met Horst in a bar, but what made us fast friends was our mutual interest in the outdoors. Especially since Horst's wife was not exactly an outdoor person, Horst and I often went on trips in the surrounding mountains or took a weekend trip all the way to San Philippe in Baja California, Mexico. There, we paddled in Horst's foldboat out on the Sea of Cortez to fish and it didn't matter to us that we mostly only caught small sharks and let them go again. I also shot jackrabbits around our camp for the owner of the cantina at the campground, and caught lizards and sometimes a snake. But when it came to catching reptiles, Horst was satisfied by being merely an observer.

This time, however, we had traveled north from our home near Los Angeles to the Kern River area and since I had long since graduated from a bicycle rider to a used car owner, we had taken my car. Looking for small critters near the river, I surprised Horst by catching a big, beautiful rattlesnake, but when I insisted to keep that snake as a pet for a while, Horst almost was ready to walk home, rather than share the car's interior with that snake. After some assuring discussion, the snake was securely tied up in a burlap sack, lying in the back of my station wagon and Horst could be persuaded to join me on our drive home. Whenever the car drove over a bump, we could hear the rattling in the burlap sack behind us, and by the time I dropped my friend off at his house, he might have been fairly near to a nervous breakdown.

California 1964

After my divorce, I had moved to a backyard bungalow in El Monte, where I had enough freedom and privacy to keep whatever kind of pets I wanted to keep. My preoccupation with exotic pets also caused me to take correspondence schooling from the North American School of Conservation, just in case I would decide to apply for a job with Fish and Game in the future. If or how I would ever make use of that knowledge and the final diploma from that school was still a big question, but at least I would improve my English while I learned more about nature and wildlife. Since I wasn't married anymore, my chances of living a more adventurous life had greatly improved, but how to get into a position to do so could only be answered if I would come to terms with what I really wanted to do with my future.

Most of my free time, outside of work and my studying, naturally went into my outdoor trips and collecting unusual pets, but after I had collected several rattlesnakes, there came a day when I decided to sell my snakes to a dealer. Even my brother, Peter, kept a small rattler in a terrarium at his place at the time, of which he had also grown tired.

Our plan was for me to pack up my snakes and then stop over at my brother's apartment for dinner, before we went to sell the snakes. While Peter still was frying the pork chops, I wanted to make myself useful and save us some time packing up his pet snake. With a leather thong loop on a stick, I lifted the animal out of the enclosure and grabbed it by the neck, a simple procedure in which I had done often enough by then without any thought of danger. Loosening the leather thong from the snake with a pencil or any other object along that line would have been the right way to handle it, but since I didn't have anything handy, I used my forefinger and thumb. Before I knew what had happened, the snake had dug one fang deep into my right forefinger.

As soon as I became aware of it, I dropped the snake, grabbed a kitchen knife and cut my finger where the fang had entered it, to make it bleed. A few minutes later, we were sitting in my brother's sports car, cruising through Pasadena, trying to find the emergency station or attract the police, so they could guide us there. We found the emergency station before the police found us. By then, my finger was hurting in a way as if it had been injected with acid and the only relief I got at the emergency station, since they didn't have any snake bite serum, was that my hand was put into a bucket of ice and I was transported by ambulance to the nearest hospital.

At the hospital, I found out how lucky I was that the emergency station did not have the serum. The doctor at that hospital obviously knew what he was doing when he barely punctured my arm with the syringe and found out that I was allergic to the snakebite serum.

"If they would have given you the antiserum at the emergency station," said the doctor, "you would be dead by now."

With that comforting thought, I was left alone lying on the hospital table in a small room, while my whole body felt like the way one's foot feels when it falls asleep, but if I moved, the feeling went away. The pain in my finger had vanished, at least for the time being. My brother, who had followed the ambulance to the hospital, entered the room with a hospital bureaucrat. As soon as it was established that I had neither insurance nor a fat bank account, I was put back into an ambulance and driven to the L.A. County Hospital.

Once assured that I was in good hands, Peter drove home and found the snake still curled up in the middle of his living room floor where I had dropped it and we had forgotten about it. He sold all the snakes the following day.

At the general hospital, the doctors were not too sure as to what to do with me. In addition to a suction cup on my forefinger, I was hooked up to an IV, which at first gave me the feeling that I was getting hungry, but then I had to throw up instead. The IV was discontinued, and soon thereafter, I felt better again. Next, I got into an argument with a couple of interns who did not believe that I was bitten by a rattlesnake.

"You guys might be on your way to be doctors," I said, "but when it comes to snakes, I probably know a little more than you!"

If that didn't satisfy those smart fellows, I suggested for them to drive to my brother's place and check out the snake that bit me, a suggestion which they did not follow up on.

During the night, the pain in my finger returned, and the nurse had to give me some painkiller. By morning, the pain was gone again, except that all the joints at my right arm were discolored and painful when I moved it.

Medically, there was nothing else that could have been done for me, but the doctors wanted to keep me for two weeks under observation. Since that would have been at my expense, plus the fact that my vacation was starting in a couple of days, I had issues with that idea.

"You have two choices," I told my doctor the following day, "either you bring me my clothes and call my brother to pick me up, or you'll find me walking the streets in this funny little shirt!"

As I mentioned my vacation to the doctor, a nurse standing next to us wanted to know where I was planning to go on my vacation. I smiled at her and said, "Into the mountains—to catch snakes!"

The nurse threw her hands up into the air and left the room. The doctor, while being more understanding to my situation, made me promise that I would call him upon my return from my vacation, just to let him know that I was still alive. Then he gave me a large bottle of disinfectant to bathe my finger in and wished me good luck.

Two days later, I was on my way to the Mojave Desert, starting my anxiously awaited vacation. At the Bowen's Ranch, to which I had been previously introduced to on a trip with a coworker, I paid a small fee to park my

Valley Man Recovers From Rattler Bite

A South San Gabriel snake collector who was bitten by a rattlesnake Monday was reported in fair condition today.

Wolfgang Hebel, 29, of 3300 Walnut Grove Ave., was bitten on the right forefinger while attempting to handle the reptile in Pasadena Monday.

He was first rushed to the Emergency Center by his brother, Peter Hebel, and later taken to Los Angeles County General Hospital.

The Independent

Vol. XXXI—No. 305   Aug. 18, 1964

Valley Man Serious After Rattler Bite

Collector Was Handling a 'Pet'

A South San Gabriel snake collector was bitten on the right forefinger by a rattlesnake Monday night while attempting to handle the "pet" reptile.

The accident occurred at 154 Mar Vista Ave., Pasadena. Wolfgang Hebel, 29, of 3300 Walnut Grove, South San Gabriel was rushed to Emergency Center by his brother, Peter Hebel.

He was taken to St. Luke Hospital by city ambulance and later transferred to Los Angeles County General Hospital.

Hebel was reported in serious condition late Monday night after administration of antivenim.

Snake Bite Victim 'Fair'

PASADENA—A 29-year-old snake hunter was reported in fair condition Tuesday at County General Hospital after being bitten by one of his rattlers.

Wolfgang A. Hebel, 3300 Walnut Grove Ave., South San Gabriel, suffered the bite Monday as he transferred the snake from one cage to another at the home of his brother, Peter, 25, of 154 Mar Vista Ave.

In the news

car at the end of their property, where the useable road ended and the foot trail into the Deep Creek Canyon started. From there, I had a couple of more miles or so to travel before I would reach the actual canyon. In foresight I had brought a couple of long bamboo poles along, from which I now constructed a travois, to drag all my gear down to the creek.

Instead of a running creek, I found only ponds and puddles along the creek bed. Above one of the smaller ponds, I established my camp by merely stretching a tarp above my sleeping bag, to create some shade and called it home for the next ten days.

Aside from some bread, I had brought along some fruit, rice, a few boiled eggs, and spices. Mother Nature was supposed to supply the rest of my sustenance, besides the peace and quiet of isolation.

It was an especially hot summer, even by California standards. Because of the heat, I spent most of the day sleeping or reading and restricted my activity to the early morning and late evening hours. The pond right below my camp was a perfect place to observe the wildlife. A flock of California quail came every morning and every evening to quench its thirst at my pond. Lizards seemed to be everywhere, but even an occasional snake came for a drink now and then. A hummingbird took a fancy to my colorful blanket and the ever-present California ground squirrel was seldom missing from the scene.

Most of the wildlife activity naturally occurred at night, when pack rats, kangaroo rats, and similar rodents rushed about. Also, tiny brush rabbits darted from bush to bush to avoid being spotted by the owls. Even deer stopped by once or twice, but the noisiest neighbors I had was a family of coyotes, of which I only got to see a single member one early morning. But the pups announced their presence in the vicinity during the night by constantly playing and fighting with one another, just like human brothers and sisters.

In full moonlight, a tarantula marched into my camp and was promptly added to my pet collection. Rattlesnakes, if they were big enough, ended up on my menu, providing a nice change from the more frequent ground squirrels roast.

On a trip down the creek bed, to the Deep Creek Hot Springs with an established campground for weekenders and trout fishermen, I found an unopened can of chicken and half a six-pack of beer in the creek. Unexpected but appreciated, my find was incorporated in my wilderness vacation diet. The only bad part about my dream vacation was that it came to an end too soon.

Deep Creek, California 1966

Deep Creek

After these long dreamed of ten days in the wild, it was no easy task to readjust to sitting at my workbench at the glassblowing shop, waiting for the next short weekend. And yes, I called the doctor to let him know that I had survived and that my finger was healing just fine.

Deep Creek California 1966

Chapter 4
South of the Border Episodes

That desert vacation of my dreams had also increased my appetite for more adventurous outdoor activity. By then, I knew that sooner or later, I had to find another way to make a living besides blowing glass from eight to five. After I received my diploma from the North American School of Conservation, I thought that the day had arrived to change my career and get a job with the Fish and Wildlife Service. Some initial inquiries at the Park Ranger offices did not bring the results I had hoped for. All what was offered to me were office jobs, often with an elderly lady as my prospective boss; my enthusiasm to get into this field of work was quickly ebbing. The more information I accumulated about the works of the strictly structured regime of the wildlife service, the less it seemed to be my cup of tea. Even if I wasn't totally disenchanted yet, I put the whole idea on ice for the time being and kept on blowing glass.

My brother, in the meantime, had moved to the state of Colorado, while my friend, Horst Stumpf, more or less took my brother's place for many of my outdoor trips. Since Horst's wife, as mentioned earlier, did not have the slightest interest in hiking or camping, Horst was always ready to head for the hills with me; sometimes, Horst's young son, Michael, would accompany us.

Outside of Horst, I also had made a couple of new friends. Neal Thomas, who was a salesman for the glassblowing firm I worked for, was, just like me, a recent divorcee, and he, too, was an enthusiast for the outdoors, and an avid photographer. While he was a somewhat moody character and a few years older than I was, I found Neal to be an otherwise very likable and quite clever fellow.

Jerry Regan I befriended in my neighborhood bar. He was a few years younger than I was and the happy-go-lucky type. Together, we spent many evenings and nights roaming through the bars in search of female companionship, but Jerry also was game to spend some weekends in the hills or the desert. His passion was fishing.

Neal, Jerry, and I (all three of us being bachelors and having roughly the same interests) eventually rented a big enough house together, so we had all the comfort we needed and room enough for our individual privacy. The main reason, however, for our moving together was our big dreams and plans for future adventures, which were to include a foldboat trip down the Amazon, or a horseback trip Through Mexico from Mazatlán to Vera Cruz. At that point, however, neither of us had the money or the experience for these long-term plans, nor did we know the first thing about horses or how to ride. But that did not stop us from dreaming. Starting out on a smaller scale, we planned to visit Mexico in a more conventional way, by car or train, in order to get a feel for the land, and get some exposure to the customs and the language of that county. At the same time, smaller trips like that were supposed to test our compatibility in unexpected situations.

It was May 4, 1967, as we drove in Jerry's Volkswagen toward the border of Mexico. Engaged in conversation about our expectations of our undertaking, we noticed too late that Jerry had taken the wrong highway. We still would arrive at the Mexican border that way, but at the border town of Tijuana, to the west of our planned destination, Mexicali, from where we had planned to take a train. Believing that we had a lot of time on our hands, we crossed into Mexico at Tijuana and headed for Mexicali along the south side of the border, enjoying the scenery and a meal at a Mexican restaurant along the way. Since our papers had not been properly checked at the usually casual border crossing in Tijuana, Mexico, we had to cross and recross the border at Mexicali to rectify the situation, necessary for our deeper penetration into Mexico.

Arriving at the Mexicali train station, we found out that our train had left thirty minutes prior to our arrival. Studying the train schedule, we came to the conclusion that the next train to Guaymas would leave at midnight. So, we had more time than we thought, and that was when Jerry decided that his car might be safer at the US side of the border. Neal and I had to agree, and with all the time we had there was no reason not to do something about it, and back across the border we went, where Jerry parked his car in front of the Calexico Police Station.

Guaymas in the Night

After entering Mexico for the third time on that day, we decided that it was dinnertime, and we ate a nice meal before slowly wandering back to the train station. But it had been a long and somewhat stressful day so far, and we were getting tired.

Too tired for barhopping and the waiting hall of that train station being not exactly the cleanest place for us to relax in, we tried to get comfortable on the lawn in front of the station. We had expected to be heading farther south into a more subtropical climate and were therefore clad in leather shirts, jeans, and moccasins only and therefore we soon got chilled to our bones while lying on that lawn. Hopping around to get warmed up didn't seem to help either, so we decided to take a taxi back to town and spent some hours in a bar after all. Our taxi driver had suggested that there might be a bus leaving for Guaymas or Mazatlán, but with our hearts set on a train trip, we disregarded that possibility under the assumption that it wouldn't be that much longer anymore before our midnight train would leave.

In spite of the upcoming Mexican holiday, Cinco de Mayo, the bars were pretty quiet and uninteresting and we soon wandered back toward the train station. That was when I had a sudden revelation: 12 O'clock in Mexico, just like in Europe, means exactly that. There is no AM or PM and midnight would actually be 00:00 hours. Consequently, there would be no train leaving till noon the next day and that meant we would have to travel by bus if we wanted to get anywhere before the weekend was over.

Arriving by taxi at the downtown bus depot, almost as if it were planned, we got there just in time to watch the bus to Guaymas pull out of the station.

"Now I really feel like one of the three Stooges!" said Neal in disgust.

"We sure as hell are one disorganized bunch," Jerry added, and I had to agree.

The next bus to Guaymas was scheduled for 10:25 a.m. and we were not taking any more chances. We sat down in the bus depot coffee shop, ate breakfast, drank coffee, and smoked cigarettes until the bus was ready to be boarded.

The traveling cost by train or by bus at that time in Mexico was about one cent per mile. If we figured out how much money we had already spent on food, drinks, and taxi fare since we entered Mexico, we could have paid for our whole trip and still have money left over. It was quite obvious even to us that any planning for any bigger adventure in the future would have to be undertaken with a lot more care and foresight.

Some miles farther into Mexico, the bus stopped at a checkpoint, where our visas were checked. There, we also took advantage of the occasion to buy a big bottle of Coca Cola each, which we spiked with some rum we already had in our hand packs. After all the confusing and the sleepless hours, it didn't take too many sips from our spiked Coca Colas before we went to sleep.

When the bus stopped next and we looked out the window, we knew we couldn't have slept very long. There was no settlement in sight, only sand, brush and cacti, and the sun still high in the sky. But everybody was getting off the bus and so we followed. Finally, it became clear to us that the bus had a flat tire and we, like everybody else, sat down in the sand waiting patiently for the tire to be changed.

"Now I know we'll never get there!" said Neal and Jerry pointed up to the sky, where some turkey vultures were circling above us.

"They are waiting for us," Neal remarked again sarcastically. "Can't you see their evil eyes?" But in spite of Neal's sarcasm, the tire on the bus was soon changed and our trip continued.

It was about midnight when the bus pulled into the Guaymas terminal and we disembarked fully rested. Filling our lungs with the fresh sea air, we were ready for action. While this old town with its romantically lit streets and buildings looked very inviting, nothing and nobody seemed to be awake at this hour. No people roamed the streets and no restaurant or bar was open.

A taxi pulled up next to us and the driver addressed us in broken English. After we told him what we were looking for, he made a long face and said, "Nothing open at this time. Maybe a couple bars on the other side of town, but no good for tourists!"

"Do we look like ordinary tourists?" I argued.

The taxi driver shrugged his shoulders and motioned for us to get into the taxi. A short time later, he stopped in front of a corner bar with western style swinging doors. As we paid our fare and got out of the taxi, the man shook his head again and repeated, "No good!"

Well, the taxi driver was most likely right and certainly entitled to his opinion, but we were here to see the real Mexico, not the tourist traps and into that place we went....

If some of the patrons in that cantina would have carried revolvers, we either would have believed in time travel or that we had entered a western movie set. There were no windows in the whitewashed walls of that room. In the corner to the left of us, there was a bar of sorts, built of raw lumber. In the middle of the room stood a pool table on which a sleeping drunk was snoring. Several of the other guests were also lying or sitting along the walls, either sleeping or otherwise removed from reality.

"Are you guys sure that we have the right address?" Jerry asked jokingly.

"Almost like home!" I answered, equally in good humor, but in reality, neither one of us felt completely safe in this establishment.

The bartender greeted us with a smile and I could have sworn to have seen the reflection of dollar signs in his eyes as he busily wiped the bar with a grayish towel and invited us to sit down.

So we fearless adventurers sat down in front of the bar and ordered three beers while engaging in a language-limited conversation with our host.

We toasted each other to our arrival in the real Mexico, when Jerry interrupted the ceremony: "I don't really want to look right now," he said, "but something below us is trying to take off one of my moccasins."

Along that bar, there was a ditch in the cement floor, which, besides the runoff from the bar, contained cigarette butts, peanut shells, and other unidentifiable refuse. As I inspected the gully for the cause of Jerry's complaint, I saw a rat of healthy proportion nibbling on Jerry's footwear. In order not to cause unnecessary alarm, I smiled as I looked at Jerry and told him not to worry and that the rat at his foot was most likely the bar mascot with an interest in the newest footwear fashion.

In time, we found out that there were at least two or three of these cute little buggers running around below our feet, but not wanting to give the impression that we were Gringo wimps, we bravely ordered a second beer before leaving this glory hole of entertainment.

From right across the street, we heard the inviting sound of Mariachi music and our curiosity got the best of us. Upon entering this place, we were surprised when we found tables with tablecloths and chairs in this, by far, cleaner establishment. But outside of the music, there wasn't any other entertainment to be found there either.

While we figured on finishing our beer and calling it a night, one of the few male patrons in the place joined us uninvited at our table. He spoke fairly good English and wanted to know all about us. But whenever Jerry tried to join in our conversation, the man got very irritated and told Jerry to shut up. After inquiring about his dislike toward our friend, he claimed to have met Jerry previously in connection with some disagreeable incident.

Even after we tried to explain to the man that Jerry never before was that deep into Mexico, he insisted that he knew Jerry and that he never would forget a nose like Jerry's!

We endured the guy's animosity toward our friend until we had finished our beers and left the establishment. Without a taxi in sight and not knowing where to go to begin with, we wandered down toward the beach. There, in front of a hotel, we bedded down in the sand and went to sleep. The high points of our adventure this far were the flat tire in the middle of nowhere, rabbit size rats in a bar, and a new nickname for Jerry, "El Nariz!"

Somewhat refreshed, we were awakened by the rising sun, took a walk through the town to take some pictures, and then had breakfast in a small restaurant. Afterwards, we returned to the bus depot to take the next bus to Mazatlán.

During the bus ride, as soon as the sun went down, we soon fell asleep again until we arrived early in the morning at our final destination. A big breakfast of fried shrimp gave us the strength for a new day of exploration.

Sea Bass - Mazatlan

We arrived at the fishing boat harbor just in time as the returning fishing boats unloaded their catch. These colorful painted boats in the morning light, the great variety of fish and the business action of the people all around us, created a postcard picture atmosphere. One outstanding spectacle was created by a man transporting a two-hundred-pound sea bass on a trailer behind his bicycle.

After taking a few photographs, we followed the beach toward the south and found an old fort to explore. An antique, rusty cannon was still pointed out to sea, as if ready to defend the fort against hostile ships, and the pock-marked walls of the fort were further reminders of Mexico's turbulent past.

With a sudden "Hello there!" we were greeted by another admirer of Mexico's history. "Where're you fellows from?"

The man walking toward us introduced himself as Gus and he proclaimed to be an experienced world traveler. Be that as it may, he rightfully had spotted us as beginners in the field. Mazatlán was one of Gus's favored towns to visit, in which he certainly knew his way around. Gus clued us in on the various dos and don'ts in Mexico and soon had us set up in one of the more reasonably priced, but clean hotels. Now, we had a place to relax, take a shower, and leave our hand packs behind during our photo expeditions through town, of which our first target was the colorful marketplace.

"Where is Jerry?" asked Neal shortly after we had arrived.

"He might have found something interesting for the camera and didn't want to share it with us," I answered. But, at that moment, we heard some angry cries not too far from us.

"*Policia, policia!*" hollered a man from near the butcher stand while waiving his fist in the air. We also caught a quick glance of our friend, Jerry, before he vanished into the crowd.

"You think he stole a sausage?" I jokingly asked Neal.

"Who knows where he stuck his nose in this time," Neal answered, chuckling.

Later, Jerry explained to us how he wanted to take a picture of the flies on the meat hanging there at that stand, but the butcher obviously didn't see the humor in it.

"He probably thought you were nosing around for the health department," I couldn't help remarking, and got another chuckle out of Neal.

Somehow, Jerry seemed to be a magnet for trouble. The following morning, when we went to eat breakfast, Neal and I thought it was time for some variety in our diet and so we ordered *huevos con chorizo* instead of our usual fried shrimp. Jerry, however, insisted on ordering his usual fare.

Neal's and my order arrived within a fairly short time, while Jerry had to wait somewhat longer, but we didn't feel obligated to let our food get cold while waiting for Jerry's shrimps to arrive, and started eating. To Jerry's relief, the waiter finally arrived with a big, steaming plate of shrimp for Jerry and Jerry dug into them with great enthusiasm. Two or three bites later, Jerry dropped his fork and leaned back in his chair. When we looked up at him, he pointed at his plate, where amid those delicious shrimp lay a fair size cockroach with his legs stretched toward the heavens.

"Think of it as a slightly burned shrimp," I teased.

"It might be just a different species of shrimp," Neal added jokingly, and with smirks on our faces, we kept on eating.

Jerry soon had recuperated from his shock; he thanked us for our concern over his appetite, then flipped the odd critter ceremoniously off his plate and started eating again.

If we liked it or not, on the following day, we had to head for home, but this time, we made sure to take in the experience of a train ride through Mexico.

The taxi driver who drove us to the train station certainly lived up to the reputation of his countrymen taxi drivers, by constantly using the horn instead of his brakes, and by the time we arrived at the station well ahead of our departure time, we were thankful to have gotten there in one piece and undamaged.

Standing around waiting for the train to arrive with the rest of the prospective travelers, we noticed a rough-looking Mexican watching us. Finally, the man came toward us and addressed us in Spanish; *"Cazadores de tigre?"* he asked while shaking our hands without a sign of doubt that we understood what he was saying. When neither of us answered right away, he asked again; *"Cazadores de tigre?"*

Finally, it rang a bell with me. Because of our attire, the man mistook us for jaguar hunters. But rather than go through the painful task of explaining our appearance to him and burst his bubble, I saw no harm in making the man happy, and nodded smiling in agreement. He proudly shook our hands once more and left.

The train rolled into the station and the masses streamed toward the doors of the coaches.

Having been brought up to be polite, we stayed back and took our time, but by the time we boarded, we almost didn't make it. Our next problem was that we couldn't find a place to sit down, especially since some people were still milling around and it was hard to tell which seats might already have been claimed. People constantly wanted to pass and we eventually stepped into a small room without a door just to get out of the way. But then it was quickly pointed out to us that we were standing in the entrance leading to the ladies room. From this situation, we were rescued by a conductor, who showed us to some open seats. Neal, however, had to sit separately from Jerry and me, but at least we didn't have to stand and be in anybody's way anymore. Relieved and relaxed, we could absorb the whole atmosphere. People from all walks of life and with a variety of skin tones seemed to be present. Across the aisle from Jerry and me sat a proud-looking, elegantly dressed man next to an Indian woman who was breastfeeding her baby. Above the woman, on the luggage rack, sat a basket, from which a string of sausages was dangling, swinging to the rhythm of the moving train. Farther down that same side of our coach, the cries of a couple of parrots could be heard coming from a cardboard box and about where Neal was sitting, a live rooster, quietly protesting, was dangling upside down by his feet....

Vendors Greet the train.

That whole scene gave us the illusion of having stepped back in time once more.

At every whistle stop along the way, the train was surrounded by vendors, calling out the goods they had to offer, "Tacos, tortillas, burritos, *cerveza!*" and so on. But any hungry or thirsty person who wanted to buy anything through the windows of the train surely had to know what he or she wanted and how to get the transaction done before the train rolled on. We for one didn't even try it, especially since we in most cases couldn't be sure what we were buying to begin with.

Around sunset, a sandstorm developed. All the windows were closed and since there was nothing else to see or do, we went to sleep. When I woke up, the inside of our coach looked like a smoke-filled bar. The fine dust in the air had penetrated in spite of the closed windows. Every passenger, no matter how colorfully dressed, now seemed to be dressed in the same color clothes. When we stood up, an avalanche of fine sand and dust fell off us to the floor.

Jerry and I had decided to go to the washroom, but this time to the men's washroom, where we were soon joined by Neal, who mumbled something about going blind while he was polishing his glasses.

After Jerry and I had cleaned ourselves as much as possible, we lit up a cigarette. Leaning at the entrance to the washroom and smoking, Neal behind us was about to dry his face with his bandana, when a young Mexican woman walked by. Her eyes got as big as saucers when she looked at us and then she started running and hollering, "Banditos, banditos!"

To find out what was happening, we followed the young lady into our coach, where we were greeted by laughter from the other passengers. The young Mexican woman, who must not have noticed us earlier, had actually taken us for banditos. Now she stood there with an embarrassed smile on her face.

"That would have put a nice, finishing touch on our trip," said Jerry, "to get arrested and spend a night or two in a Mexican jail!"

Neal nudged me in my side and remarked that Jerry most likely would have to spend an extra few days there, because of his unforgettable nose.

But we all arrived safely back in Mexicali and, a short time later, we were back on U.S. soil, sitting in Jerry's car on the way to our home in El Monte, California.

A couple of weeks later, we made another long weekend trip to Mexico, but only as far as Guaymas, where we swam and fished in the ocean, took more pictures, and ate like kings on the delicious, reasonably priced seafood.

At work, however, dark clouds were on the horizon. Our southern excursions were not looked upon with the same enthusiasm or understanding. A day or two late back for work didn't matter much to me, especially since I felt underpaid and thought I should have some kind of freedom as an equalizer. Promises for a better future with the firm had lost their attraction for me as time passed. But my boss didn't quite agree with my viewpoints and things between us came to a head, which ended with my immediate resignation, in spite of the fact that I had no idea about what I wanted to do next.

Neal came home a little later that same day and with a smile on his face, he congratulated me for having quit my job.

"Word gets around fast, doesn't it?" I asked.

Whereupon, Neal told me that he heard about my quitting as he returned from his sales trip. When he openly agreed with my decision to terminate my employment, the foreman criticized his attitude, which caused Neal in turn to hand in his resignation as well.

Then Neal and I shook hands, and he put a bottle of Jim Beam on the table, and heated some water for a coffee royal. While we talked, smoked, and sipped our beverage, it became clear that we both seemed to have long-standing grievances about our former employer. Feeling justified in our decision to quit our jobs, neither of us brought up the obvious question of, "What now?"

Chapter 5
El Beasty

When Jerry came home from work on the day Neal and I had quit our jobs and found us sitting around drinking coffee royals, he knew right away that something unusual had happened. After we had explained our situation to him, Jerry asked the question which at least I had not dared to ask myself yet. "And what are you unemployed characters planning to do now?"

"Why don't you give us a couple of days to answer that one," said Neal, before I could open my mouth.

Neal's reaction was true to his character, and I had to conclude from it that he was up to something, but for the rest of that night, the subject of our future did not come up again. Instead, the three of us went out for dinner as if nothing had changed. In fact, a day or two passed when Neal came home with a fresh bottle of Jim Beam and I was determined to get to the bottom of Neal's behavior. In a teasing manner, I said: "Either you have received a substantial inheritance, or you have found a new high-paying job."

Neal laughed as he set the bottle on the table and put on the kettle for hot water. But I wanted my answer and kept on digging. "Okay," I said, "you're just training for the lifestyle of the homeless!"

"None of the above!" Neal finally answered. "But I have some ideas and would like to hear what you think of them."

Now, we were getting somewhere. When the coffee was done and the coffee royal was served, we sat down in the living room and lit a cigarette.

"For a horseback trip through Mexico," Neal took up the conversation again, "we are totally unprepared, since we can't even ride a horse yet. Nor do we have the money for a foldboat trip down the Amazon. But how does a trip to Alaska sound to you?"

Alaska had been the last place in my mind, but I had to admit his suggestion had potential. Alaska sounded adventurous enough and our getting there quite feasible even for our limited means. To me personally, anything along that line sounded better than a search for another job as a glassblower.

When Jerry found us studying maps when he came home from work, he right away made another smart remark by asking us if we were planning to rob a bank now.

"No," answered Neal. "Instead of breaking in, we actually are planning to break out of this humdrum, civilized existence we are living here."

After serving a coffee royal to our friend, we explained our whole plan to him and told him how we planned to fix up Neal's old pickup, which he had already converted into a homemade camper of sorts. Furthermore that, we planned to sell most of our belongings and then head north toward Alaska, or as far as that old vehicle would take us in that direction.

Typical for Jerry, he just smiled and kept his thoughts to himself for the moment. It was not until the following evening, when Jerry suddenly turned to Neal and asked, "Do you think three people could sleep in your camper?"

In reality, Neal and I had expected something like that, but now we both looked at each other like we were surprised.

"Did you lose your job, too?" Neal asked him.

"Not yet," Jerry answered, "but the more I think about it, the less sense does it make to me that I work my ass off while you two clowns are having all the fun."

"If you're serious about it," said Neal, "we'll make room."

Ready for Alaska

We still had three weeks before we would have to pay rent again, and that also gave Jerry enough time to give notice at his job. In the meantime, we had to get our act together, sort out and sell our belongings, work on our vehicle, and clean the house in order to get our rent deposit back. Jerry and I also had to prepare our present girlfriends for our upcoming vanishing act. If Neal even had a girlfriend, we couldn't tell, since he never brought a girlfriend around and usually kept his love affairs to himself.

But in no way did we feel pressured for time and we often went out to dinner or to play a couple of games of pool in the evenings. We also studied maps of Alaska, to look for and pinpoint suitable locations for a life in the wilderness, while we had no idea about what lay ahead or what the conditions might be wherever we would end up. In my case, it certainly increased my enthusiasm to get started and to test my ability to survive under primitive self-sustaining conditions in the wilderness. Sitting in a comfortable home thousands of miles away from our goal and making plans under the most favorable situations was easy enough. Many things could happen before we even got there, but then again, that was what adventure was all about. If, for instance, our truck should break down, we would have to find work wherever that would happen until we were financially in a position to continue our venture. Therefore, all the planning was nothing more than dreaming. We were starting a totally new lifestyle of a day-to-day existence and hoped that our friendship and our happy-go-lucky attitude about the whole thing would hold out.

Cleaning the house was the last item on our "have to do" list, because we couldn't be sure to satisfy or landlord in order to get our cleaning deposit back. For the moment, we had a more personal issue to solve. In discussions about our trip, the suggestion came up that our truck should also have a name, but what should it be? In memory of our Mexico trips and our original plans to head south, we thought of a Spanish name, but couldn't find anything fitting with the right sound, but eventually, we came to a conclusion and the following day I painted the name "El Beasty" on both sides of the camper. "El Beasty" was born.

Finally, everything was done and we were ready to leave, except that the cleaning of the house as we had expected was not done to the liking of the landlord, even though in our opinion, we had left the house in better shape than it was when we moved in. Figuring that the landlord just didn't want to give us our deposit back, we didn't see any point in wasting our time and brought most of our gear to Jerry's parent's house for temporary storage in their garage. Early in the morning on the following day, we locked the house, dropped the keys in the landlord's mailbox, and drove to our favored location into the mountains of the Mojave Desert at the Bowen's Ranch, where we made camp.

The reasons for driving to our old high desert hangout was because we wanted to get used to living with El Beasty as our only home and see how we got along under those conditions. Outside of that, we felt the need to say good bye to our old stomping grounds, not knowing if we would ever see the place again.

My friend Neal - Deep Creek

Once we had camp set up, we visited the Deep Creek Hot Springs, near the place where I had spent my ten-day vacation after my snake bite incident, and we hunted rabbits and rattlesnakes for our field kitchen.

On the third day at our desert camp, we were visited by my friend, Horst, and his son, Michael. While Horst had brought a case of beer along, we supplied the hamburgers.

Since Horst was very well acquainted to my ways, it was to no surprise that he pointed at the bowl of ground meat from which we made the hamburger patties and asked, "What kind of meat is that?"

"That's our Deep Creek special," I answered, "the best cuts from rabbits, onions, and Mexican peppers mixed in."

"Tastes good!" he replied after another bite from his burger. Then he pointed to the bowl of which I just had stopped grinding the meat.

"That looks lighter," he stated, "what kind of meat would that be?"

"That's our extra special!" Neal replied before I could say anything.

"And what makes it so extra special?"

"It is exactly like the other," I explained, "only that rattlesnake meat has been added."

"That's exactly what I was worried about," Horst said. "None of that for me, please!"

If it wasn't hard enough to assure Horst that there was no rattlesnake meat in the burgers we had served up to now, there was absolutely no chance convincing my friend to try one of the extra special burgers. His son, Michael, on the other hand, had no objection against trying one of these burgers and found it to be even tastier than the other.

I certainly could have spent more time in the desert camp, but after our visitors, Horst and Michael, had left again, we, too, had to think of getting on our way if we ever wanted the slightest chance to make it to Alaska that year.

On our way back to El Monte, where we had lived, we stopped at a pet store and sold some lizards that I had caught. Three freshly caught kangaroo rats and my Townsend desert ground squirrel, which I had kept as a pet for the last two years, had to wait until we got to Santa Barbara. Since it was illegal for pet stores in the Los Angeles area to carry these rodents, we decided to donate them to the Santa Barbara Children's Zoo, along with an old bird egg collection I had when we got there.

For now, we were fully tanking up and loading the rest of our belongings onto El Beasty, and spent another night at Jerry's parent's house. Early in the morning on July 7, 1967, we took the first serious step toward our undertaking and headed north.

My optimism as to how far we would get was not too high, since our overloaded vehicle swayed like a ship on the ocean at every turn. But Neal and Jerry seemed to be full of confidence and in an especially good mood, when they started to sing our newly-adapted theme song, "Born Free"!

I then figured if El Beasty was able to endure our singing, it was possible that she also might survive the whole trip to Alaska. Stopping at the museum at Santa Barbara as planned, we visited one of Neal's old time acquaintances and made our presentations of wildlife and bird eggs, of which the latter was greatly appreciated by the ornithology department.

By 11 p.m. that night, we stopped at Neal's parent's trailer home in San Jose. This stop took a little longer than I had expected, but after all, Neal had not visited his parents in a while and, for some reason, my companions didn't seem to feel the urgency to travel on like I did. So, for a few days, we lay around at the swimming pool of the trailer park, behaving like retired people, while I even received a visit from a former girlfriend, who drove down from San Francisco just to see me one more time before I vanished into the wilderness of the north.

Neal works on El Beasty

On July 14, we resumed our drive to the north and made camp at the Russian River that night. Jerry caught a big carp in the river for our dinner and, afterward, we sat by the light of our gas lantern to make notes in our diaries. The following day was a very hot one and since our unsophisticated vehicle did not have an air conditioner, we visited the redwoods and a Tillamook cheese factory during the hottest hours. By evening, however, we retreated from all public places, into some wooded side road, where we could enjoy peace and quiet and maybe get a chance to catch some more fish or shoot a rabbit. After all, without any income, we had to stretch our funds as much as possible.

One morning, after getting up particularly early, I returned to camp with a couple of cotton tail rabbits. Neal was just climbing out of his sleeping bag and congratulated me on my successful hunt before explaining to me in an apologetic way that he had been awake since a while, but didn't dare sticking his nose out of my sleeping bag because the whole camper was filled with a buzzing sound.

"Why should that keep you from getting up?" I asked.

"Because it sounded like a four-pound wasp flying around in there," he answered.

But when the buzzing didn't want to stop, Neal finally took a peek and saw that it actually was a hummingbird he had been so scared of.

"That bird just couldn't understand," I replied, "why you two lazy bums are wasting the morning hours of such a nice day."

Camp on the Russian River - Neal and Jerry

That evening, we found a nice patch of raspberries and while I started picking them for our dessert, Neal and Jerry, full of anticipation, collected firewood to cook our rabbit dinner.

Soon, a loud holler interrupted my concentration on the berries and as it turned out, while picking up firewood, Neal had disturbed a wasp nest and promptly got stung, but he was very glad that the wasp was not of the four-pound variety.

Before we crossed the Columbia River, from Oregon into Washington, we visited Fort Clatsop, of which the original had been built by the Lewis & Clark Expedition in 1805-1806. But soon after the fort was turned over to the local Indian chief when the expedition turned back, it fell into decay. Many years later, the present day replica of the fort was rebuilt.

As soon as we entered the state of Washington, it started to rain. The dirty streets under that gray sky of the first small towns, often leading past buildings that looked like deserted factories with blind windows, got us in a depressed mood. Luckily, that lasted only until we entered the Olympic National Park. By then, the rain had stopped and the tatters of mist lying over the wild, rocky coast were a quite picturesque sight.

Inside the park, we were required by law to camp within any campground limits and naturally could not hunt for small game. So we chose to stay at the

Solduck campground, where we befriended the park ranger, Robert Krear, and learned a lot about these 1,314 square miles of parkland.

When we told the ranger that we were headed for Alaska, he envied us, since he himself had spent some time there with the well-known naturalist, Olaus J. Murrie, and the arctic traveler, George B. Scholler.

Fort Clatsop

While enjoying the company of Robert Krear, we also took advantage of the campground facilities by taking a shower and to clean out our crowded camper. Then after crossing the Hood Canal, we soon arrived in Seattle, where I still had to pick up some money from a canceled life insurance policy. At first, it looked like as if I would have difficulties collecting my money, unless I shaved. Apparently with my beard and the long hair, I did not look like the guy on my driver's license or on my passport anymore. But, finally, I had been asked to sign a bunch of insignificant pieces of paper, until it dawned on me that the folks at that bank just had their fun with me. I'm not so sure whether the smirks on the faces of my friends were over the joke which was played on me, or if they smiled over the extra money we now had to spend on our trip.

After this little amusement at my expense, we stopped at a smaller town to do our laundry, a little shopping, and even splurged on a glass of beer from my latest income. Then we made camp somewhere in some meadow, where cows and deer grazed next to each other. The next day would be a new milestone on our journey, when we would reach the border and cross into Canada.

El Beasty entering Alaska 1967

Chapter 6
North to the Future

On July 25, we crossed the border into Canada from the town of Blaine in Washington. High in spirit, we felt ready to start this new leg of our journey. The customs officials were friendly and helpful, and right on the other side of the border, we went to the tourist bureau, where we were able to find the current phone number of my old acquaintances, Gerhard and Anita Laschkowsky in Vancouver. But before we went to the town of Vancouver, I wanted to introduce my travel companions to another fort which I remembered visiting five years earlier.

Fort Langley, with a history of mishaps caused by fire and by Indians, used to be an important trading post for the Hudson Bay Company until the year 1880, when the paddle wheeler, Surprise, was able to get 78 miles farther up the Frasier River. From that day on, Fort Langley lost on significance, but was partly preserved and restored as a tourist attraction.

Heading toward Vancouver after our visit of the fort, Neal said to me, "Now that you have introduced us to another piece of history, could you introduce us to a good restaurant?"

"Will do!" I answered, and gave directions to the well-known Robson Street in Vancouver, where I hoped to find the Europa Café I used to frequent. There, we enjoyed a delicious German style dinner and then called Gerhard and Anita, where we were promptly invited to eat dinner later that night.

That the home of my acquaintance was located at a dead-end road in the outskirts of town turned out quite convenient for us later on. After our second dinner for that night and many hours of conversation with our hosts, we drank quite a few beers before we turned in for the night and climbed into our camper. After all, there was no need to burden our hosts for sleeping accommodations, since El Beasty offered all we needed outside of a bathroom. Because of all that beer we had consumed, the brushy slope on the other side of the dead-end street proved quite handy and soon, one or the other of us, dressed in no more than our skivvies, slipped out to cross the street and vanish into the bushes.

While our hosts had to work the following day, I took my friends around town and showed them whatever else of Vancouver had left an impression on me. Even though I only had lived in this area for less than a year, I still felt quite at home, especially around the Stanley Park and the growing zoo within. Later on, we also visited the Vancouver Museum, with its large collection of local Native artifacts.

The evening of that day was almost a repeat of the night before—with good food, good conversation, and the following effects of the many beers. In the morning, we said good bye to our gracious hosts and traveled on.

We followed the road along the Frasier River to Cache Creek, and, from there, we took highway 97, steeply into the mountains to about 4,000 feet. In spite of the elevation and the latitude, the temperature was 95 degrees Fahrenheit in the shade. So, by the time we reached the campground at Lake La Hache, we looked forward to a refreshing swim in the lake. Jerry was also able to make use of his British Columbia fishing license and supplied us with a few squaw-fish for our dinner. I, on the other hand, was surprised to find a big tiger salamander along the lake shore. This was quite meaningless to my companions, but I had not expected to find this amphibian this far north.

Wolf and El Beasty, Canada 1967

Dark clouds threatened us with rain as we pulled out of the campground the next morning, but this time, the bad weather was not able to dampen our spirits as we pushed northward. We soon noticed a lessening in signs of human activity, and when we stopped at Pine Pass, we could see nothing but woodland in all directions from this point, but also made the acquaintance of the small biting flies called gnats, which showed little or no respect for our mosquito dope.

July 31 was a very rainy day in Dawson Creek, as we took a picture of Neal driving El Beasty past mile post zero.

Alcan Highway

From this point on, the miles along the Alcan Highway count upward in both directions, because this point is generally accepted as the spot where the Alcan Highway was completed. However, the two crews working from the north and from the south actually met on October 23, 1942, at mile post 588.1.

Besides taking that picture of our camper passing this point, we had a couple of more reasons to stay a little longer in this town. First of all, we needed to do a little shopping and while walking around the town in the rain, Neal and I were quite well protected by our broad-rimmed western hats. Jerry, on the other hand, always worried to look too much like a cowboy, had never bought himself a hat like that. It was now that Jerry had to admit to the practical side of such attire and with a little urging from us, he finally broke down and bought a western hat. While Jerry needed some time in the store to decide on just the right style of his head cover., Neal took advantage of the situation to do some shopping for Jerry's birthday, which Jerry probably thought we had forgotten about. By the time Jerry had made his choice and came out of the store with his new head gear, Neal had returned from his secret mission, his absence undiscovered by Jerry. But Neal and I had to restrain ourselves from making any remarks about Jerry's new acquisition; Jerry with his tall, slender figure probably was now the only one among us who really looked like a cowboy.

By the time we made camp at the Kiskatinaw River, the rain had stopped, and I invited Jerry to check out the river with me for fishing possibilities. When we returned to camp a short time later, Neal had set up a kind of birthday table, with a cake and candles, a steaming pot of coffee, and a bottle of whiskey. We sang "Happy Birthday to you!" and the surprise party was a success.

At Mile 85, the pavement of the highway came to a sudden end. From there on, we would have to drive on gravel until we reached Alaska. In the beginning, the gravel road was still wet from the latest rain, which kept the dust to a minimum for the time being, but later on, whenever we were met or were passed by another vehicle, we were left in a cloud of dust, which made it almost impossible to see where we were going—especially when we were passed by a semi, which also heightened the danger that a rock might be hurled into our windshield.

At a town called Trutch, we had to gas up again, stretch our legs, and maybe enjoy our daily blueberry pie, but there were so few buildings that we had to wonder if this town even had a coffee shop. Outside of the old gas station attendant, there seemed to be no people around this settlement anywhere.

"I wonder if there is a coffee shop around here," Jerry asked loud enough for anybody to within normal earshot to hear, but the gas station attendant either couldn't hear or wasn't the talkative kind. The man showed total indifference toward us and not a word was passed from his lips during the time he filled our truck or while we paid for it. Jerry just smiled and shrugged his shoulders and we went on to find the coffee shop without the attendant's help.

As we entered the place, we found it totally empty; not even a waitress or waiter was within. So we sat down and waited. Just as I wanted to make a remark about this place possibly being a self-service establishment, a very pale-looking waitress appeared and came toward our table at a snail's pace. After we placed our order, the girl mumbled something that neither one of us understood, but eventually we were served. The coffee was barely warm and the pie was at least three days old. Before we could complain about it, the waitress had vanished again.

"Maybe there has been a death in this community," Neal suggested.

"I don't care what it is," replied Jerry, "this place gives me the willies!"

With these words, he got up to put a coin into the music box and it was to nobody's surprise that the music box didn't work.

It was Jerry's turn to pay for our daily splurge, so Neal and I went outside ahead of him and lit up a cigarette. After what seemed quite a while, Jerry came out of that coffee shop, recounting the coins in his hand.

"Didn't I know it!" he called out and turned around to reenter the place. About another five minutes or so went by before our friend reappeared and explained to us that the girl had tried to charge him double for our luxury meal.

Our camp next to another river that evening was quite refreshing in comparison to our coffee break stop that day. A big patch of wild strawberries gave us the opportunity to make up for the dried-up blueberry pie and a small herd of half wild horses nearby was a more pleasant company than we had during our visit to that town called Trutch.

On the following day, we crossed the highest point on our trip at Summit Lake, 4,250 feet above sea level. Since we had left our home in California, we had driven 3,100 miles and, from this point, we had another 826 miles of unpaved road to drive before we would reach the Alaskan border....

Visiting the Liard Hot Springs along the way was something interesting to see, but the tourists and the trash lying around the place prompted us to travel on to look for a quieter place. We hadn't gone too far yet, when we heard a suspicious noise and Neal brought the swaying truck to a halt. We all knew that we had a flat tire, but how much trouble we were in for none of us could have guessed at this point.

It was getting late and El Beasty was sitting in the middle of the road. Neal couldn't drive the vehicle toward one side or the other, since the top-heavy truck might have tipped over. Therefore, we would have to hurry with our tire change and hope that no semi would approach from either side.

By the time we had jacked the truck up to a certain point, the Handy Man jack started to bend under the weight of its load and the truck was nowhere high enough yet for us to take off the wheel.

"What now?" asked Neal.

"We'll have to unload!" answered Jerry.

That was not what Neal wanted to hear and it would have taken us till dark to accomplish that feat.

"Maybe we could get the truck a little higher with some kind of lever," I suggested and went on to explain what I meant.

Then, as I had suggested, we searched for a manageable boulder and a small tree trunk. With the tree trunk under the truck, we pushed it over the boulder and while Jerry and I balanced ourselves on the outer end of the trunk, we were able to get the truck high enough for Neal to remove the wheel. But there still was not enough room for the air-filled spare tire to fit.

"What now, professor Hebel?" Neal asked in a tone mixed of humor and sarcasm.

"Dig a hole!" I answered matter of fact like.

Fraser River

Neal and Jerry looked at each other in surprise over my quick solution, but then they got out the pick and shovel and before we knew it, we were back on the road again. Thankful that no semi had arrived during our ordeal, we cleared away the boulder and the tree trunk and filled in the hole in the road.

At mile post 627, at the Iron Creek Lodge, we entered the Yukon Territory of Canada, where we also renewed our fishing licenses before we drove on to Watson Lake and made camp again. To keep away from the swarms of gnats and mosquitoes as much as possible, we chose a brushless stretch of shoreline of the lake to park El Beasty. The water temperature was just right for us to take a refreshing bath and the water was so clear that we could see schools of grayling swimming around us, but all our angling efforts remained fruitless.

The following day, Jerry took a walk in the near surroundings and returned to camp in the company of a man by the name of Jerry Shaw. Jerry Shaw was a local of the Watson Lake Community, and he pointed out to us that we were camped on the end of a military runway. The only reason we had not been blasted out of there by the noise of departing planes was that it was a weekend.

Jerry Shaw's suggestions about angling for grayling, however, did not improve our luck either. So he took us out on the lake in a small motor skiff, from which we at least landed a couple of pikes before the thick swarms of vicious insects drove us back to shore, because neither of us had remembered to bring the mosquito dope along.

Camping at Swift River the next day, we cooked up the last of our pikes for dinner. I also had found some mushrooms, but while I was preparing them, Neal asked, "What kind of mushrooms are those?" That was a question I couldn't answer, since I had forgotten the name for those mushrooms in German and I never had known it in English. All I knew was that I ate those mushrooms before, but that did not satisfy my friends and I had to eat all the mushrooms by myself. Jerry at least promised me a proper burial after I would croak, but to the surprise or the disappointment of my friends, I was still alive and well on the following morning.

This day being a very windy one, we drove for 35 miles along Teslin Lake, whose total length I can't remember. During a conversation with a gas station attendant, we were informed that the lake was inhabited by twenty to twenty-five kinds of fish. This would have been useful information under different circumstances, but due to the windy weather, it would have been senseless to try our luck fishing.

A little later, we stopped in Whitehorse, but only long enough for our blueberry pie and coffee. Afterwards, we drove only nine miles farther, to Marsh Lake, to get away from the big city atmosphere.

This time, it was my turn to be surprised when I returned to camp after a little exploration of our surroundings, because my friends had put up a birthday table for me. If it would have been my birthday, it wouldn't have been much of a surprise to me, but it was one day too early. My companions knew that, but their excuse was that they had already purchased a new handle for my hatchet and that they were afraid that on the next day, when we planned to return to Whitehorse to do our laundry, I would buy my own hatchet handle. I accepted their explanation, but I had the suspicion that my dear friends just needed a reason to bring the whiskey bottle back out to wet their whistles.

By the time we had done all our chores in the city the following day, most of the day was gone and we drove only fifty miles out of town to an established campground and called it a day. There Neal, and Jerry got into a conversation with some guy who was returning from Alaska, and they listened to a lot of tall stories about the sky-high grocery prices to which we had to look forward to.

If I liked it or not, the vote was two to one, and so we visited Whitehorse for the third time on the following day to buy some bulk staples. Not only was I reminded of our badly planned train trip through Mexico, but later, we also found out that the price scare was totally unfounded.

In Whitehorse, Canada

After making camp that evening, I explored our camp surroundings as I often did, because up to this point we had not encountered any big game since entering Canada and I was anxious to at least catch a glimpse of a moose or a bear. I found a sign of big game all right, in the form of a skeleton of a killed or starved moose and had to chuckle to myself when I planned to tell my companions about the starving Wildlife of the north. At that moment, I almost became big game myself, when a hunter obviously mistook me for a bear and started sneaking up on me. I took cover and started to whistle until I saw the man relax and lower his weapon. Then I stood up and greeted him with a hello!

"I hoped you might be a bear!" said the hunter, showing clear disappointment.

"No, thanks!" I hollered down to him, "I like myself for what I am." We both laughed and went on our way.

Silver City used to be a wagon train stopover along the way to Dawson City on the Yukon River from 1904 to 1924 and it also was used as the headquarters for the Royal Mounted Police for some time. But by the time we visited the place in 1967, all that was left of it were a few crumbling log houses by the shore of Kluane Lake.

Silver City, Canada

As we left this historical curiosity, we started counting the many ground squirrels along the roadside. These animals usually would stand near or on the road in upright position until our truck got too close to them. Then, with a flip of their short tail and a shrill whistle, they would vanish into their nearby dens.

One of these squirrels decided to be different. It stood right in the middle of our pass and showed no sign of wanting to surrender its position.

"Tough guy!" said Neal, and slowed down the truck until El Beasty came to a halt, only about six feet from the animal. Carefully, I started to roll down the window, in the hope to get a picture of the little hero. But at that moment, a sharp whistle, a flip with its tail, and off toward its den it went.

"Either the animal was nearsighted," said Jerry, "or he had a bet with his friends that he could stop a truck!"

"Yea," answered Neal, "and a dummy like me fell for it!"

Technically, El Beasty had kept up its part of the bargain as we pulled up at the first Alaskan coffee shop. This old truck had brought us to where we wanted to go and only with one flat tire along the way. It was time to celebrate with blueberry pie and coffee.

So, we parked and Neal got out, then Jerry got out, but I seemed to be stuck for some reason. Only after some extra efforts was I able to break loose and climb out of the vehicle. That was when we established that I must have had picked up some tar while I sat down somewhere at the border crossing to take a picture. I didn't feel like digging for a pair of fresh pants in the camper, but neither could I go and sit in the coffee shop with the tar on my pants.

"Bend over!" said Neal and, without hesitation, he pulled his Bowie Knife to scrape the tar off my rear end. Jerry, in the meantime, got a gasoline moistened rag and finished the job.

"That dumb s.o.b. can't even wipe his own butt!" he remarked jokingly.

"When you have servants," I answered, "why do the dirty work yourself?"

"Right," said Neal, "and now you may pay your servants by buying us some pie!"

Still joking around, we approached the coffee shop and became aware of a car full of tourists who had been watching us all that time with amusement, all the while being unaware of the fact that we were spreading joy among our fellowmen.

Chapter 7
End of a Carefree Summer

Now that we had arrived in Alaska, we planned to drive to Fairbanks. But before driving right back into human society again, we needed to spend a couple of days to fix and clean some of our gear as well as the inside of El Beasty.

After buying our Alaska fishing and small game hunting license in the town of Tok, we pulled off the highway into a wooded trail at the little Gerstle River and made camp.

The idea that our trip and with it the fun of a free and careless life was nearing its end was something that started only slowly to sink in. The thought of reentering civilization also seemed to bring on some tension, especially between Jerry and Neal. I had the feeling since the beginning of our trip that Neal really wasn't too enthusiastic about taking Jerry along, but I hoped to be wrong about it. In Neal's mind, an alliance with other people generally had to be of some advantage to him, like for instance my companionship, which came with a lot of outdoor ability. In Jerry's case, Neal looked upon him more like an extra fun to have around when all went well, but in no way necessary. While Neal always had very strong opinions, Jerry in his independent ways was always ready to listen and learn, but did not like to be dependent on others in any way, or feel like a second fiddle to anybody else.

Fully aware that neither one of us was perfect, I tried to be more diplomatic and tolerant toward either one of my friends while ignoring Neal's superiority complex. I treated Jerry always as an equal; after all, we all were individuals and loners in our own ways, but we certainly had enough in common and should have enough intelligence to work things out between us.

The camp we had chosen as our first camp in Alaska was practically surrounded by raspberry bushes loaded with ripe fruit, of which we certainly would make good use.

Neal and I had gotten up early to see if we could find some kind of camp meat. Fishing had been already ruled out, because the Little Gerstle River was at flood stage and fish don't bite when the water rises. The only game we encountered on our little excursion were tree squirrels, of which there seemed to be one or two of these animals in every big spruce tree. So, we started shooting squirrels, which had been on our menu before. Enough of these little critters in the split pea soup would make a mighty fine meal. Returning to our camp and looking forward to our meal, we also hoped that Jerry had picked enough of the wild raspberries for our dessert. Jerry, however, was just getting up as we arrived and apparently had not picked any raspberries. To me, that was not a big deal, but Neal, who, for some reason, was already in a bad mood, started to argue with Jerry. I had an idea that Neal's anger flare up had little or nothing to do neither with the unpicked berries nor with Jerry. More likely, it was the fact that Neal had become brutally aware of the fact, just as I did, that we had arrived at our destiny, were out of financial resources, and had no prospects or plans for our immediate future.

At any case, I knew Jerry well enough to know that he is not the most forgiving person on the planet, and, therefore, I was pretty sure that irreparable damage had been done to whatever friendship had existed between my companions.

It was not until we ate our squirrel stew that night before the camp atmosphere was somewhat back to normal and even some jokes were told. Some mushrooms I had picked on that day were even eaten and appreciated by my companions.

Right after Delta Junction, on our way toward Fairbanks, we crossed a small bridge. Near the bridge stood a high-water marker, submerged in the flood of that creek except for the uppermost part, on which some joker had written the words "TOO DAMN HIGH!"

High water in the Tanana River 1967

From the looks of the Tanana Valley to the left of us, the joker certainly was right. The whole valley looked like an endless mangrove swamp, with only treetops here and there sticking out of the water. Reaching Harding Lake, we had the feeling that we were driving into a refugee encampment, and the reason for that was that the road to Fairbanks was closed because a couple bridges had been washed out. We were told that even Fairbanks itself was partially flooded, and that it might take two weeks after the water starts receding before the road to Fairbanks would be open again. That was not what we needed. Camping for two weeks at that spot with a bunch of disgruntled travelers was nothing we were willing to endure. We turned El Beasty around and drove back toward Delta Junction, but when it started to get dark, we turned into a dirt road toward the Clear water campground.

"What the hell was that?" asked Neal, as he stepped on the brakes, almost sending us into the windshield. Jerry and I had seen it, too, but it took us a few seconds to realize that we just had encountered our first big game in Alaska as two moose crossed the road in front of us.

Contrary to our expectation, the campground was totally empty, which was surprising but welcome. In the morning, we could see many good-size grayling swimming in the creek and I wouldn't have minded at all to stay in that camp for a couple of days and fish. But since my two friends were in no mood for fishing, the vote was two to one. Overnight, Jerry had in fact decided that he wanted to be dropped off at the town of Delta Junction and start taking his future in his own hands from there. Neal probably would have been glad to get rid of Jerry, but seemed to feel some remorse about his behavior toward him and talked Jerry into sticking it out till we got to Anchorage via the Glen Highway.

We barely had pulled out of the campground road when Neal once more hit the brake, backed up the truck a few feet, and asked, "Buffalo what?"

"That's what it says," answered Jerry as he read the sign, "Buffalo crossing!"

There was another thing we didn't know about: Alaska actually harbored several herds of wild-running buffaloes.

Anchorage Alaska 1967

Matanuska Glacier

The community of Delta Junction in 1967 was so small that even Jerry had to admit that his chances to find a job there would have been less than slim. Therefore, he gave in to Neal's and my urging to stick with us for now. In Delta Junction, we turned right, onto the Glen Highway toward Anchorage. The scenery along the roadway was as pretty as a postcard. Mountains and glaciers provided the right background for a few more moose encounters, and while driving through some mountain passes, we even encountered some Dall sheep. After this display of wilderness, there seemed to be a sudden increase of homesteads and small communities and before we knew it, we found ourselves in the middle of Anchorage, the biggest town in Alaska.

To find ourselves in a city of that size was quite a shocking experience. We felt totally out of place and eventually decided to turn around, drive back for fifteen miles, and make camp at the community of Eagle River. We parked El Beasty at the Eagle River Campground and called it home for the time being.

Food was not an immediate problem for us at that point and the camping weather would most likely hold out a while longer. But there was no doubt about it that winter would come sooner or later and make living out of the camper impossible, which meant that we had to find jobs.

Jerry, still driven to be on his own and to get away from Neal, was the first of us to hitchhike to town and look for a job. As for Neal and me, we still were not quite acclimatized to a change in our lifestyle and strolled along the Eagle River to mentally prepare ourselves for whatever changes may lay ahead. Somehow, we found ourselves in front of a bar, on the other side of the highway from the campground.

"How much money you got?" asked Neal, digging in his own pocket for some change.

I found a few coins in my pockets and into the bar we went for a beer. The room was almost empty as we sat down and I laid the hatchet, which I had playfully carried along, next to me on the bar.

Recognizing us right away as newcomers to the state, the bartender asked where we were from. We gave him a Reader's Digest version of our trip while we drank our beer; then the bartender refilled our glasses for free and said, "Welcome to Alaska!"

Dressed in leather shirts, with long hairs and beards, we soon attracted some of the newly arriving patrons of the place and had to retell our story a couple more times, while the free beers kept on coming. We were in deep conversation with some of the other guests while nursing our fourth or fifth beer, when the bartender took my hatchet off the bar and smilingly said to me, "I'll keep it safe for you!"

It must have been at least midnight before we left the establishment, and neither one of us was anywhere near being sober. Neal didn't even want to walk all the way back to the camper anymore; instead, he wanted to sleep in the bushes near the road. Several times, I had to pull him back onto the road, while he argued that we would not be able to find our camper anyway. When I finally had convinced him that we didn't have much farther to go, he started hollering into the night, "Jerreee! Jerreee!"

Jerry did not answer, but he certainly was amused about our condition, especially when it took us a few more spills and giggles before we climbed into the camper and eventually went to sleep.

I woke up with a raging headache, and, by the looks of things, Neal couldn't have felt much better than I. Jerry clued us in about our comical stunts of the night before and then he told us about his first unsuccessful search to find work. He also had found the address of my old-time friend, Karl Engelke, who lived in Anchorage at the time. But Karl was not home and Jerry had left a note on his door, to explain where we could be found.

That same afternoon, Karl and his fiancée, Marlyse, came to visit us and invited us to dinner, but as far as work was concerned, Karl couldn't be of any help to us either.

A couple of days later, we got a surprise visit from a Don Muetz and his family. Neal and I eventually remembered faintly that we had met Don at the night we got drunk on our last pocket change. Again, we were invited and were offered a chance to shower, shave, and even get a haircut if we wanted it.

After Neal was all cleaned up and had his hair cut, he looked awfully unfamiliar and funny to me. Somehow, it was almost a painful process to go through such a radical change within such a short time and all of that just to fit back into society again. But one thing was clear even to us; by the time it was over, we certainly had improved our chances to find work.

Don explained to us afterwards that he had some property nearby with an old empty trailer home on it and if we would fix it up a little, we would be welcome to use it until we found something better. How was that for luck? Naturally, we thankfully accepted this offer and soon we moved into our new home.

For the next two weeks, we improved our temporary abode, searched for jobs, and hunted grouse and squirrels in the surrounding woods in order to get some meat on our plates. It was the first time for me that something positive came out of getting drunk and every time I think about it since, I'm left with a shameful feeling that, because as far as I know, none of us ever thanked Don Muetz and family for helping us out during that time. I'm sure that none of my companions had made a greater attempt to keep in contact with the Muetz family; that idea just got buried in our individual battles to start a new life in Alaska, but it should not be an excuse for such an oversight.

Neal had been the first to find a job, when he became a salesman at the Stewart's Photo Shop in Anchorage and moved in with his newly befriended coworker somewhere in town.

I don't quite remember how soon after that Jerry moved out, or what kind of work he had found. I only know that Jerry got somewhat serious with the daughter of his next landlord and eventually, he got married to her. But before Jerry got married, I had lived at his place for a short time in order to be nearer to town. When my old friend Karl Engelke and his fiancée got married as well and went on their honeymoon to Europe, I moved into Karl's trailer home right at the outskirts of Anchorage and found a job as a helper at an Anchorage upholstery firm. But just as I expected, the employment only lasted for about two weeks before I got laid off again.

So I tried to get something closer to my profession as a glassblower and contacted the only manufacturer of neon signs in Anchorage. Their business was not exactly thriving at that time and they were more in need of a designer for their neon signs, rather than in need of another glassblower. Designing neon signs was not totally outside of my ability, but in order to work there, I also would have had to join the electricians' union. Since I'm not much of joiner and couldn't afford the high union fee, especially for just a part-time job, that idea fell through as well.

With winter upon us by then, I was thankful not to live far out of town and therefore was able to generate some income in any way I could without owning a vehicle. Posing as a commercial artist, I painted signs and murals on the walls of bars or even at the cantina of the nearby Air Force base. The strangest job I was asked to do was to paint a tiger on the wall of some lady's bathroom. Today, I'm still not totally convinced that the tiger painting on her bathroom wall was the only reason for my invitation to her house, but that was all she got for her money. In this way, I made it through my first winter in Alaska.

During that time, I also had found a more or less steady girlfriend. But when spring arrived, so did my thirst for adventure.

Karl and his wife had returned from Germany and Karl suggested that this was the right time for me to try and get a real job with the oil companies. He might have been right, but I couldn't see myself working at a job I had no interest in, nor talent or qualifications for, or even respected. As an adventurer and lover of wilderness, I looked at oil companies as an adversary and promoter of civilization.

While my two companions with whom I had come to Alaska were more or less back into a similar situation which they had planned to escape from, I felt that I owed it to myself at least to see some more of Alaska before making any plans to settle down. So I bought the foldboat from my friend Horst in California, which he had offered to me for a price I couldn't pass up. Then I would somehow get to the Yukon River near the Canadian border and paddle down the Yukon from there.

At an evening on the town with my girl friend Alice, an Eskimo girl from Nome, Alaska, I explained my plans to her and then asked her kind of jokingly, if she wouldn't rather quit her job at the post office and come along than stick with her postal career. When she decided enthusiastically to accompany me on my adventure instead, I almost fell from my bar stool.

2nd Avenue, Anchorage Alaska 1967-1968

Chapter 8
My Childhood Dream Becomes Reality

Alice did in fact quit her job at the post office and was now included in my summer adventure plans. By the time the foldboat had arrived from California, we also had adopted a Husky pup, whom I named Minado. The name for the dog means "demon" according to some Indian story I had read sometime, somewhere. That name turned out quite fitting for the animal in the future.

Besides the boat and the dog, we had accumulated quite a bit of equipment we thought useful or necessary for our adventure at that time. As soon as the weather was warm enough, we moved to the (to me) already familiar Eagle River Campground and lived in our tent, while testing our gear and making sure we wouldn't overlook anything of importance. Then we arranged a good-bye party for our friends, which at the same time was supposed to be our engagement party. When a heavy thunderstorm crashed our festivities prematurely, it struck me almost like an omen, either concerning our planned trip, or for my union with Alice. Well, it was merely a fleeting thought, because there was nothing which would have changed my mind at this point for either case.

By the end of May, 1968, we thought to be ready for takeoff, but, as usual, some technicality of which I cannot recall the details delayed our departure till June 8.

The bus to Tok Junction 1968

On this date, Neal arrived with El Beasty at our camp to load all our gear and drive us to his place for a good bye dinner. Afterwards, we spent the evening in discussions of what might lay ahead for us, while we drank a few coffee royals until the late hours.

Early in the morning, Neal drove us to the bus station in downtown Anchorage, where we encountered our first unforeseen problem. We had no kennel for our puppy and neither did the bus company. Since Minado had to ride in the luggage compartment, he was supposed to be in a kennel, but the best substitute we could come up with at this time in the morning was a sturdy cardboard box, which we had found in a dumpster in a nearby alley. Then it was time to say good bye to Neal. We thanked him for his help and he wished us good luck for our adventure.

A short time later, we sat in our upholstered seats and admired the spring-time scenery along the way. Now and then, we could hear the whimpers of our puppy from below in the luggage compartment. At the halfway point on our way to Tetlin Junction, we were allowed to let the dog out for a short time and discovered that he had long since chewed his way out of his cardboard prison. Since this particular luggage compartment was filled with our gear only, we were allowed to lock Minado back in there without a box for the rest of the way.

The whole trip from Anchorage until we arrived at our destination in Tetlin Junction took a total of twelve hours, but this was also as near as we could get to the Yukon River by public transportation. From Tetlin Junction, we had another 161 miles of dusty field road to travel, before we would get our boat into the water at the village of Eagle.

With our 400 pounds of gear, we certainly could not continue on foot. Our only alternative was to hitchhike. The fact that not many vehicles drove in our direction was further complicated by our enormous pile of gear. The vehicle that would give us a ride needed to be a pickup or a van with enough room for all our stuff.

It wasn't totally unexpected that we had to spend our first night next to that road in between our packages and bundles, which we had arranged into a windbreak. But we went to sleep that night with high hopes for the following day.

In the morning, as soon as the nearby coffee shop was open, we left our belongings under the watchful eyes of our dog and went for breakfast. Returning to our stressful task of watching and waiting for a possible ride, we kept our eyes on a gas station along the highway. It was about noon when I took a picture of a red pickup, which just had stopped at that gas station. In response to Alice's questioning look and to keep up her spirit, I told her that we might want that picture of the truck that took us to the river.

To our surprise, the truck turned our way and stopped to pick us up. As soon as we were on our way, Alice asked, "Why didn't you start taking pictures earlier?"

"Well, the red truck wasn't there earlier!" I answered.

Even though this particular truck took us only halfway and dropped us off on a turnoff to a gold mine or something like that, we didn't give up hope while we sat there in what could truly have been called "nowhere." Soon, a dust cloud appeared in the distance and our second transport had arrived.

It was quite a bumpy ride and I don't remember how many hours it took to get to the village or small town of Eagle. It was about midnight when we pitched our tent only a few feet from the river and next to the main street in Eagle, on the church lawn. While Alice wanted to catch up on her sleep, I was too restless and fired up and I went to work on putting our boat together.

In Tok

In the morning, we put the boat into the water and loaded it with our belongings almost to the limit of its capacity and tied Minado up next to it, while we made a final round through town to mail some letters, buy a few small items, and visit a couple of historic sites.

In 1898, the gold fever had brought 3,000 people to Eagle. At the time we were at the settlement, there was only a fraction of that population living there. It was from this town of Eagle, from which Roald Amundsen in 1906 telegraphed his message about his discovery of the Northwest Passage to the outside world. The cabin in which he had lived for a while was still standing during our visit.

Most of the inhabitants of Eagle seemed to be of Caucasian descent, but we were told that a Native village was located three miles farther up river. We, however, were planning to head downriver and I was anxious to get started. The moment had arrived for us to make discoveries of our own and start our adventure. In 1968, it was not yet a common thing to have people traveling the mighty Yukon in a canoe or a fold boat, and, for that reason, we had a lot of onlookers and well-wishers around us as we pushed our boat off shore under a cloudless sky and waved good-bye to our audience. This really was the moment my childhood dreams had turned into reality.

The full length of the Yukon River would have been more like 2,300 miles, but we figured that 1,875 miles, which we now had ahead of us, were enough river miles to cover during the short Alaskan summer. After all, it was not our goal to eat up the miles or win a race. The idea for me was to be out in the wilderness, away from civilization, and self-reliant, a situation I always had wished for.

We barely were out of sight from Eagle when we saw the first moose wandering along the riverbank. The animal probably enjoyed the cool air in between the leftover ice blocks which kept the bothersome mosquito swarms to a minimum. Getting to see our first big game right at the beginning of our river trip seemed to be a good sign, but we were surprised to still see the big muddy ice blocks along the riverbank during this time of the year, especially since it was quite hot on the river.

Our dog, Minado, had not been aware of the moose, since he was half asleep lying on top of our gear. Then he stretched himself, rolled over, and promptly fell into the icy waters of the river. I had the dog tied up on his chain and quickly pulled him back on to the boat. To thank me for my quick reaction, he shook himself and gave me a refreshing shower.

This incident made me realize how much of our safety and our survival was now dependant on my knowledge and ability. Any wrong decision could spell disaster for either one, or all of us.

At my estimation, the river was at this place about one mile wide, but we paddled closer to shore, not so much for safety reasons; rather than that, we wanted to have a better view of the shoreline and hopefully encounter some wildlife. A small stand of tall spruce trees made an inviting stop for us to stretch a leg and follow nature's call. Trying to live off the land as much as possible, I kept my eyes on the trees, to shoot a squirrel for Minado's dinner. All the while, the dog was running freely up and down the shore, getting his well-deserved exercise. When he heard me shoot and discovered me in between the trees, he ran straight toward me, paying no attention to a water-filled ditch covered with dry floating leaves. There was a big splash and a surprised yelp as Minado took his second bath for the day.

Beginning our river trip

Alice, in the meantime, had discovered bear tracks along the shore and I found out how afraid my fiancée was of these animals. When it came to making camp that night, it was to my companion's great relief that we had found a small island with a good oversight in all directions. It wasn't only that Alice felt safer there from the bears, but a warm breeze also kept down the mosquitoes on that island. Because of the warm weather, we didn't even bother setting up our tent that night and just slept on our blankets.

"What are those?" Alice asked, as some finger-long, green insects landed all around us.

I had to admit that I wasn't sure. These insects looked like caddis flies, but I never saw any at that size, nor that colorful. Later, we actually identified them as Giant Stone Flies, commonly called fish flies by the natives.

During our second day on the river, some deserted settlements attracted our attention. The first of these settlements, according to our outdated map, should have been the old village of Nation. The whole place was overgrown with high grass and brush, so that from afar, only the gables of the buildings were visible. While some of the cabins and sheds were near collapse, others were still in useable shape with tools and tubs hanging on the walls of the porches. In one cabin, we found a pan on the stove and plates with mummified food rests still sticking to them on the table. The only living soul we encountered in this ghost village was an exited squirrel on a collapsed shed, which strongly protested our presence.

Minado says, "Nobody Home"

Some big, old, decaying boats lying in the willows near the beach led to our discovery of a second deserted village. The trails in between the buildings still seemed to be well traveled and most of the cabins or even the sheds were locked. Since Alice claimed that this place gave her the creeps, I kept our exploration of this place to a minimum....

Okay—fear of bears, the creeps at deserted places, what would be next?

I never had encountered a bear in the wild either, but I respect any animal especially in the wild, but fear would have and should have been a good reason for me or anybody to stay home in civilization.

We hadn't paddled much farther when our first encounter with a bear or bears was upon us. Two black bears were grazing on a hillside. Pointing the animals out to Alice, I said, "Look there, a couple of your friends!"

Because the animals were far enough away, plus the fact that we were in our boat on the water, Alice's reaction was not what I would have expected. She looked at them and replied in a cool and collected manner, "That's the distance at which I don't mind seeing them."

Bears, however, seemed never far from my companion's mind and, therefore, she was very happy when we found an unlocked trapper's cabin to spend the night in.

On the following evening, we again found some signs of human activity when it was time to make camp, but there were no buildings at all, it was just a well established camp spot, next to a clear-running stream.

Since we couldn't ask for a better spot, we made camp there and spent a peaceful night.

In the morning, however, the excitement started when I was loading up our boat. I was on my way back from the boat to the camp, when Minado rushed past me from behind and I noticed Alice's scared expression as she called out to me, "Look Wolf, a wolf!"

My Winchester just happened to be within reach of me, leaning against a tree to my right. I grabbed the rifle while I turned to look. A few feet behind me stood a wolf, and in a split second, I had the rifle on my shoulder and fired. The animal fell dead and all danger, if there ever was any, seemed to be over. A little later, when I had time to think it all over, I felt rather ashamed for having been so quick on the trigger. At the time, the thought of protecting my travel companions, or at least to prevent Minado from being killed, had led me to act the way I did, but the eyes of that obviously young, inexperienced wolf expressed nothing more than surprise. I certainly didn't feel threatened by it and it was the animal's bad luck that I was as inexperienced as the young animal itself.

Well, it was too late to change anything about it now, so I went to work and skinned the wolf. At that time, there was still a fifty-dollar bounty on the wolves in Alaska, which, in spite of it all, would come in handy for us.

Still within sight of the last camp, a cow moose with calf swam toward us from across the river, but when the animals became aware of us, they turned around and crossed the river once more. It was almost as if they just wanted to make sure about who or what we were.

During the occasional stop along the way, we could only marvel at the quantity and variety of animal tracks in the area, but since many of these tracks were bear tracks, Alice got so nervous about it that I found it hard to talk her into making camp anywhere. My fiancée insisted on another small island, without much brush or trees.

"Bears can swim, too!" I couldn't help teasing her.

To find an island to Alice's specification was easier said than done. Finding a good camp spot was often hard enough without preconditions. In spite of my aching arms, I paddled on until Alice pointed to an island ahead of us, which seemed to be covered by only shoulder-high willow brush. "This one seems to be a good one!" she called out to me and I was certainly ready to oblige her. I steered our boat straight toward the island until we were about twenty yards away from it. At that point, I had noticed a yellowish lump in the middle of all the willow brush and before I could voice my suspicion, a fair size grizzly stood up to his full height, looking at our approach with intense interest.

While I started digging for my camera, Alice reached behind her, grabbed my paddle, and started paddling as fast as she could.

"What's the matter?" I teased her. "I thought you wanted to camp on this island?"

"Are you nuts?" Alice answered almost angrily.

"Then where would madam like to bivouac tonight?" I kept hacking on her, knowing very well that I would have a long night of paddling ahead of me.

The sun vanished behind the hills for a short time, which indicated to us that it must have been midnight when my hurting arms got a well-deserved break from paddling. A porcupine was walking the shoreline and porcupines were on our grocery list. Alice still wasn't ready to leave the safety of the boat, but I could persuade her to grab some branches to hold the boat in place while I got out. Picking up a strong piece of driftwood, I hunted down my prey. After securing the slain porcupine behind me on the boat, where Minado couldn't reach it, I climbed back aboard and we paddled on.

A couple miles farther down, we saw a campfire on the opposite side of the river.

Many miles of the Yukon lay before us

"Would you like to go visiting?" I asked Alice, in the hope to finally getting a chance to rest my arms. When she agreed, I ask her to dig out her own paddle and start paddling, if she wanted to reach the other shore before we passed the camp. In spite of our determination, we soon had to admit that we wouldn't make it in time, the current was too strong. Our efforts to reach the other side of the river were noticed, and soon we heard a motorboat start up and saw it coming toward us.

After we landed with the help from the motorboat in front of that campfire, Minado was the first on land and showed us his instinct for self-preservation by running straight toward a frying pan near the fire and helping himself to a portion of fried duck. Luckily, our hosts were amused by the action of our dog, as he headed with part of their meal into the near brush. The three young Indians at this camp, Jack, Al, and Paul, were from Circle City, about another twenty miles farther downriver. The boys had been looking for a bear to shoot, but up to this point they were unsuccessful.

We introduced ourselves and answered some questions about our plans, while we were served hot coffee, which we gratefully accepted.

The trio had made camp to wait for the sun to reappear from behind the mountains before driving farther up river in the hopes to find their bear. But while we still were all waiting together, I butchered and cooked the porcupine I had hunted down and then invited our hosts to join us and we all ate the tasty meal. Even our thieving dog ate some more of the less palatable parts and bones of my prey.

Then we drank more coffee until the sun reappeared, and our hosts invited us to go along on the bear hunt. We probably should have tried to sleep, but in between all that coffee and the experience of a motorboat ride, we decided on joining them. While it was interesting to us to go upriver and see the landscape from a different perspective, the only bears we encountered were a grizzly sow and her cub. I don't know if our new friends would have tried to shoot them as well or not, but I was glad that the animals had enough sense to take flight early.

Returning to the original camp, the boys figured on hunting for black bears on the way home and asked us to come along again. Since the motorboat wouldn't be able to go fast enough while pulling our boat without endangering it, we loaded it and our gear on to the motorboat on the way toward Circle City.

Around the next river bend, Al hollered from the bow of the boat, "A bear, a bear!"

Sure enough, a big black bear was walking the beach without paying any attention to us.

Jack steered the boat straight toward the animal, while the other two boys started firing. This actually was an illegal action, but as we later found out, it seemed to be common hunting practice of the natives in Alaska.

By the time the boat ground up on to the gravel beach, the bear had run up a steep, brushy hillside. We all agreed that the animal must have been mortally wounded and Al took his rifle to go and search for it, but Al climbed that hill somewhat to one side from where the bear had climbed it to get a better vantage point, just in case the bear was still alive.

For a short time, we could hear Al climbing and then there was the sound of breaking branches, followed by absolute silence. When our calls for Al remained unanswered, the other two boys started getting a little nervous about the situation.

"I really don't like the idea of following that bear with a rifle up that hill through all that brush," said Paul, and his partner Jack didn't seem too enthusiastic about it either.

I could see where a rifle would be somewhat cumbersome under those circumstances and therefore I suggested that I should go with my 44-caliber handgun to see what the situation was.

"Be careful!" warned Alice, like she really needed to tell me that.

For me, this was a totally new game, but in spite of the inherent danger, I felt fairly sure about what I was doing. With the revolver in hand and ready, I climbed up that hill, stopping every few feet to listen for any heavy breathing noises of the possibly mortally wounded bear. Finally, I saw the hind paw of the animal sticking out of the brush above and somewhat to the left of me. Again I listened, but I only could hear my own heartbeat. Taking a deep breath, I cocked my revolver and tugged on that paw. This caused the dead animal to roll down the hill, until it came to a halt in front of my companions.

We had the bear, but where the heck was Al?

The other two Indians started skinning the bear, when we finally heard Al climbing on the hillside and Paul hollered up to him, "What the hell are you doing up there? The bear is down here!"

"I'm looking for his wallet!" Al returned in good humor and without hesitation. Once he was back down on level ground, the boys got into a slight squabble over "who really killed the bear." In the hope to prevent an all-out argument, I suggested that the bear had been alive until I caused it to roll down the hill and he broke his neck. That made everybody laugh and the boys came somehow to terms with it. As it turned out, the skin of the animal was all the young hunters were interested in and I only took the liver and a good size roast for our needs.

A short time later, we pitched our tent at the riverbank right in front of Circle City. After a refreshing bath in the nearby slough, we retired to our shelter and finally got our long deserved sleep.

Leaving Eagle 1968

Indian with a black bear 1968

Chapter 9
Up the Creek without a Paddle

A waking refreshed in Circle City, we cooked up our bear meat and liver
to fill our own and Minado's hungry belly. Then we made a list of things
to be done before continuing our trip, which included sending the wolf fur
to the proper authorities. For the next three days, we washed clothes, mended
what had to be mended, sent out some personal mail, and did a little shopping for necessities. Knowing that this town, as so many other settlements
along the Yukon, had its start as a gold mining camp, we also tried our luck
with the gold pan along the riverbank. Sure, we found a few grains of gold,

but it took many a pan, many hours, and a sore back to come up with the tiny flakes, barely visible in a small vial of water. The profitability to mine the gold in this area had long since expired, and all that was left of these glorious times was some rusty machinery standing there like abstract sculptures, silhouetted against the midnight sun.

In spite of some threatening, scattered rain clouds, the Yukon beckoned us. The wide expanse of the so-called Yukon Flats lay now before us, a basin of many river channels, sloughs, and islands, 180 miles in length and 70 miles wide. There were no more mountain chains or bluffs on either side of the river to follow and no more clear streams to camp beside. Instead, there were steep cut-banks with layers of frozen earth and trees threatening to fall on anybody passing too close to shore. Submerged drift logs and strange currents and eddies had to be taken in consideration as well. Sand and gravel bars appeared when we least expected them, and sudden winds would come up while we were crossing the wider parts of open water, creating high waves with whitecaps.

By the time we had left Circle City, it was already afternoon and outside of a couple of sprinkles, we were lucky with the weather. Knowing that the next settlement, Fort Yukon, would be to the right of us, we held to that side as much as possible without entering into any dead-end sloughs, or narrow winding channels, which might take us on long detours far inland. Palatable drinking water was not easy to come by, since the water from the ponds and lakes was stained by the rotting plant material. Even boiling the water didn't improve the taste of it. The best water turned out to be the river water left behind in the depressions of the gravel bars, where the silt had settled out. And if we felt like it, we even took a bath in these sun-warmed ponds after filling our drink-water containers.

In search of a good camp spot, we went through one of the narrower sloughs. Right at the entrance of the slough, we were greeted by a whole group of fledging great horned owls. They all sat on a dead tree looking at us with great curiosity as we paddled by. Toward the end of that slough, Alice pointed toward something afloat in front of us, which I at first thought to be a beaver dragging willow branches. But as we got closer, we saw a young owl in between some branches, with its wings spread on the water. I rescued the bird by scooping it out of the water with our fishnet and then wrapped it into a towel.

After we made camp at the end of that slough, the bird didn't look too good and I decided to keep it warm in a dry towel for the night. In the morning, the owl was sitting on top of its blanket, where the sun shone into the tent, but I didn't think that the bird was ready to fly and take care of itself. The right thing to do would probably have been to paddle back up the slough and deliver the bird to that family of owls, to which it most likely belonged, but my fascination with the owl didn't even let that thought enter my mind in time. Instead, I constructed tethers from a leather thong and gave the bird a place of honor on the bow of our boat. Alice laughed about it and said, "Pretty soon, we'll look like a traveling circus."

Time for a bath

On this day, we also expected to reach Fort Yukon, but before we saw any sign of it, we heard a strange, haunting noise coming from across the river and Alice asked, "What is that?"

Old trapping camp

Fishwheel

It almost sounded like a particularly sad loon to me, but then we discovered the source of these mournful cries. Across the river channel from us, a fish wheel obviously was turning on an axle which had not been properly greased, but its presence was a sign to us that we must be reasonably close to Fort Yukon.

A fish wheel is a contraption which had been used in China since at least the last 5,000 years already, and I was told later on that a Dutchman might have introduced this unique device to the North American continent. It consists of a raft, which carries from two to four wire baskets on an axle. The raft is anchored to the shore at a spot where the water depth and the currents are favorable. The current of the river then turns the baskets on the axle in a windmill fashion and scoops the upstream running fish out of the river. From the baskets, the fish slide into a collection box on the raft, where the fisherman will collect them twice a day. The trick in catching fish with this device, particularly salmon, is to know the right spot where to place the fish wheel and how to adjust the baskets according to the depth of the river.

The town of Eagle on the Yukon

Soon after the discovery of the fish wheel, our foldboat was gliding under a blood red sky on the glass smooth surface of the river toward the silhouettes of Fort Yukon. It was midnight again, but nevertheless, we were greeted by several children and some loose dogs at the shore. Out of consideration for our own animals and the possibility of sticky fingers, we decided to paddle across a bay and set up camp away from all the hoopla. In the morning, I visited the town alone, to check for mail at the post office and to get drinking water from a public well.

Located eight miles north of the Arctic Circle, Fort Yukon started out as a trading post for the Hudson Bay Company in 1847, but by 1968, it was well established as an Athapaskan Indian village with about 700 inhabitants.

Because of the heat of the day and the many swallows, which feasted on the swarms of mosquitoes, it was hard to come to terms with the thought that we were so far north, or to imagine winter temperatures down to minus 70 degrees Fahrenheit.

Two days later, we paddled on and passed the mouth of the Porcupine River, which is one of the larger tributaries of the Yukon. All signs of human activities were behind us again and we started encountering more and more waterfowl, from ducks to geese and cranes. The geese seemed to be especially watchful. They spotted our little craft from more than a mile away, walked slowly to the edge of the water while starting to cackle. At first, only a few birds started cackling, then more and more geese joined in, stretching their necks higher and higher, until suddenly the whole flock took flight under an almost deafening honking noise.

On one of these occasions, we saw how one of the birds, right after takeoff, splashed back into the water and got left behind.

"There is our next dinner!" I said to Alice as I steered the boat into the direction of the disabled goose. But as soon as we got close enough to it for me to take a shot at it with my 22-caliber rifle, the bird dived and came up behind us.

"So, that's the way you want to play it?" I mumbled more or less to myself, and gave chase. I paddled forth and back and every time, the bird dived just in time to save itself.

It was no easy task to keep track of my prey, but I was determined to eat that bird before a hawk or a fox would get it. As the diving times of that goose were getting shorter, I finally got the break I needed to shoot it.

By that time, Alice was in tears—no, not because she felt sorry for the bird, but from laughing too hard about my paddling and turning the boat.

"What's the matter with you?" I asked.

"It's you," she answered, "as fast as you paddled, you looked like one of those Disney cartoons!" and then she wiped her tears.

With our next dinner secured, we entered a slough and came upon an inviting gravel bar. The heat of the day under the cloudless sky and the exhaustion from my goose hunt was catching up with me. I needed a break, and Minado, too, announced his urgency for a pit stop and we pulled over.

When several Arctic Terns made diving attacks on Minado while he was doing his business, it became clear to us that this gravel bar was a breeding colony for these birds. Breeding colony or not, I was a little too tired to move; besides, we would had no plans to interfere with the birds. I pulled the foldboat two thirds up on to that gravel bar, unloaded a few things to get to our tent, and set it up to create some shade for us and our pets. Alice, in the meantime, had started the coffee water. As soon as I had placed George, the owl, on the shady site of the tent, Minado came running and made repeated attempts to invite the bird to play with him. But just as it had happened during his earlier attempts, Minado got a peck on the nose and from then on decided to leave that owl alone.

In spite of our coffee, we felt too tired to travel on during this heat and decided to wait for the cooler hours. Lying down on the floor of the bare open tent, we promptly fell asleep. I had no idea how long we might have been sleeping, but by the time I woke up and looked out of the tent. I couldn't believe my eyes. The shoreline was now only a few feet from our tent and where in hell was our boat?

"That's nuts!" I mumbled.

"What is it?" asked Alice in a sleepy voice.

"Our boat is gone!"

Believing that I was making a bad joke, Alice came to see for herself and came to the amazing conclusion that the water had risen.

"At least by two feet!" I replied, while getting out of the tent to look for our boat.

The boat was nowhere to be seen, but I hoped to find it hung up somewhere in the shallows. So I told Alice to stay put, and without waiting for her reply, I grabbed my Winchester and jogged along the beach. The nice gravel beach, however, ended soon at a fifteen-yard wide side slough, but there was our boat just ahead, drifting from the slower flowing water toward the faster current along the high cut bank. Without thinking twice about it, and self assured that I would get our boat back in a few minutes, I stepped out of my footwear and took off my pants, held my rifle up above my head, and waded into that stagnant ditch. About halfway across that slough, I became aware of a black bear and her cub, swimming toward the same point of land as I was heading for. The animals got there first, climbed ashore, shook the water out of their fur, and then watched my approach with interest. Not about to let a couple of bears stop me from getting my boat back, I shook my rifle at them and swore at them in German. It helped! The bears must have thought that I was crazy enough to attack them. They turned and ran into the woods along that same high cut bank I now had to follow myself, but my progress over fallen logs and through the wild rose bushes was far slower than that of the bears or my boat, which drifted now in the faster current along the high cut-bank.

It had been my experience that the boat with one or two persons in it would usually get hung up on the branches of submerged or overhanging trees unless it would be steered away from them. To my surprise, the empty boat avoided all obstacles, as if it was steered by remote control and was in no way slowed down.

Not to be able to gain on the boat gave me another bright idea; if I would swim where the boat was only floating, I should be able to catch up with it in that way. I after all always had been a good swimmer. So I leaned my Winchester against a tree, hung my T-shirt up as a marker, and jumped into the water, just to find out that the water was so cold that I was unable to breathe. I told myself that it was just my excitement which didn't let me breathe and gave it a second try. The result was the same and I had to return to shore. Still hoping that the boat might get hung up yet, I ran or rather limped along the riverbank a while longer and even crossed another muddy, stagnant ditch, but when my boat was no more than a dot on the water in the distance, I had to admit defeat.

While starting my way back to camp, my lungs were burning; I felt dizzy and became fully aware of my cut and bruised bare feet. Twice I had to climb down the cut bank to quench my thirst on the muddy Yukon water and the distance on the way back seemed a lot farther than I could remember. I was already afraid to have passed the tree where I had left my Winchester, when I finally saw my T-shirt hanging there. While my feet might have been hurting, what was hurting the most was my pride as a woodsman. Rising water or not, boat half out of the water or not, neither one was an excuse, I should have tied up the boat down nevertheless.

Crossing that ditch back over to the gravel bar where our camp was soothed the pain in my feet. I only put on my pants and carefully slipped the socks over my hurting feet. My shoes I carried, without even trying to put them on.

Limping toward our tent, I found Alice with my 44 on her hip and a big fire in front of our tent. Alice's face lit up when she saw me, since she had almost convinced herself that a bear, which had come from my direction right after I had left, might have killed me. According to her, I had been gone for four hours. That I returned without the boat was of little importance to Alice at that moment. She had started the big fire after the first bear had come in her direction. A second bear came swimming across the slough next, and parked himself right behind the tent in the willow brush. That bear had left only a few minutes ago as I approached the tent.

I was proud of Alice that she, with all her fear of bears, had held together the way she did, but for now we had to think about our situation.

While I doctored up my feet and covered them with several pairs of socks, Alice was making coffee again and then asked, "What now?"

"Well, we have two choices," I replied. "We can sit here and wait to be found, or we can try to build a raft and go on."

Since we were not on the main river channel and didn't feel like sitting around feeling sorry for ourselves, we decided on the raft. And while still sipping our coffee, we started by taking inventory of our possessions, which, thanks to the fact that I had removed them from the boat to get at our tent, were quite numerous:

1 tent
2 sleeping bags
2 blankets
1 .22 caliber rifle with one cartridge
1 Winchester with seven cartridges
1 .44 caliber revolver with a full cartridge belt
2 knives
1 machete
50 feet of rope
1 camera
Half a box of Pilot bread
Half a jar of jam
Half a jar of peanut butter
2 sticks of regular butter
Some pots and pans,
Some coffee and sugar
Matches
One dead goose

The rest of our belongings were on an independent journey in our boat. But to be honest about it, I did not feel that we were in any particular bad shape.

After all, unexpected difficulties belonged to a real adventure, and wasn't that what at least I had been seeking?

My memories about my childhood fantasies at the ditch in the cattle meadow included mishaps as well, but somehow our present situation was more realistic.

How Alice felt about the whole thing I couldn't really tell, but at least she didn't lecture or blame me, nor did she seem to be particularly stressed.

While she cooked our goose (like our goose wasn't cooked already) I was stumbling around in my socks in search for suitable logs for a raft in the driftwood piles. Cutting the logs to a manageable length with the machete, I dragged them to the river. Thanks to that nylon rope, I eventually produced something that resembled a raft and after covering the raft with a layer of brush, I set the tent upon our ark.

At 4 a.m. and in good spirit, I hollered, "All aboard!"

The raft

As soon as the gear and the pets were loaded up, we took one more look around to make sure that nothing stayed behind, and then went on our way, at least for about fifty yards. Stuck in a shallow spot, it took us another hour to get free and be able to continue. The next miscalculation came to light when we arrived at the high cut-bank, where our tent was promptly kicked down by the first overhanging tree. Well, putting that tent up on the raft seemed to be a good idea at the time, but not to be discouraged by such minor incidents, we used the tent as a carpet on our craft.

Building the raft with only a machete put my hands in somewhat the same condition as my feet were. As I inspected the blisters on my hands, I said to Alice, "Look at it from the bright side—we could have had rainy weather on top of it all."

I could not tell how much Alice thought of my sense of humor, but again, at least she didn't whine or complain, as I would have expected.

Even Minado was as polite as he could be. When he had to do his business again, as if he knew that we couldn't land the raft for that, he went out on the longest log to do it, while we just hoped that he wouldn't slip and fall into the river.

Naturally, I was still hoping to find our boat somewhere hung up and tried to stay awake, but as all the hard work and the excitement threatened to catch up with me, Alice offered to watch out for the boat and urged me to take a nap.

It seemed to me that only a very short time had passed before Alice woke me up and it was not because she had found the boat. Instead, our raft was caught in a small whirlpool, going in circles about twenty yards across with a one foot deep funnel in the middle. My homemade rudder, oar or paddle, whatever one would prefer to call it, was not too effective the tool for the job and therefore it took me a quite a few rounds of hard work to get us out of the merry-go-round.

By that time, everything on the raft was in a state from damp to wet and we both were ready to make camp just about anywhere. Coming around a bend, we saw a deserted village, which would have been the perfect place to stop and improve our ark, but the current was so fast, and we saw it too late. Before we knew it, we had missed our chance to stop. There just seemed to be no easy way to stop that raft, so we used a blanket as a makeshift sail and let the wind drive us toward a small island. Tying both ends of the raft to some willows, we hung all our belongings in the bushes to dry, pitched the wet tent, and fell asleep on the bare floor of it.

Chapter 10
Rescued

I awoke to the sound of a motorboat. Still half sleepy, I stumbled out of the tent and saw people on a sand bar not far from us. Reaching for my Winchester, I shot into the air, but apparently our camp had already been discovered. A few minutes later, we were greeted by Cliff and Babe Adams, a Native couple from the village of Beaver. Several people from that village had been searching for us as far as forty miles upriver.

George

As we loaded all our stuff, including the owl, into the boat of our rescuers, Cliff pointed at the bird and asked, smiling, "Would that be George?"

With that question, Cliff had steered my own curiosity. How could he have known that the name of our owl was George? On our way to Beaver, which was only about eight miles farther downstream, Cliff and Babe told us how a white trapper from their community, a Jay Eisenhart, had found our fold boat on a sand bank and had pulled it back to Beaver. When Jay and some friends searched through our belongings in the boat, they found my log book, and since one of the entries mentioned that George still had to be fed by hand, it caused those people to think that we might have an infant with us. In horror of that assumption, they notified the National Guard, which was scheduled to look for us on the following day.

Cliff smiled as he looked at the owl again, and said, "You know, our chief's name is George as well." But what was even funnier to us was when we looked at some maps at Cliff's and Babe's house and found out that the island at which we had lost our boat was called Dead Man Island.

Cliff couldn't quite understand how we could have slipped past all the people searching for us and then he remembered that he should call the National Guard back and cancel the search for the following day. At Jay Eisenhart's log cabin, we were invited for coffee and had our foldboat including its contents returned to us. Right across from Jay's home, we pitched our tent at the riverbank and planned to stay a few days, at least until my hands and feet had healed some.

Forgotten town on the Yukon

Our pike harvest near Beaver

The village of Beaver had a nice romantic atmosphere. Most of the buildings were log cabins and there were no beat-up trucks or other discarded machines sitting around to clutter up the surrounding. All the inhabitants, outside of three Caucasian trappers, were a mixture of Eskimos and Indians, which made us feel welcome and comfortable among them in this village. As in most settlements, the kids of the village took great interest in us and it didn't take long before we had befriended the chief, George Weiner, and his family, so that there was no particular reason for us to hurry and travel on. A last paycheck, which Alice still expected, should be waiting for us at the post office in Stevens Village, which was the next village on downriver, but that money would not last for long either. The fact was we were flat broke at this point and had to live off the land as well as we could manage. Outside of a snowshoe hare, which I shot near the village, I managed to shoot some pikes with bow and arrow in a nearby clear running ditch. We ate pike boiled, fried, and mixed with mayonnaise on pilot bread crackers, which we had purchased at the local store with our last pennies. Even George the owl had to live off pike for the time being and didn't seem to mind it. On one occasion, I accompanied some natives on a hunt, but had no luck and we returned empty handed.

Twice, we had been invited to dinner at the chief's family, but even these meals consisted of fish. When we finally were ready to travel on, George Weiner arrived with an arm full of groceries at our camp, and talked us into staying a few days longer so we could experience the fourth of July celebration in Beaver.

The festivities of that day consisted mainly of games for the children and a shooting contest for the grownups. Some of the teenagers also participated in some kind of water skiing, during which an old car hood on which a daredevil kneeled, would be pulled behind a motorboat on the river. But the high point of the day was a potlatch with good food and afterwards even a bottle or two of whiskey were rotating in between the men. Everybody seemed to have some fun on that day and for us, it was a nice way to conclude our visit in Beaver.

We had said our good-byes and were ready to cast off, when George Weiner brought us some more groceries and gave us a letter of recommendation to the chiefs of the next two villages. "Just in case you should need some help," he said. Thankful to the village of Beaver for the kindness shown to us and to have gotten our boat back, we were ready to go. But we hadn't paddled too far, before a motorboat caught up with us and offered us a ride to Steven's village. Since we felt we had some time to make up and also were anxious for our mail waiting at that village, we accepted the offer. Again, we loaded our boat, gear, and pets on to the motorboat and arrived at Steven's Village before nightfall on that day. A little tired of the Yukon Flats in general, we were anxious to get back to hills, bluffs, and clear water streams. At Steven's Village, we now would be that much closer to have these wishes fulfilled. The native who had offered the ride in his boat to us was Jeffery Adams, the son of the local chief, who also offered us a cabin to stay in during our visit. But since we didn't plan to stay at this place for long, and because of our pets, we respectfully declined the offer and pitched our tent.

In Beaver

The village had about a hundred inhabitants at the time, but it was in many ways a more modern community than the village of Beaver. It had a generator that produced electricity for the whole village, a big school, a store, and a regular post office, where we received our mail, including Alice's last check.

Jeffery, rightfully very proud of his heritage, showed an old spear to us, which was once used by his grandfather to hunt bears. He described this old-fashioned way of hunting to us in the following way: The object was to enrage the animal to provoke an attack. The hunter would then ram the dull end of the spear into the ground, while he held the shaft in just the right angle, so that the attacking bear would impale himself on it.

Yukon Flats 1968

Yellow Warbler nest near Ft. Yukon

Jeff Adams with spear

I'm sure that such a feat of strength and courage could not be found nowadays among the so called sport-hunters, who rather shoot their game with a high-power rifle and scope from a safe distance.

During that night, George the owl had freed himself from his tethers and had taken his leave. We did not search for him too seriously, figuring that he might have gotten tired of eating fish anyway. Then, in the afternoon, a

Native boy came running to our tent, explaining to us that our owl was sitting on the school's radio antenna and that some kids were throwing stones at it. Grabbing my fishnet, I followed the boy and soon managed to recapture the bird. While George might have been ready to be on his own, he did not know that not all people liked owls and I was reminded not to let him go near a village.

A few miles after Stevens Village, the river seemed to be one straight channel toward a mountain chain and since we had the wind in our backs again, we remembered the improvisation from our raft and put up a blanket as a sail once more. All I had to do was to use a paddle as a rudder and soon we were in between mountains and rocky bluffs we had missed for so long. It almost felt like coming home.

Wherever clear running streams would flow out of the mountains, we often would see fish camps, where whole families sometimes spend some time during the salmon season to capture and process their fish for the winter. Most people at those camps invited us for tea and conversation. At our departure, they often presented us with smoked, fresh, or half-dried salmon. The smoked and half-dried salmon tasted so good that we ate it like candy while traveling. If the salmon was fresh, it was a question of how hungry we were and sometimes we stopped just around the next river bend, to make a fire and cook the fish. The bears, too, like salmon and therefore, we saw them now quite often as they patrolled the shoreline downriver from the fish camps for the occasional discarded salmon or washed up scraps of fish from the camps.

Since we had left Circle City, all settlements along the river had been on the right side of the river, because those were original Indian settlements, established there because of the longer exposure to the sunlight. Approaching the village of Rampart, however, we had to hold to the left side of the river. The reason for that was that this was another settlement established as a supply port for the gold miners. During its heydays in 1890-1898, Rampart had about 1,500 people living there, but by 1968, only 49 souls called this place their home.

In front of the small community store, we met a part-time mine worker, who invited us to visit one of the last working gold mines in the area. Not being on a set travel schedule, we welcomed the opportunity to get to know yet another lifestyle from the gold rush days in Alaska.

Old mining equipment, Circle City 1968

1968

Leaving Fort Yukon 1968

After having been assured by the people of the village that our tent and boat would be safe during our absence, we accepted the offer and soon were on a bumpy Jeep ride into the mountains.

Young Athabaskan Indians from Circle

Chapter 11
Then There Were Two

For about one week, we were the guests at a small family operated gold mine, a few miles into the mountains south of Rampart, where an extra, empty log cabin was allotted to us by the miners. Not only were we allowed to observe the whole operation, but also were encouraged to try our luck with the gold pan at various places on the mine. The idea behind that was that it would give the miners an inkling about how rich the ground might be at any given spot and if it was worth buggering that ground into the sluice box.

Now and then, we came up with a few tiny flakes of gold, but for the work it took, it would not be a way to make a living. I'm also sure if we would have found anything bigger than the tiny flakes that only could be appreciated in a vial with water, the owners of the mine would have changed the rule about it for us to keep what we found.

We soon thought it more profitable for us to pick our share of the abundant blueberries in the vicinity until our hosts decided on a visit to Rampart and returned us to the river.

As we readied ourselves to travel on, there was a lot of talk about the upcoming Yukon Rapids. Some people gave us more advice than I appreciated, since it made Alice unnecessarily nervous. One person even suggested that we tie a log to either side of our foldboat in order to make it a safer craft. Obviously, this person had never paddled anything like a foldboat. I for one had no real concerns about the situation and did not even consider any of those ridiculous ideas.

Young porcupine at Bear Creek

On the evening we left Rampart, we made camp at a clear-running stream called Bear Creek, just above these so-called rapids. A trapper's cabin next to that creek could have saved us from setting up the tent, but a bear had played interior decorator in the cabin and had rendered it quite useless for human occupation. The weather was nice enough and the creek supplied us with fresh grayling. We also received an honorary visit from a young porcupine, which was too young to be considered game, but it presented a good photo opportunity instead.

"Are you absolutely sure we will be all right?" asked Alice nervously as we started out in the morning.

"Don't worry," I answered, "if those nutshells, which they call riverboats around here make it through there, there'll be no danger to our foldboat!"

As suggested to us, I held to the left side of the river, from where we were able to identify the big rocks to our right, which we were to avoid. As we went over a couple of bigger swells, the current had brought us back to the middle of the river again. To the right side of the river we had just passed a fish camp; after I steered our boat into a big eddy, the current took us back to that camp. A Native stood in front of that camp watching our approach and I asked him where the rapids would start. He, laughing out loud, replied, "You just came through them!" Then he invited us for tea.

During our tea conversation with the man and his family, we received the sad news that since our departure from the village of Beaver, George Weiner's youngest son had fallen into the river and drowned.

George Wiener family in Beaver 1968

Our spirits somewhat dampened by the shocking news, we paddled a little farther before stopping to cook the salmon that had been given to us at the camp.

About forty miles or so after the rapids, we reached Tanana. The boarded up old buildings at the front street and the rusty, broken down cars standing around did not make a good impression on me, but I found a brushy corner near the riverbank were we could set up camp without being in the middle of the unpleasant things.

In 1880, the Alaskan Commercial Company had started a trading post at this old settlement, which was then known as Nuklukayet. Over the years, the name of this settlement had changed many times before it finally became known as Tanana, named after the Tanana River that enters the Yukon across from the town. In 1968, about four-hundred people of mixed races lived there and the town even had a hospital, as well as a small plane airport.

Not too enthusiastic about this settlement, I was looking forward to our departure from it on the following day and so was Alice, but she had a different direction in mind. Even today, I can't tell what caused Alice's sudden decision to quit the adventure and fly from Tanana to Fairbanks to visit her sister. Was it the bad news from Beaver, the episode during which we lost the boat, or just the hot weather? Well, it was her money and her life and I didn't ask any questions. I accompanied my fiancée to the Tanana airport, where we said good-bye, and since Alice had not offered any further explanation for her decision, I considered our affair as closed.

As soon as I returned to the camp, I packed up and went on downriver in spite of the 95 degrees in the shade. Somewhere near, there must have been a forest fire raging and not a breath of air was to be felt under the smoke-filled, yellow sky.

Lazily, I drifted with the current, paddling only enough to keep the boat straight. As soon as all the noise from town was behind me, there was absolute silence. No birds were singing in the woods. Not even the usual distant cry of a seagull or the cawing of a raven was to be heard. This atmosphere was more than fitting to my mood while I was trying to adjust mentally to the loss of my travel companion.

Again, I told myself that it was all part of my adventure, but I had to admit that I missed Alice's company. Looking over the rest of my crew, Minado had withdrawn into the shade under the bow of the boat, making use of the now vacant accommodation and George the owl, without a doubt tired of the heat, showed a lot of interest in the wooded shoreline.

"You're right, my friend," I said. "It certainly must be time for you to be on your own."

Just before Tanana 1968

Tanana 1968

Crawling to the front of the boat, I carefully cut the tethers off the bird's feet.

If George was aware of his freedom, he didn't show it at first, but after a little more than an hour, he suddenly spread his wings without hesitation and flew toward shore and vanished into the woods.

"Good luck!" I called after the bird and then turned to Minado and asked, "Did you want to leave, too?" In response, the dog only wagged his tail lazily and that brought the crew of our vessel down to two.

Drifting through a short channel, we came upon an inviting sandy beach of an island to our left and I decided to stop and give the boat a good cleaning and rearranging for a brand new start. After unpacking, brushing the sand and dry mud out of the boat, as well as washing the owl droppings off the bow, I rearranged the cargo more to the comfort of Minado and me. By then, it was late enough to make camp and since I couldn't wish for a better place, I just spread a blanket out on the sand, made a cooking fire, and called it home for the evening. There seemed to be no chance for rain, it was warm enough, and the smog in the air had chased all the mosquitoes into hiding.

In the morning, nothing had changed as far as the smog or the weather was concerned, and it promised to be another hot and windless day. I started early, but my enthusiasm for paddling diminished under the rising heat. The sun was merely an orange ball in the yellow sky and the river surface without as much as a ripple, not a sound was to be heard and the whole atmosphere felt depressingly odd.

How fast time passed was hard to tell as I mostly drifted downriver and slowly became aware of a distant thunder. Judging by the weather conditions, a thunderstorm was out of the question; besides, it almost sounded more like cannon fire than thunder claps and jokingly I thought to myself, *Maybe World War III had started.* In fact, it gave me a feeling like I was one of the last survivors after a world catastrophe.

During that time, the thundering came closer or rather that I had drifted nearer to it, but the origin of it still was a mystery to me. After the next loud crash, I heard the mournful cry of a seagull and I was happy to hear that there still was life out there after all! That was when I also noticed a foul smell in the air, which at first added to the mystery, until I saw the faint outline of cliffs through the smog. With the next thunderclap, water splashed at the base of those cliffs, and suddenly, it all became clear to me. Big chunks of sand were breaking off those cliffs, crashing into the river, and one of them close enough to me that the waves caused by it rocked my boat. I took that as a clear warning for me to keep my distance from those cliffs.

But what caused that awful smell?

Minado 1968

Wolf 1968

On my map, this place was marked as the Palisades, but it was not until some years later when I found out that these frozen cliffs of sand and mud were also called the bone yards, because of the Pleistocene fossil remains it contained, which, together with some rotten vegetation, would have explained the foul smell.

But not having all that information at the time, I was anxious to leave those cliffs behind me and started paddling faster. If nothing else, this stretch of river had broken the monotony for a short time and near the end of it, I even got to see a bald eagle take wing from a tilted tree high up on the upper edge of the cliff.

I settled back into a comfortable position again and to let the boat drift along. Sometime, somewhere, I had dozed off and when I awoke, I was drifting along an island, with a moose watching me float past. Carefully, I dug for my camera and took a picture, but it was the last exposure on that film. While I was pulling the boat toward shore to reload my camera, the moose disappeared. Since Minado came out from under the bow, indicating that he might need a pit stop, I decided to disembark with my dog and see where that moose went. Keeping Minado close to me, I looked all over the island for the moose, but no luck, in spite of the fact that the island was covered only with fairly young willow grows. Not aware at that time yet how well these large animals could hide themselves, I was puzzled and climbed back into the boat and paddled on. A few feet from where my dog and I had stood, the moose stepped out of the brush and followed us along the shore to the end of the island.

Kokrines 1968

123

The next morning, I awoke to a blue sky, but a very windy day. While the world in general looked friendlier again, the river with its two-foot waves did not. If the immediate surroundings of my camp would have looked a little more interesting, I might have waited until the wind died down, but since that was not the case, I paddled on against the wind, as close to the shore as possible. Progress was slow, until I got around the next bend. From there, the paddling was not only easier, but I also saw what could have been signs of a settlement called Kokrines, which was the next village marked on my old map. As I got closer, it became obvious that the white patches on that hill were graves on a cemetery. Still, a cemetery should indicate that there also would be a village within a reasonable distance. Stopping and checking out the cemetery, I found no road or even a well-used trail that could have connected the place to a village.

About a quarter of a mile farther downriver from that cemetery, I discovered a single boat without a motor at the beach. Tying up my boat, I followed some narrow steps up the steep riverbank. From the top of the bank, I could see the gables of some log cabins sticking out of the tall grass and brush that surrounded them. A short distance along a trail through the high grass, the landscape opened to a well-kept garden in front of a cabin and some dogs started barking, but no human soul was in sight. With Minado by my side, I walked toward the open door of that cabin and hollered, "Hello there, anybody home?"

There was no answer and I walked closer so I could look inside. I then saw an elderly Indian, totally absorbed with eating a stack of pancakes in front of him. Knocking at the door frame, I said again, "Hello there!" And, finally, the man looked up at me with big surprised eyes, but froze in position. I had to repeat my greeting once more before the man hesitantly rose from his chair and asked me to enter. Whereupon, I introduced myself and asked if this place was all that was left of Kokrines. The man nodded and then introduced himself as Frank Titus. Frank's mannerism gave me the feeling that he either was afraid of me, or embarrassed about the whole situation. When he offered me food, I politely refused, but accepted a cup of tea, while I offered him a cigarette. This seemed to relax Frank and he started telling me a few facts about the remains of this old village.

Frank and his life partner, Josephine Corning, who had kept herself in obscurity up to this point, were in fact the only full-time residents left at this place. Josephine, obviously very shy toward strangers, didn't speak much English either, but Frank was not only articulate, he also gave me the appearance of an all-around, well-informed human being.

We talked for a long time, until the wind had slowed down and I was ready to travel on. Frank escorted me down to the river to take a look at my boat, where we smoked the last of my cigarettes before we said our final good-byes. As I paddled on, I was left with the feeling that I had entered into a lasting friendship with this old Indian named Frank.

Frank Titus 1970

On a now calm river, I reached the village of Ruby by about midnight and made camp on the lower end of the village, near the bluff. As usual, in spite of the late hour, some children found their way to my campsite and bombarded me with the usual questions.

"Where you come from?" and "How far you gonna go?"

Right after these first inquiries came business offerings to get drinking water or firewood for me, but since I was broke, there were no deals and most of the would-be panhandlers quickly lost interest and left.

One eight or nine-year-old boy by the name of Leroy stayed around and wanted to share his candy with me.

"You always offer candy to strangers?" I asked.

"No," he answered, "but you are my friend and maybe someday you'll help me."

There was no doubt in my mind that I was dealing with a very sharp boy, and during the next days, we actually became friends of sorts.

Leroy also followed me on my hunting forays to find hares, grouse, or even squirrels to shoot. That somebody like me would eat squirrels was hard for Leroy to understand and there was no way I could persuade him to try the meat, but he showed no hesitation if I had grouse or hare for dinner. In return for eating with me, he would haul the drinking water for me from the village spring.

The community of Ruby came into existence around 1911 as a gold miners' town, and with a population in the thousands, even the hillsides to both sides of the village were covered with shacks and house tents at that time.

While there were still some active gold mines in the back country of Ruby during my first visit there, the actual village population had fallen to about 250, of which most were more or less natives, and many of them had moved there from the old village of Kokrines or from other villages along the river

Traveling along the Yukon and living from hand to mouth had its attraction for me and the history of the settlements along the river certainly is interesting, even having no money was not so bad at this point either, but the summer wouldn't last forever. Sooner or later, winter would arrive and no matter where and when that would happen, all I could hope for was that I would find some kind of employment from here on downriver. In my opinion, things usually had a way to work themselves out and, therefore, I was in no particular hurry to leave Ruby.

Probably because of my leather clothes and because of the way I lived, the children in this village had taken to calling me David Crockett, but it seemed my friend, Leroy, had his own way of looking at things. One evening, when he visited me at my tent, he said, "When I grow up, I think I will grow a beard like you!"

I smiled about his remark and replied, "You'll have to wait and see about that, most Indians do not have very heavy growths of facial hair."

Leroy stared at me in surprise and asked, "You're not an Indian?"

"No, I'm from Germany."

"Don't they have Indians in Germany?"

"We are the Indians in Germany." I answered, chuckling, and then proceeded to explain to him in as simple terms as possible about the different races of the world. How much the boy understood of it was hard to tell, since his world ended about a hundred miles up or down the river.

Checking the post office for mail the next day, I got an unexpected package from my friend, Neal, with some film for my camera and a five-dollar note, which was a pleasant surprise, but an even bigger surprise was a letter from Alice. In that letter, she stated that she would be waiting for me in the town of Galena, which was the next village fifty miles farther downriver. Alice gave no explanation for her action now, or for her reason to have left our expedition at the town of Tanana. To say the least, I felt a little taken for granted, since I had settled on the idea that we were done. By the time I got to read her letter, I had to assume that she already arrived in Galena about a day ago, so how could she be so sure I hadn't passed that village yet? Well, I couldn't just let her sit there, so I said good bye to Leroy and broke camp that same afternoon.

Ruby 1968

Still relying on my old map, it looked to me as if the Ruby Slough, right below Ruby, would reenter the main river after a couple of bends and thereby would save me some time, so I took a chance on that shortcut. Fifty miles should not be a problem, and sometime during the night, I should be in Galena.

A fairly good current took me into the Ruby Slough, but then it soon slowed down. After the first two bends into the slough and the feeling that I had made a mistake was soon confirmed when, after a couple of bends, there was no opening to the main river. Well, maybe the next bend, but again, no such luck. It also seemed that the water in the slough was hardly moving at all and if I wanted to make progress, I had to keep paddling all the time with the realization that I would have to paddle that slow winding waterway all the way to the Yuki River, which then in turn would enter the Yukon about halfway between Ruby and Galena. Bend after bend without end, it some-times felt like I was making complete circles. To top things off, it started to rain and when the rain mercifully stopped again, it got windy. The funny part was, no matter in which direction the slough turned, the wind always seemed to come from the front.

When it started to get dark, the wind slowed down, but the water was at times so shallow that a big bull moose walked in the middle of the slough ahead of me. As the water got deeper again, the moose veered off into the woods, and owls sitting on the drift logs and dead trees probably wondered why some dummy would paddle around this ditch in the middle of the night. I got so close to one of these birds that I almost could hear it asking, "Lost, are we?"

Beavers, too, swam around me and sometimes close enough to me, that when they dived and slapped their tail on the water, I got sprayed. All this entertainment did not change the fact that I was getting tired, but camping was out of the question since the steep, muddy banks of the slough seemed impossible to climb without getting totally covered with mud.

Then I saw the silhouette of a beaver sitting in the willow brush and figured that I earned one of those critters for my next good meal. Pulling out my .22 caliber rifle, I aimed as well as I could in the light available and shot. The animal fell over, making a sound that was very familiar to me. Even before I was able to pull the carcass with my paddle within my reach, I knew I had killed another porcupine instead of a beaver. But meat was meat; I just had to secure my game on the back of my boat again, where Minado couldn't reach it to get himself in trouble with the quills. Without a chance of finding a camp spot, much less a place to butcher my game, I had to find a solution to still my hunger. So I let the boat drift where it wanted to and dug around in my gear for my white gas cooker. A short time later, I had a pot full of what looked and tasted like milk rice, ate half of it, and gave the other half to Minado. Then I stretched out in the boat as comfortable as possible and went to sleep.

One time, when the branches of an overhanging bush tickled my face, I awoke, but since the boat wasn't really drifting anywhere and I didn't feel rested enough to care, I went right back to sleep, till the cool morning air penetrated my clothes.

It had not been the most comfortable night I ever spent, but I felt somewhat refreshed. Paddling soon warmed me up and limbered my stiff bones. After only about two-hundred yards, I entered the Yuki River and had real current under my boat again. It took only minutes to reach the Yukon, where the sunlit bluffs beckoned from the other side. Paddling as straight across as I could, I landed the boat and hurried to collect my firewood, before Minado marked every piece of it along the shore. After cinching the quills of my spiny game, I skinned and cut it up. The fried liver followed by a pot of coffee made a good breakfast, while I checked the possible mileage I had before me.

About twenty-five miles more to go should not be too bad, but there was no more room for errors, otherwise Alice might assume that I had already passed Galena, or think I was trying to avoid her.

Since nothing goes as smooth as we wish, I had a couple of stretches with strong headwind and waves to battle against, but nothing prepared me for what was happening when I finally came within sight of Galena. I could have, and should have, followed the shoreline that made a big bend to the right, but in my anxiety to make up for lost time, and with the river looking quite calm at this point, I aimed straight ahead toward the outline of the houses in the distance. About at the middle of the river, the wind picked up again. At first, there were only big swells like on a big lake or out at sea, but as the wind started to blow harder, white caps started to build up on top of the swells.

Minado had already withdrawn below deck into the front of the boat and I was trying to get back closer to the shore by holding into the waves and paddling my boat sideways. It seemed the wind and the waves were coming from all directions, and by the time I was close enough to shore, I also was right in front of the settlement.

Completely exhausted, I tied up the boat and the dog, when I overheard some natives up on the road who apparently had been watching my arrival.

"If I wouldn't have seen it, I wouldn't have believed the guy would make it!"

Looking back out on to the river, I myself could hardly believe I had escaped that caldron of angry, foaming waves.

"Do you know of an Eskimo girl by the name of Alice?" I said as I approached the three men on the road. Their facial expressions reminded me of the way Frank had looked at me when I stood in the open door of his cabin in Kokrines, but I was assured by the people that Alice was in town, but where I could find her they didn't know. Then they went on their way and left me standing there.

As I turned and looked around trying to decide which way I should start searching, Alice came out of the house in front of me. After our initial greeting with a hug, I told Alice that I had the feeling that the people here were afraid of me. Alice laughed and said, "You should see yourself in the mirror, the way you're dressed and your big gun on your hip, you don't exactly inspire trust."

Wolf on the Yukon 1968

Chapter 12
Even Childhood Dreams Have to End

Because of the persisting winds, we decided to stay for the night and made camp at the end of the town. That the community of Galena also had an Air Force base made it just that much less attractive to us and with the wind settling down overnight, we lost no time in the morning to paddle on, in spite of threatening rain clouds. In general, it seemed the nice weather was coming to an end. Up to now, we had been spoiled by a very sunny summer and had been used to waking up to a sunny sky. So we really didn't have a reason to complain about the weather then, but barely back on the river, we found something else to complain about. A couple of guys in an Air Force helicopter, lowering themselves right in front of our boat to check us out and if the noise from that machine wasn't irritating enough, the wind from that machine curdling the water all around us didn't make me love them anymore. In the hope that the pilot would get the point, I gave him the bird. When that didn't bring the on the expected result, I pulled my revolver out of the holster. The helicopter took off and did not wait for me to point the weapon on them, which I wouldn't have done anyway, much less shoot at the helicopter. But the bluff had worked, because the pilot knew that his action was illegal to begin with.

Koyukuk 1968

Twenty miles or so downriver from Galena and about one mile or so into the mouth of the Koyukuk River lay the village of Koyukuk, which we wanted to visit. But to avoid having to paddle against the current of the Koyukuk River, we paddled up a slough, which led us into the Koyukuk a short distance above the village, and from there, we drifted down to the settlement.

Only about fifty people lived at this old Indian settlement at the time, but most of those people were out in their fish camps because of a salmon run.

We made camp right below that village, just in time to get out of the rain. It was the time of the year when it started to get dark at night again and the cloudy sky made it even darker, which meant, to us, that from now on, we had to make use of every bit of traveling time in between the rain showers. In the morning, the rain had stopped and we traveled on. At this stop, we also had noticed an increase of the tiny gnats, locally called NO-SEE-UMS, which seemed to replace the mosquitoes during the later part of the season. Not that those little pests were biting as much, but they got into our eyes, our ears, and under the hairline, irritating the heck out of us.

Nulato 1968

Back on the river, a fine rain started up again, but rain or no rain, the abundance of raspberries we encountered at some places just beckoned to be picked. So we made several stops to pick our share of the delicious fruit before we went ashore at the village of Nulato.

Nulato is one of the oldest villages along the Yukon, about which I had already read as a young man in Germany in a book by Peter Freuchen, called *Larion's Law*.

The Russians had built a trading post there in 1838, which was destroyed by the Indians in the same year and then rebuilt in 1839. After the Indians burned it down once more, Vasili Derzhvin was sent to Nulato by the Russian-

American Company in 1841 to rebuild the post as a fort with palisades. Ten years later, however, a surprise attack by the Koyukan Indians resulted again in the destruction of the fort and in the death of all of its inhabitants, including Vasili Derzhavin and an English Marine officer, Lieutenant Barnard. Three years after that incident, a new fort was built two miles farther upstream, but it, too, was totally decayed by the time of our visit.

It was the eighth of August when we set up our tent at the Nulato River and then went to the post office to check for mail. To our surprise, we found a letter with a check for fifty dollars from the Fish and Game Department. It was the bounty for the wolf I had shot earlier on the trip. While I still felt a little bad about that, the money sure came in handy for us and since it also was my birthday on that day, I looked at it as a birthday present.

So we went right on to the village store to buy some sorely needed staples and even splurged on a candy bar.

The fish in the clear-running Nulato River seemingly knew nothing about our need for fresh meat, nor did they care that it was my birthday; they just didn't want to bite. To get our fish dinner, we had to find a stagnant slough nearby, were we shot some pikes with my small caliber rifle.

Later that day, as I returned after having successfully tracked down a porcupine, a canoe with two Caucasians landed in front of our tent. Two young men, Don and Dave, from the lower forty-eight states, had started their trip in Whitehorse, Canada. Their goal was to paddle the Yukon all the way to the mouth of the river during their timely-limited vacation. In order to accomplish that, they always paddled in the main current and only stopped at villages long enough to take some pictures. Since entering Alaska, the two young men had heard about us traveling ahead of them and they had been looking forward to catch up with us, but our conversation with Don and Dave was quite short. They took some photos and filmed us, and then hurried on downriver.

In Nulato, we naturally also had children around our tent again, and one of the boys in particular followed us around, even up to that slough where we had shot the pikes. Near there, we had found the biggest paper wasp nest I had ever seen. But when we went there the next day to check on the wasp nest, without the boy, the wasp nest was already destroyed. It might only have been a wasp's nest, but the one thing I had noticed by then was that the children in the bush villages were always quick to destroy things, and generally showed little concern for distress or pain in animals.

Somewhere along our way to the village of Kaltag, which was only another twenty or twenty-five miles downriver, we also did a little misbehaving ourselves. On a high cut bank, we found a landing for helicopters. The army supply rations which were sitting there reminded us of the Air Force helicopter that almost blew us out of the water.

We now decided that it was our chance to take revenge and opened the rations to remove all the cigarettes and all the chocolates before climbing back into our boat and paddling on.

At the village of Kaltag, we had better luck with our fishing and also picked a bunch of blueberries. But since we didn't stay around long enough, we did not get much information on the community itself. According to our map, we had two-hundred miles of wilderness ahead of us before we would encounter another settlement. Not that we didn't relish the thought of it, but we probably would have enjoyed that stretch of river at lot more if it wouldn't have been for the almost constant rain. The country on both sides of the river was fairly flat and therefore somewhat monotonous. An occasional bluff and a couple of deserted fish camps were the only changes in the scenery. Even the wildlife seemed smart enough to stay out of the rain, except that during one night, the wild barking of Minado woke us up. Almost sure that we had a bear in camp, I stormed out of the tent with a flashlight in one hand and my .44 caliber handgun in the other. Ready to fight the villain who dared to disturb our serenity, but instead of a bear, I found myself confronting another porcupine. Since we had enough to eat at the time and were anxious to get back to my sleeping bag, I chased the animal into the willows and got out of the rain.

With all the nice weather we had in the beginning of our trip, we had left our proper tent poles behind in order to have more room in the boat. We figured on cutting new poles wherever we camped and needed to put up the tent. Now we paid the price. Being one of the cheaper tents to begin with, the constant rain didn't help and keep our tent from leaking. All our things in the boat in general had reached a state from damp to wet and camping to stay out of the rain had become senseless under those conditions. So we kept on paddling till we came upon the next fish camp where in spite of some tied up dogs and several cabins, no human soul was to be found.

We moved into one of the totally empty shacks, made a fire in the barrel stove, and hung all our belongings, including the tent, inside the cabin to dry. Then we heated some water and took a long needed bath before going to sleep.

Old Church in Kaltag

Good catch near Kaltag

By morning, there still was no sign of the owners of the camp and nobody came to take care of the dogs. Outside of a few tatters of fog over the river, we had blue skies above and a promise of a nice day ahead. As soon as we were all loaded up, we paddled on. One loose dog in that camp had fallen in love with our Minado and followed our boat as far as the beach allowed him to do so, then he woefully howled after us.

"There is a forest fire ahead of us," Alice pointed out. Sure enough, there was thick smoke rising from the beach ahead of us, and since we had seen a distant fire during the night of the porcupine incident, I had no reason to disagree with Alice; but as we got closer, we could see some people at the beach and we discovered that we had come upon another village that was not marked on our old map. A short time later, we talked to a young engineer from Norway. He was in charge of the airplane runway construction for this new village called Grayling. This settlement was only five years old at the time, which explained its absence on our map. The smoke we had seen came from the big piles of brush that had been cleared off the land for the runway and were now burning.

A few miles further downriver from Grayling, we reached the village of Anvik, where we stopped for just a few minutes to look around, when an elderly man approached us to give us advice about the dangers of the river, because it was quite windy again. When we inquired about his concern about us, he told us that only a few days ago near this village, the canoe of two white guys got swamped and one of them had drowned.

Trading post in Holy Cross

Right away, we knew that the man could only have been talking about Don and Dave. Even though we did not really get to know those two young men, it was sad news once again, and another reminder that traveling this river had to be taken seriously at all times.

We entered a slough or very slow flowing creek with the intentions of catching a pike for our dinner. Instead, we came upon a family of otters at play on a muddy riverbank. The animals seemed to have a lot of fun by climbing up an old beaver house along the steep bank and by repeatedly sliding back down the beaver's slide, back into the water. When we tried to carefully paddle closer, hoping to be able to get a picture of the animals, we were quickly discovered and the show was over. The otter that we conceived to be the mother of the family swam toward us to draw our attention, while the younger animals fled upriver. A short time later, mother otter had vanished as well, and we returned to the Yukon without trying to get our pike. Soon after, we paddled up a larger slough, which brought us to the village of Holy Cross. Since this was a slightly larger village, we decided that it might be as good a place as any to start looking for work. After all, somehow, somewhere we had to earn some money in order to get back to Anchorage.

The cabin we stayed in in Holy Cross

Holy Cross had about two-hundred and fifty inhabitants, of which almost all were Indians and Eskimos, or a mixture of the two. The people were generally friendly toward us, but during a short fishing trip, some kids went into our tent and stole most of our last provisions. When the store owner, Harry Turner, heard about it, he sent some other kids down to us with a whole cardboard box of groceries.

On the following day, I was introduced to the local priest, Father Andrew. Father Andrew was an exchange priest from Canada, but he was born in Hungary and even spoke some German. But what was of greater importance to me was that the Father offered me a job. Holy Cross, once a good size Catholic Mission, had been considerably downsized and modernized. Because of the ensuing changes in progress, I got a job as an all around handyman for two dollars per hour and we now had an income. I shoveled gravel, played electrician, and painted Christmas pictures on sheets of plywood. Sometimes, Father Andrew would work alongside me and we sang German songs or told a lot of jokes. At one time, I was hired out to a local Indian in order to help him level his cabin. When I went there early in the morning, the owner of the cabin was not home and I had to wait around for a while before he finally showed up. Then he pulled a bottle of whiskey out of his coat and invited me for a drink. I argued that we should get the work done first and then maybe we could have a drink together afterwards.

Wolf's artwork on the school in Holy Cross

Wolfs art in Holy Cross 1968

"It isn't right anyway," said the man to me, "I should be working for you, not you for me."

"Where in the hell did you get an idea like that?" I asked.

"That's just the way it always has been," he replied. "The white man has jobs to be done and we work for them.

"Well, those days are gone and you better change your attitude about that. We're all the same and now you have a job for me and I'll work for you!"

I practically scolded the man before we went to work, and only after his cabin was leveled did we have that drink together.

Before the first snow fell, that Norwegian engineer from Grayling bought our foldboat for fifty dollars and an Eskimo by the name of Willi offered his cabin for us to live in, since he was moving out to his trapline early. Willi even came back to town a couple of times during hunting season to bring us some bear and moose meat. With another of the local natives, I went on grouse and duck hunts, which also kept us from spending my hard earned money on food.

But winter was coming and the first snow fell on September 26. It gave the whole surrounding a totally new atmosphere. Alice had already left for Anchorage in October, hoping to find work in town, while I had decided to stay as long as my job with the mission would last. My faith in finding a job in Anchorage was not that great, and I didn't want to spend the money I had earned on rent for a place in town.

Waiting for the plane back to civilization 1968

It was November 17 when I, too, was sitting with my dog, Minado, in a small airplane, heading back to civilization. For me, it was the first time in my life that I was flying, but then again, there had been many things during that year I had done for the first time. It had been the most exciting and interesting year of my life up to date, and now my childhood dream was coming to an end. But as I looked out of that bush plane at the setting sun over the snow-covered wilderness below, I knew that I would have to return to the Yukon River sometime soon.

Chapter 13
An Intermission from Adventure

When I arrived in Anchorage, my buddy, Jerry, met me at the airport and took me to his home. Where Alice was I had no idea, and I guess Alice had no idea when I would be arriving from Holy Cross. Anchorage still being a town of comfortable size at that time, it probably would only be a matter of time when Alice and I would bounce into each other. Why we had no closer contact I really can't remember. I had not been able to write to Alice since I had no address of her, and Alice apparently hadn't gotten around to writing to me before I left Holy Cross. Maybe this time it was Alice who figured that our relationship had run its course; who knows about women?

Jerry was not really in the position to have me stay with him and his family. So, when a day later or so I got in contact with Neal and he offered me to stay with him in a trailer home he was renting at the time, it seemed to be the perfect solution for me, at least until I figured out what I wanted to do next.

All my friends and acquaintances in Anchorage wanted to hear about our big adventure on the river and I was constantly invited to dinner. As predicted, I also met Alice and found out that she, too, was living with a friend and had not found a job so far. Her only income consisted of unemployment benefits, but that was more than I could count on. Alice acted like nothing had changed between us, and I cannot remember if we ever even talked about the period during which we had no contact with each other.

The reason that Alice often was not included in my invitations to dinner by my various acquaintances was probably due to it that some people didn't look at our relationship as a serious one, especially since I was staying with Neal and was not in constant contact with her. I also suspected that racial prejudice might have played a role in some cases, but, for the time being, I couldn't let that worry me too much, since I did not feel independent enough while living at Neal's place for free. First of all, I had to get an idea about what options I had for my immediate future.

After selling a few of the artifacts that I had collected along the way and the money I had saved from my meager income in Holy Cross, I still had accumulated more money than I had since coming to Alaska and, subconsciously, I already knew what I was going to do. Never having had the money to do so, I had not been back to visit my folks since I had left Europe in 1961. Not knowing when I ever would have the money for a trip to Europe again, I decided to take that opportunity and do just that.

I'm sure Alice wouldn't have minded at all to come along, but she had no money to spare and I wasn't quite rich enough to take her along on my expense. But once the idea of me going back for a visit to Germany had taken hold, there was nothing that could change my mind. I had no big preparations to make other than to find a place to stay for Minado and he was welcomed with some friends in Rabbit Creek, near Anchorage. After that, I was practically packed and ready to go.

One day before Christmas Eve, I once again sat in an airplane, but this time it was a big airliner with all the comforts of civilization on a flight across the North Pole to Europe. Jet lag might have come in to play later on sometime; for now, I was still trying to readjust to the civilized world all around me. When the plane finally arrived in Frankfurt, Germany, somewhat later than it should have, my connecting flight to Hannover had already left. I was told that the next flight to Hannover was already overbooked, and the following flight after that was not leaving until the next day.

Naturally I was angry, since due to the time zones it now was already Christmas Eve and I had figured on arriving at my parents' house that night. In fact, I was so angry that I didn't even bother to speak German when I asked the person at the ticket counter, "And what am I supposed to do now?" It then was suggested to me that I could take a train or go to a hotel overnight and take the first flight in the morning, but the expenses for the hotel, or even for the train ride, would be mine.

"Listen here!" I replied, "I bought a ticket to Hannover and I was scheduled to arrive there tonight. So, until I get there, all occurring expenses will be the responsibility of your airline."

To make the story short, room was found for me on the next flight to Hannover, overbooked or not. From there, I took a train to Braunschweig and continued by taxi to my parent's home, where I arrived exactly at midnight on Christmas Eve.

As I entered the house, I was greeted by my overjoyed parents and my sister and her family. Needless to say, that the reunion with my folks was a happy occasion.

Showing up at the doors of unsuspecting friends during the following days was also a lot of fun and there always were a lot of questions to ask and to answer from both sides. Too many things had changed in my hometown during the years of my absence, and I felt more or less a stranger to my once so familiar surroundings. Financially, I was not in great shape either and was not able to travel around enough to visit everyone, especially my friend Wolfgang Wegener, to whom I still felt indebted and therefore I didn't cherish the idea of showing up on his doorstep totally broke. Hoping to repeat my visit to Germany in a financially better shape before another seven or eight years would pass, I returned to Alaska during the month of March of 1969.

Arriving in Anchorage, Alaska, late at night, financially speaking, I certainly was worse off than before I had left. I had no job, no more money at all, and as far as I knew, I didn't even have a place to stay. Thinking about my situation had made me about as grumpy as the customs official who checked me back into the country.

"What is your address?" he asked in an unfriendly tone as he leafed through my passport. All I could give him was my Anchorage post office box number.

"You cannot live in a post office box," he replied in an even angrier tone and repeated his question as to where I was living.

"I don't know yet," I answered.

"Then where did you live before you left?"

"On the Yukon River."

"Where on the Yukon River?"

At that point, I started to be amused about our little game and smiling at him, I said, "Pick a spot, I was traveling a lot."

Accompanied by a vicious look, the official handed my passport back to me, but I was sure that if he would have wanted to take the time, or wasn't so anxious to get home himself, he would have loved to spend some more time with me. Sure, I could have been a little more obliging, but I always get a kick out of getting under the skin of unfriendly or grouchy public servants, who too often think of themselves as above the ordinary citizen, or like in my case, even a foreigner.

The greeting with my fiancée, Alice, in the airport lobby was considerably warmer.

During my absence, Alice had found a job as a desk clerk with an oil company and she had rented her own apartment. At least for that night, I had a place to stay. The conditions set by Alice for me to stay in her place longer or even permanently were that we would get married, and so we did on March 14, 1969.

In August, right on my birthday, I also made my U.S. citizenship final, and my friend, Neal, and our friends in Rabbit Creek, who had taken care of my dog Minado, gave us a big party for all three occasions.

While all of this was really nice, I still didn't have a steady job. Again, I had tried to make a living in any way I could, which ranged from repainting hotel rooms to playing bodyguard for a German businessman on a trip to Nome, the hometown of my wife. It was certainly interesting to see that community, but I already knew then that Nome was not a place where I would like to live permanently.

Eventually, I found a somewhat steadier employment with the infant Alaskan Children's Zoo as an animal caretaker. The zoo, pretty much in its beginning stage at the time and I being the only caretaker for a variety of animals from chickens to black bears, was not an easy job. Insufficient funds caused a lot of corner-cutting and that included extra working hours for me.

Under better circumstances, this job could have developed into another one of my childhood dreams come true, but it wasn't meant to be.

Expected to be at the zoo every day, including during the visiting hours on weekends, caused an incident on one particular weekend, when I took an hour-long picnic break with my wife. Upon my return to the zoo, I was threatened with the possibility of dismissal by one of the zoo directors. Threats evoke the same reaction in me as do unfriendly public officials. So I got my belongings together right then and there, handed in the keys, and wished the director lots of fun feeding the animals and cleaning their cages.

A day later, Alice lost her job as a receptionist at the oil company for which she had been working. There we were, both of us unemployed, and winter was just around the corner.

While we were sitting at home one night contemplating our situation, our friend, Neal, came by for a visit. After we told him about our dilemma, Neal said, "Don't feel lonely. My job, too, will end by this month."

"Well, that's just great!" I answered sarcastically.

"You two have any idea yet what you might be doing?" Neal asked.

"No," I answered, "do you?"

Instead of giving me an answer, Neal asked, "What do you think about going trapping?"

I was more than startled. Neal might be adventurous, but I could not really see him as a trapper. I also told my friend that I didn't know the first thing about trapping and that he should stop making jokes like that.

"That was no joke," answered Neal. "Didn't you say something about empty cabins in Kokrines?"

I nodded and thought about the promise I had made to myself that I would return to the Yukon some day. At the same time, I had the suspicion that for whatever reason Neal wanted to go trapping, he must have an alternate reason for wanting to disappear into the wilderness, and it certainly wasn't for his love of trapping. When it came to trapping or anything concerning wildlife, Neal's knowledge was limited and his interest usually restricted to photography. Already, in California, on our mutual outings, the hunting and everything that goes with it was generally left to me.

But one thing was for sure, our immediate future in Anchorage did not look too rosy and Neal's reasons for going trapping were his own concern, but he knew me and he knew how to push my buttons.

"Even if we won't get rich that way, just think of the adventure," Neal said, just as I was thinking the same thing. I had to admit that Neal's idea was better than ending up homeless in town for the winter, so I agreed to think about it, and Neal then put a bottle of Jim Beam on the table and I asked Alice to put some coffee water on.

Alice had been quiet during all this time and had just listened to us, but now she suddenly asked, smiling, "And what about me?"

Somehow, I had taken it for granted that Alice would come along. However, my dear wife didn't seem quite ready to do that, even though she knew me well enough to know that I might go no matter what. So she suggested that she would accompany us to Fairbanks to visit her sister and if she couldn't find a job there, then she would fly to Nome and spend the winter with her parents in her hometown.

That solution was okay with me and I'm sure it was preferable to Neal that way.

Sitting in a warm room and toasting each other to our uncertain future as trappers, it was easy to dream of the romance of this kind of life, but little did we know what lay ahead. Our plan, however, was set and sealed before the night had passed.

Chapter 14
Return to the Yukon

In 1903, a private firm had begun laying tracks for the first train in Alaska, but it went broke in 1908. The Northern Railway Company then continued with the construction of the railway in 1910, and a 71-mile stretch of track was laid, from Seward to the Turnagain Arm. Because of neglect, this stretch of track became useless by 1915. At that point, the state took over the operation, and eight years later, 470 miles of track from Seward to Fairbanks were finished, and came to be known as the Alaska Railroad.

Now it was 1969, on a rainy November morning, as the three of us—Neal, Alice and I—sat at the Anchorage train station. Minado looked somewhat worried as he sat in his homemade transport kennel in between our sizable luggage pile. Our uncertain venture was about to start with a twelve-hour and four-hundred mile train ride from Anchorage to Fairbanks.

By the time we sat comfortable in our seats and the train slowly started to roll out of the station, I had to think back to our train ride in Mexico and Neal must have had similar thoughts when he suddenly said, "While ducks and geese are flying south, idiots like us are heading north!"

Alice

The drab, fall landscape soon started to show patches of snow as the train headed farther inland. By the time we crossed the three-hundred-foot deep Hurricane Gulch over the 918-foot long bridge, the whole surrounding was covered with snow. Mt. McKinley National Park, which would have offered the most interesting vistas, was still miles away and by the time we reached the area, it was already too dark to see anything, much less the double mountain peaks of 20,320 and 19, 470 feet high, the highest points on the North American continent.

Alice's sister, Rose, and our brother-in-law, Dale, met us at the train station in Fairbanks and took us to their home, where we stayed for the next two days while shopping around town in order to complete our outfits. Here, we got the gear we thought we needed and could afford, and Dale also gave us two pair of Canadian snowshoes, which we knew would come in handy, and thankfully accepted. The following day, it was time to say good bye to Alice and to my relatives.

It had started to snow as Neal and I climbed into the Twin Otter airplane, which was going to take us to the village of Ruby. There were not many passengers on that plane outside of us, but most of the space in that plane was taken up by our gear, including Minado, who sat in his kennel again with an indefinable expression on his face.

The inner windowpane at my seat had a small crack and some joker had put a band aid on it, which caused Neal to point out to me that the copilot, who had just locked the back door of the plane, was securing the lever of the door lock with bailing wire.

"Now I start wondering," I said, "if our pilot is still on crutches from his last mishap."

In spite of my suspicions, our plane lifted off without hesitation, climbed through the clouds, and headed west under a blue sky. The clouds below us thinned out more and more the farther west we went, and exposed for us a view of the endless winter wilderness below us. Time went by fast as we admired the wide expanse of the land below and before we knew it, it was time to land again. While the landing, too, went very smooth, an unexpected icy wind greeted us as we climbed out of the plane. There was no airport lobby or any structure at all on this landing strip to find shelter in and we started wondering how we would get with all our gear down the hill to the village. At that moment, a beat-up pickup came laboring up the hill, driven by Gilbert Cleaver, the postmaster of Ruby. Apparently, it also was his job to pick up the occasional passengers, along with the mail.

To my surprise, Gilbert recognized me right away. "What are you doing here, at this time of the year?" he asked. I introduced him to Neal and then told Gilbert that I had written to Frank in Kokrines about us spending the winter there to try our hand at trapping.

According to Gilbert, it was twenty below, the first real cold day for Ruby during this season. Neal and I took that little news item as a personal welcome for us, so we would get the right attitude about our new lifestyle.

Ruby Trading Post

The postmaster dropped us and our gear off in front of the Ruby trading post and went on his way. As we stepped inside the store to warm ourselves at the crackling barrel stove, I was recognized again by Harold Esmailka, the store owner. Harold invited us to a cup of coffee and then he put us in contact with Johnny May. From Johnny, we rented a cabin for five dollars per week and made ourselves at home. Our landlord even supplied us with kerosene for the lamp in that cabin and firewood for the first two days. From then on, we would have to fend for ourselves, but even for getting our own wood, we received an old dog sled from Johnny.

Winter had not been the season I had in mind when I had promised myself to return to the Yukon, but for better or worse, there I was. It took us a couple of days to get adjusted to our new surroundings, for Neal probably more so, since he had lived fairly comfortably in Anchorage. Since Ruby was on the south side of the river and our destination, Kokrines, lay thirty miles upriver on the north side, we had to wait till the river was properly frozen over and safe to travel on before we could hire somebody to bring us to our destination. Trying to be as patient as possible, we talked to some local trappers to pick up some tricks of the trade. With Minado's help, we got our daily firewood and, in the evenings, we often were visited by my friend, Leroy, and some other kids who bombarded us with all kinds of questions, or tried to make money off us by offering to haul drinking water or sell us a stick of firewood. Sometimes, Neal and I would go across the river to hunt for grouse and squirrels. For crossing the river on foot, right in front of the village, the ice was strong enough by then, but nobody wanted to take a chance yet to go on a snowmobile trip up or downriver. There always were some spots of open water on the river which froze over later than normal and it takes experience to recognize such places. For us to start setting traps within walking distance of the village was senseless, since the more driven children of Ruby had already done that and thereby claimed it as their trapline. November is the best month for trapping marten and that month was almost over. We knew already that we wouldn't make a killing in trapping, because without having any experience at all, we also had far too few traps. Our more realistic outlook on the situation was to learn and survive this winter as well as we could and maybe get even some enjoyment out of it.

Ruby in the Winter

After we heard that Gilbert had made it by snowmobile to Kokrines without taking us, I had the suspicion that he wanted to make sure that Frank really wanted us there. But it also stands to reason that breaking a fresh trail would not have been easy while pulling a loaded sled with all that gear and a couple of greenhorns. At any case, Gilbert didn't seem to have time after his initial trip, and nobody else who had a snowmobile was interested in doing so. If at that time we would have had any experience in walking on snowshoes, we might have walked the thirty miles or so, but besides, there was our gear and supplies we would have to pull. On the other hand, we were getting tired of hanging around in Ruby and a way had to be found to get us to Kokrines. When we mentioned our predicament to Harold Esmailka, he offered to fly us to Koknines for fifty dollars as soon as he had the time, which, after his estimate, would be most likely by the upcoming weekend.

Ruby 1969

Chapter 15
Greenhorns in a Cursed Village

We couldn't and wouldn't expect Harold to drop everything right then and there just to help us out when he promised to fly us to Kokrines. But now at least we knew that we would be getting there. The time of our departure was set for Sunday morning and we looked forward to it.

It was December 1 and we got up early, as excited as kids on a holiday to get going. We packed the rest of our belongings and walked to the general store. There was no sign of life at the store or at the living quarters in the upstairs of the building. It took all our determination to bang on the door for quite a while before we were able to drum our Good Samaritan out of his bed.

By the time we had loaded our gear onto Harold's pickup and he drove us up to the landing strip, it had been snowing pretty hard. During the loading of Harold's Super Cub, it quickly became apparent that it would take two flights to get us and our gear to where we were going. As Harold took off on his first flight with our gear, Neal and I settled back into the pickup in order to keep warm and watched the heavy loaded little plane as it labored into the air to vanish into the snowstorm. Anxiously we waited for what seemed to be hours, before we finally heard the plane returning. It was with great relief to us that the weather had not discouraged our pilot from making the second flight to get us there.

I had to climb as far as I possibly could into the back of that plane and hold my dog half on my lap and half next to me. Neal had to sit on my knees, kind of folded over toward the pilot and up into the clouds of snow we went. My head was twisted to my left, which gave me a great view of our snowshoes, tight to the wing straps of the plane. Beyond that, I only could see a wall of flying snow, and I had to wonder how Harold could see where he was going.

Actually, Harold had to make several passes to find the old village of Kokrines and its partially overgrown and snowed in landing strip. But Harold proved to us that he really was the expert bush pilot he was known for, and he landed us safely. He taxied the plane next to what looked like a snow-covered beaver house, but in reality it was our pile of gear that Harold had unloaded there after his previous arrival.

While we helped Harold to turn the plane in the right direction for a takeoff, Frank came to greet us. I introduced Neal to him and then Frank invited all of us into his cabin for a cup of coffee.

Frank's common-law wife, Josephine, was already busy cooking, but she took a short break to greet us and to exchange a few words with Frank and Harold in the Athapaskan language. What they were talking about Neal and I had no idea, and we didn't worry about it either. After Harold had said his good-bye and we had watched him take off, barely missing the roof of the outhouse, Neal and I became fully aware of the fact that we were now stuck in the winter-wilderness of Alaska with an elderly Indian couple and little knowledge about that which lay ahead of us.

Since I first had met Frank on my river trip, he had a stroke, which had left him a little wobbly on the legs and with a weakened voice, but otherwise he seemed to be in good spirits and happy to have us there.

Kokrines home from 1969–1971

Frank's cabin in Kokrines 1969

"You can have the little cabin next door," said Frank, "but you have to fix it up some and find a stove to put in there. Till then, you can sleep here," he added, as he pointed to one of the big double beds in the cabin. We thanked Frank for his hospitality, ate what was served, and talked to our hosts till it was time to go to sleep.

Josephine Corning 1970

The following day, we went to work on our housing project. The measurements of our home-to-be were twelve feet by nine feet on the inside. The furnishings consisted of one bed frame without a mattress, one small table, and one shaky old chair.

The small porch on the cabin amounted hardly to no more than an elongated entrance with a very low ceiling.

After sweeping the place, we had to tighten all cracks in between the logs with old insulation or moss, and then we refitted some of the small window panes in the only window in that cabin. We naturally had no putty to hold the window panes in place and therefore used small nails and wet, mashed newspaper to do the job. Thankful for the relatively warm weather we had, we felt even luckier when Neal found an oil drum under the snow near the cabin which already had once been made into a barrel stove. It gave us the feeling that the gods were on our side. While I built myself a bed frame out of small aspen poles and rawhide, Neal constructed a stove door out of some scrap metal and by the time Josephine called us for dinner, we had made considerable progress toward our independence.

On the next day, we installed our stove with some extra stovepipe from Frank, heated the place up, and moved into our own home. Sure, there still was a lot to be done to make it more comfortable, but in time everything would fall into place.

Soon, we had a routine established for all the necessary chores to run our household. The drinking water, for instance, was procured by cutting blocks of clear ice on the river, which we stored on the roof of our porch. According to our needs, we chipped smaller chunks off these ice blocks to fill a bucket, which hung at the wall behind the stove and from that bucket, we then filled and refilled the teakettle on the stove. Woe to the person who would forget to refill either one of these containers.

The low entrance to our home was literally a headache to us in the beginning. Since not only the door frames but also the ceiling in between was very low, we often forgot about it and bumped our heads.

"Darn those short Indians!" we would mumble, knowing only too well that the entrance was built so low to prevent the heat from escaping during entering or leaving the cabin.

Supplying our home with sufficient firewood was the most time-consuming business of all. We had to find the driftwood under the snow along the riverbank, standing deadwood in the surrounding woods, or logs from fallen in cabins. Once we had brought our wood home, it still had to be cut into blocks with a regular handsaw, since the acquisition of a chainsaw had never crossed our minds; but we did not complain that we had to cut our firewood by hand—after all, the old Indian lady cut her wood with a handsaw as well. So, we young and supposedly tough adventurers should be able to handle the situation. Eventually, we found out that Frank actually had a chainsaw, but didn't use it because he didn't know how to sharpen the chain. At that time, I certainly had no idea at all about all this modern, technical stuff. Neal, on the other hand, went right to work on sharpening the chain, or at least, so he thought. It seems, while he generally was more up to date on technical things in general, he lacked the experience with chainsaws as much as I did. At any case, cutting a log with that chainsaw took just about as long as cutting it by hand. I didn't feel that I was in the position to criticize Neal's chain-sharpening technique, and kept quiet, but soon, we all kept on cutting our wood by hand again.

In between our regular activities, I even had found some time to set some traps within the near surrounding and almost as expected without any results. Neal and I also had cut a trail wide enough for a snowmobile through the rough ice, all the way across the Yukon, since we wrongfully assumed that anybody coming upriver from Ruby would follow the south side of the river before crossing it. Proudly, we had put up a sign with an arrow pointing toward Kokrines and the inscription, "Kokrines, pop. 4." As it turned out, outside of Neal and me, only some wildlife might have read the sign and therefore probably knew to stay away.

Our hope that Gilbert Cleaver or somebody else from Ruby would soon come over that trail and bring the rest of our supplies, which we had been expecting to arrive by mail from Anchorage, remained in vain. The main item we sorely missed at that time was our kerosene lamp. Frank had no extra kerosene lamp to lend to us and the candles which we had been burning up to now were just about gone. To burn the candle stubs and the wax droppings, we constructed a device with a floating wick in a jar lid, in which we soon burned almost anything of fatty consistency that we could find.

To help us out before we could go hunting, Frank had given us a frozen moose neck from his fall moose. Assuming that we were expected to shoot a moose sooner or later and pay him back with fresh meat, we had made our first futile attempts to hunt as soon as possible. But game of any kind seemed to be especially scarce during this particular winter, and all we had seen up to that point were the tracks of snowshoe hares. In spite of all my efforts to at least catch some of those critters, I had not been able to even catch one of them.

Just as it had been between Neal and me in California, the hunting for our meals was left to me again. Neal did accompany me now and then, especially in our effort to find a moose, but his interest lay closer to photography during our mutual outings. This was something I had expected anyway, and I didn't mind it at all.

Neal had more or less taken over the chores of cutting firewood and doing the dishes while I was out setting traps and searching for game. Most of the cooking was my department again, since I was the better cook, but it would have been a lot nicer if I had something to put in the pot or frying pan.

With my trapping efforts, it didn't look any better than with the hunting. Up to date I had caught one ermine, of which the pelt had a value of about a dollar at the Ruby Trading Post. All these shortcomings and the fact that our expected supplies refused to materialize created a lot of stress and tension. The effect of our discontent surfaced when Neal had found a square five-gallon can and reconstructed it into a slop-bucket, while I went to check on my traps. Neal was handier in the construction of useful items than he would have been on the trapping trail anyway; he even had manufactured a baking oven out of one of those five-gallon cans and had baked some rolls for our breakfast, as long as our flour lasted.

When I returned from my unsuccessful hunting and trapping trip that day, I found Neal in the process of putting a handle on the bucket and he greeted me with the words, "Charley is dead!"

Charley we had named a vole, who visited us every night.

"What happened?" I asked, whereupon Neal explained to me that Charley must have fallen in that five-gallon bucket during the night and just died.

Since I have an interest in all kinds of wildlife, I wanted to take a closer look at the dead vole and asked Neal what he had done with it.

"I put it on the shelf in the porch." answered Neal and I went to look at it.

As soon as I saw the vole, I knew that it wasn't Charley, since the vole in the porch was totally mummified.

"I know it was Charley," argued Neal, "because there was no dead vole in this can when I brought it in here."

"Did you wear your glasses?" I asked in good humor, but knew at the same moment that my reply had not came across the way I had intended. Neal gave me a dirty look and said, "Don't get cocky with me now!"

Knowing only too well that Neal couldn't stand to be in the wrong, I kept my thoughts to myself for the moment, but when later that night Charley came for his regular visit, I couldn't hold it back and said, "Look, here comes Charley's ghost!"

The look I got from my friend that time did not exactly express admiration. It was clear to me, if I wanted to preserve what was left of our home atmosphere, I would have to avoid further incidences of this kind, at least until Neal's spirits had recuperated; but that probably wouldn't happen until I put some fresh meat on the table.

Even after following expert advice from Frank, the snowshoe hares avoided my snares and traps. On a clear, full-moon night, Neal and I decided to take a hike along the quarter-mile trail, I had recently reestablished, to the cemetery, in the hope to get to see and possibly shoot one of these evasive creatures. Arriving at the cemetery without encountering any game along the way, we sat down on the fences, which the natives of Alaska often build around the individual graves, and lit up a cigarette. Not a breath of air was moving and the smoke from our cigarettes rose straight up toward the sky. Behind Neal, on the edge of a steep slope down to the river stood a good size birch tree, which for some reason still had most of its fall leaves on its branches. Suddenly, those leaves started shaking as if there was a gust of wind. But we didn't feel any wind and the smoke from our cigarettes was still moving straight into the air.

Surprised, we looked at each other and then Neal said, "Let's get the hell out of here!"

So we went home from another unsuccessful hunting trip.

In the evenings, I often visited Frank to exchange differences in our respective cultures and listen to Frank's old-time stories. It also was a way for me to avoid Neal when he got too moody for my taste. That particular night, I mentioned the incident about the birch tree at the cemetery to Frank, and so had steered our conversation for that evening in the direction of the supernatural. In spite of Frank's well rounded self-education, he believed in unexplainable and supernatural incidents to an extent that he would not cross a cemetery at night, unless his life depended on it. Then I asked my friend about the rumor about the curse of Kokrines, about which we had heard from the people in Ruby and Frank then related the following story to me:

"Quite a few years ago, when Kokrines still was a village, there used to be a lot of drinking and gambling going on here, which had started when the people from Kokrines took jobs in the mining town of Ruby to make some money. But while earning that money, they also took up all the bad habits of the life in that gold rush community and brought them back here. Anyway, it got so bad with the drinking that some people broke into the church and stole the sacramental wine. If that was not bad enough, they also used the entrance to the church as a bathroom. At that point, the priest had enough of it. He packed his belongings and before he left the village, he called out, 'Grass shall grow in the streets of Kokrines!' Right after that, all hell broke loose. During a big night of drinking and gambling, it came to a shoot-out. After that night, four people were dead, three of them were shot during the fight, but the fourth man, after discovering that he had shot his own brother, hung himself. Since then, the people started moving away from this village and grass started to grow in the streets of Kokrines. If one would dig up the ground in between the cabins, he would find the old wooden sidewalks under the thick layer of grass roots."

"Maybe that is the reason all the game left after we moved here?" I suggested after Frank was done with his story.

"Maybe!" replied Frank with a smile and then in a more serious tone, he added, "There are years like that, when game is just awfully scarce."

Well, curse or no curse, I kept on trying out new ideas to catch the snowshoe hares. Since nothing had worked up to that point, I scratched a hole from the side under the hare's trail and shoved a set marten trap into it. The following morning, I found that the hare had broken through his trail and got caught in my trap.

Neal's eyes lit up when I came home with my prey. Even though we still had some of that frozen moose neck left, which we ground up in our meat grinder to make hamburgers, it certainly was a nice change for us to have a nice tender hare for dinner.

Now that I had figured out how to catch them, I hoped to repeat my success, but when there were no more fresh tracks afterwards, it became clear to us that I had caught the only hare in the neighborhood. Some time later, I caught another hare on the opposite side of the village, and thereby wiped out the whole hare population all around the old village site.

Next, I took a trip with Neal along the riverbank in the hope to find some grouse to shoot.

It was an all around nice day and Neal suggested that we better practice walking on our snowshoes. I agreed at first, but after I had stumbled a few times, I decided to continue my training to walk on snowshoes at some later time, when the snow would be deeper. At this point, snowshoes were not yet really necessary to get around, but my friend, determined as usual, kept walking on his snowshoes in spite of the stumbles. When we reached a spot along the riverbank where the overflow from a little creek had built up a kind of frozen waterfall, I knew that Neal would spend some time trying to get a good picture of it. This natural ice sculpture with its greenish and turquoise colors looked real pretty in the sunlight and Neal was trying to find the right angle. But, in the process, he stepped on some snow-covered ice, fell on his butt, and slid all the way down to the river. I had to struggle with myself in order not to laugh out loud, because if anything would have happened to Neal's camera during the incident, he would have thrown a fit, and my amusement would only have made things worse. As it turned out, Neal had managed to hold the camera up out of harm's way. He got back on his feet, rubbed his rear, and mumbled something about not wearing the right gear for downhill skiing. It was then and not before that I, too, allowed myself to make a remark about Neal's ballet attempts.

Soon, we continued along the riverbank and actually scared up a couple of grouse, which I followed up the steep riverbank into the woods, but I could not find them again. In the meantime, I heard Neal shoot down at the river and hoped that he at least had found one of the birds. Upon my return to the river, I found out that Neal had mistakenly shot a gray-jay. When I mentioned that the gray jay was too small to be mistaken for a grouse, Neal said that he thought that it was a young bird, which almost made me laugh, but in order to prevent another altercation, I kept my thoughts to myself and preserved the atmosphere between us. Right after this outing, it snowed for two days, which gave me the feeling of a fresh beginning for our life in Kokrines. After the snowfall, it would be easier for me to read fresh animal tracks and would allow me to reset my traps to better locations. Fresh moose tracks would also be easier to identify and follow. Sooner or later, a moose had to come along and it did. I stepped out of our cabin and saw a moose, upriver from us crossing toward the cemetery on our side. I ran back into the cabin, grabbed my Winchester, and told Neal about the moose. Then I was on that trail toward the cemetery. There had been no time for putting on snowshoes and I had chosen to follow that trail through the woods, rather than along the river in order to stay out of sight. I knew the moose couldn't see me on that high riverbank, which he would have to climb before he could vanish into the woods. Just in case I stopped now and then to listen for breaking branches. When I didn't hear any such sounds, I was hopeful that the animal still would be below me at the river, but then I saw fresh tracks in front of me leading from the edge of the riverbank straight through the woods toward the hills. Not ready to throw in the towel just yet, I followed, hoping that the moose would stop now and then to check out what, or who was following him. My hopes to catch up with my prey finally vanished when, after some time, I stood on top of a hill with an open valley before me. The tracks of my potential prey led straight across that valley into another heavy wooded hillside. It was time to face reality and for me to return home.

My trapline - Kokrines

Arriving at our cabin, I found my friend in his underwear, hanging some of his clothes up to dry. In his haste to follow me, Neal had not even put socks on his feet before stepping into his boots. By the time he had reached the spot where my tracks merged with those of the moose, his shoes had filled with snow and his freezing feet forced him to return.

Frank was not surprised that I hadn't gotten the moose; over the years, he had gotten used to disappointments of this kind. There was no blame to put on anybody and no lectures to be given. Frank's only advice, or what he called pointers, was as simple as it sounded: "If you want to catch a marten, you have to think like a marten. If you want to hunt a moose; you have to think like a moose!"

It certainly made sense, but it would be helpful to me to encounter more of these animals, get to know them, and study their behavior. But as my elderly Indian friend had said earlier, "There are years like that, when game seems to be scarce."

While still without our expected supplies, we even ran out on burnable materials for our floating wick lanterns, but we had a full can of kerosene and that gave me an idea. I constructed a lamp out of a small medicine bottle by sticking the lower half of a ball point pen through the lid of that bottle, through which I had threaded a piece of yarn as wick. Now, we had a device to burn kerosene, which gave us about the same amount of light as a candle. Because of the missing glass chimney, the wick had to be kept trimmed down to keep it from smoking too much. Neal later constructed a larger model of my invention, but the flame would still have to be kept as small as possible at his lamp to keep the smoking down and the soot out of the air. With our lighting problems somewhat resolved, by each of us having our own lamp now, and therefore a little more light, we had more time to concentrate on all of our other shortages, like our need for groceries, and since we both were heavy smokers, tobacco, or the lack of it also contributed to our irritability. To keep this tension to a minimum, I kept to my trapping trails in the day-time and to visiting Frank in the evenings. My real reason for visiting Frank was not so much the tension between Neal and me, but as already mentioned, I enjoyed his company as much as Frank enjoyed mine.

Our need for fresh meat had turned our conversations often to hunting, which in turn caused Frank to tell me stories from bygone days about his ancestors. Frank's theory was that I, according to the old-timers belief, might not yet have earned the honor for one of the moose people to give itself to me. According to the old time Athabaskans, a long time ago, all the animals lived in tribes and could speak, just like people. For that reason, some people of the older generation along the Yukon addressed the animals as moose people, bear people, and so on.

"One thing the old-time hunters used to do," said Frank, "was to watch the ravens. When a raven would fly in a straight line, then make a roll in the air or drop a few feet, while keeping the original direction, that meant that the hunter would get his game within a week."

Frank either saw the smile on my face or he read my thoughts, because he, too, smiled before he added, "Now I don't know if that would work for white people, too!"

Believing in it or not, from that day on, I couldn't help but pay attention to the ravens when I walked my trails.

168

On December 22, Gilbert arrived in Kokrines with his snowmobile pulling a loaded sled.

We greeted his arrival with great anticipation, but soon found out that most of the load on Gilbert's sled were supplies for Frank and Josephine. For Neal and me, he had a small package for each of us and a few letters.

Now, we could only conclude that our friends in Anchorage either had a very high opinion of our survival skills, or that they hoped never to see us again. For the moment at least, even the letters and the little unexpected packages lifted our spirits. My package was from Alice and contained a pair of sealskin slippers for each of us, which she had sewn herself, plus a carton of cigarettes and some sweets. Neal's package was from his parents and contained a salami, cheese, and some sweets as well.

As I handed Neal his pair of slippers, I said, "Now, at least we can starve to death with warm feet!" And after putting on our new, fancy footwear, we lit a cigarette and read our letters.

On Christmas Eve, we ate from the puny remains of our moose neck and celebrated late into the night with tea, bullion, coffee, and cigarettes.

On Christmas Day, we were invited to dinner by our neighbors. Josephine had spared no effort to present us with a real feast, while she most likely had no idea that we would have been happy just to taste potatoes and homemade bread again.

Christmas or not, some of the old Indian customs were not broken in Frank's house. That meant that Josephine would set the table just for us men and then withdrew to her corner. To Frank, actually every meal was a ceremony, but this feast was special, and started already with the placement of every pot and plate on the table. Loading up his plate also seemed to have a system with my old Indian friend. After that, Frank loosened the top button on his pants before he sat down and stripped the suspenders off his shoulders. Then, finally, he reached for his knife and fork and started eating. I never before saw a person taking so much pleasure in preparing for, or eating a meal, but what really surprised me was that Frank was holding and keeping his knife after European fashion in his right hand all throughout the meal.

There had been very little conversation during the time we ate, while Josephine seemed content to pick around on some bones in the background, until we had finished our meal. Then she removed the pots and the plates from the table and filled her own plate from the leftovers to eat away from the table contently by herself, while we men started a conversation over tea and cigarettes.

Kokrines 1968

Chapter 16
Then The Raven Spoke

By the end of the year 1969, I kind of felt that I had passed some kind of woodsman apprenticeship. I had spent more time outside in all kinds of weather than I had ever before in my life, and I had mastered walking on the snowshoes to the point that I was jogging while wearing them. The reason that I didn't have much success with my trapping or getting a moose, I contributed to the strange year without much game we were experiencing. Mother Nature must have thought about it a little different, she probably saw me as a student and certainly had a couple more tests in mind for me. On my next unsuccessful run of trapline across the river from Kokrines, I had taken my Winchester along in the hope that I might encounter the sorely needed moose. Since my trail had been well established, I didn't even see any need for snowshoes on this trip. It was cloudy but nice, and fairly warm that day. But when I arrived at the end of my established trail, I didn't feel like turning back already; instead, I decided to enlarge my trapping trail toward a big grass lake, as the natural meadows are called around here. I followed the slough to my left for a few hundred yards and then turned north to enter the meadow, surrounded by a belt of the usual willow brush, which makes them the perfect feeding ground for moose.

I was not lucky enough to encounter a moose or any other game, except that I discovered a fresh moose track leading straight out across this open area, back in the direction toward the Yukon. Having nothing better to do, I followed the tracks, which should bring me eventually back to the river within sight of Kokrines. Even if I should not catch up with the moose, I would still get to know a little more about our surroundings, which never could hurt. All fired up with the idea that I might be successful this time, I marched enthusiastically ahead, without snowshoes, through the knee-deep snow. But soon, some fresh snowflakes started falling. I didn't let that bother me, until it was snowing so heavily that it was hard to see the woods to my left anymore. Convinced that these conditions might give me a better chance to get close to my prey without being discovered, I put another half a mile or so behind me before I became aware of the fact that it also was starting to get dark.

I knew then I had to break off my pursuit and forget about the moose, but I did not feel like walking all the way back the way I had come. To keep on walking in the direction I was going was not a good idea in the vanishing daylight, since I didn't know the terrain ahead of me and with the dark upon me, I could be asking for trouble. Figuring that I had been walking parallel to my trapping trail in the opposite direction, all I had to do now was turn left and eventually I should end up on my original trail sooner or later.

The snowfall had slowed down again, but it was really getting dark fast, especially after I entered the woods to my left. Walking through that deep snow without snowshoes started to take its toll and I was getting tired. Knowing from experience that distances under those conditions always seem longer, I kept my anxiety in check while trying to keep my direction, but there came a point in time when I calculated that I should have reached my trail. I cursed myself for letting the trees and thickets throw me off from walking in a more or less straight line and not being able to see more than a few feet ahead. I knew that the only safe thing to do then was to make camp.

The root of a fallen tree next to me would make a good reflector for my campfire, so I leaned my rifle against a tree and started breaking dry branches of the spruce trees nearby. While stepping through some heavy brush in order to reach a promising source of firewood—surprise! I stood on my trapping trail. Well, I certainly was happy about it and, in a flash, I had retrieved my rifle and trotted along the well-packed trail toward home. What could have been a very uncomfortable night turned out to be all right, but most of all it made me proud that I had figured correctly after all. I had been a little too impatient with my estimation, but otherwise I had made all the right decisions. Reaching the edge of the woods, I could see the distant lights of the cabin windows in Kokrines on the opposite side of the river. I barely had started to cross the Yukon, when, ahead of me, the figures of a man with a dog appeared.

"I'm going to have to talk to your momma about your staying out that late!" Neal greeted me, while my dog was all over me for happiness. Neal had learned a long time ago not to worry about me, but Minado had barked like crazy, and since Neal also knew that animals have a sixth sense for situations when things are not quite right, he listened to the dog and came to check on me. A short time later, when we sat in the warm cabin and I drank a hot cup of tea, I told Neal my side of the story.

Had I really gotten lost, it would have hurt my pride, but since my calculations were right, I felt great. All I had to do the next time was to walk a few steps farther, or better yet don't put myself in a situation like that to begin with. One question, however, remained, which only Minado could answer: How did he know that something was out of order?

New Year's Eve had arrived. Our festive mood and excitement rivaled just about any other of our festive occasions. We ate the absolute rest of the moose neck, drank tea and bullion for the remainder of the night, while we cleared the air between us. Neal and I told each other what irritated us about the other one's behavior and then we shook hands to wish each other a healthy and happy new year for a fresh start.

The New Year, however, didn't quite see things the same way. Neal woke up with a stomachache and spent most of that day making trips to the outhouse. By evening, he felt somewhat better again and I teased him by telling him that he shouldn't have drank so much during our New Year's Eve celebration....

Neal's stomach condition improved further on New Year's Day because of the ingredients of our holiday dinner, which consisted of no more than plain boiled rice without milk, sugar, meat, or any other condiments, due to the utter lack of it. So, there was really nothing that could have made it worse.

"Boy, that was great!" I said sarcastically as I pushed the empty bowl away from me and patted my belly like I just had finished a gourmet dinner.

"Look at it this way," commented Neal, "it can't get much worse."

The following morning, I wished Neal wouldn't have said that. Things might have looked better for him, but now it was my stomach that started acting up and the temperatures outside had fallen to sixty-five degrees below.

Frank and his dog

During weather like that, there wasn't much else to do but keep the fire going and find something to read or keep otherwise occupied. No matter how occupied I might have been, I had to manage several trips to the ice-cold outhouse. Lucky for me, by the evening, I felt good enough again to pay Frank another visit. Naturally, the cold weather and the lack of game became the topic for that night and Frank told me another story about his younger years.

"In the earlier years, even more than now, a man's survival depended upon his success as a hunter, and when years like this one came around, things started to get pretty tough. I was trapping at the Nowitna River during one of those years and all I had caught in my traps was an otter. After skinning the animal, I hung the carcass outside to cool off because I was thinking about eating that otter, since all I had left to eat was dried fish and I was hungry for meat. Otter meat is normally not good for human consumption, but my mother used to have a recipe that would make even otter meat edible. I tried all night long to remember that recipe. By morning, I still wasn't sure about it. But intending to cook the carcass anyway, I stepped outside to get it. To my surprise, the carcass was gone. According to the tracks in the snow, a wolverine had stolen the otter and probably ate it without worrying about my mother's recipe. In a way, I was glad about it, because I didn't have to cook it anymore and could spare myself some disappointment. I ate my dried fish instead and was contented."

Two days later, the temperature had risen to twenty below and Neal and I were amazed how warm that felt after the cold snap. There was another thing I had learned during that cold snap: it was that splitting wood with a double bladed axe at sixty-five below has its hazards. While the wood splits much easier when it is cold, one should preferably use a slitting mall. If one has to use a double bladed ax, it should be kept inside the cabin so it will stay warm, because if the steel of an axe gets that cold, it also gets as brittle as glass. At the first imperfect hit, one half of the blade of my double bladed ax whistling past my head certainly scared the heck out of me.

But now that it was warmer again, it was time for Neal to replenish our wood supply and time for me to get back on my trapping trails. Even with my trail being packed by now, it was necessary to pack down the fresh snow as well, so I used my snowshoes. I had learned that because of one of Frank's pointers again, in which he indicated that animals like to follow nice, clean, and straight trails. It made sense to me, but the bad part was that also the moose liked an established trail and sometimes made a mess of it. But since we were in dire need of a moose, these animals would have been more than welcome to mess up my trail, as long as they would stick around for me to get a good shot at one. My traps, however, had remained empty, except for an unlucky squirrel or a gray jay now and then. After discovering fresh marten tracks where I didn't have a trap, I reset one of my traps to that spot and on my return trip, while I still had not caught a marten, I had at least a snowshoe hare in my freshly set trap.

Trotting along my trail and looking forward to the meal of fresh meat, I scared up a flock of grouse. But I had my Winchester instead of my .22 rifle, because I had hoped for an encounter with a moose. Carrying both rifles with me at all times just was something I was not willing to do. Hoping the birds would stick around and no moose tracks anywhere near my trail, I took my small caliber rifle the next day. Naturally, there were no grouse to be found, but farther up the trail, I heard crackling noises and, carefully, I sneaked through the brush, hoping to get near a flock of feeding birds.

Instead, I suddenly stood about fifty yards or less in front of a moose. I could have cried for anger, but it wouldn't have changed the facts and all I could do was to withdraw and hope the moose would hang around.

My search for that moose on the following day took hours and was in vain. Then as if to rub my nose in it, I encountered the grouse again on my way back home. But this time, I was in no mood to ignore them. I lined up on the neck of the first bird and dropped it like a rock. I missed the second bird, but shot one more before the rest of the flock flew away.

The first bird I shot was minus a head, but I could not find any damage at all on the second bird. Either my bullet had passed its head so close that the shock killed it, or it died of fright. At any case I was bringing home the bacon again, even if it was very lean bacon for the price of the 30-30 cartridges.

One thing I had not figured on was that my shots had been heard across the river in Kokrines and Neal was already sharpening his knife, believing that I had shot that moose I had been looking for.

With the hare already eaten up, Neal was watching me impatiently as I prepared the grouse for our evening meal and as soon as he heard the frying pan sizzle, he said;

"If those funny birds are not done within ten minutes, I'll eat mine raw!"

However small my recent successes might have been, they did a lot to lighten our dreary camp atmosphere; so much so that I even got Neal back out on the trail and together, we made a snare set at a beaver house in the slough near the end of my trail. Not having any experience along that line, as well as not the right equipment for the job, it turned into a little bigger job than it should have been. We chopped a hole in the ice with an axe and when the hole filled with water before it was big enough, we got quite wet while finishing the job. By the time it was done, our pants legs were covered in ice, but we went home with a feeling of having accomplished something. Three days later, when I checked on our accomplishment, the beaver had thankfully chewed on our fresh birch poles, but he had avoided the snares. So I went to work and renewed the set by myself, while wondering if it was worth my efforts. As payment for my toil, I found my first marten in one of my traps on my way home. Determination seemed to pay off!

"Things are looking up," said Neal when he saw our first valuable fur. "If you keep it up now, we might even be able to pay our store bill in Ruby."

At that time, a marten fur was worth about ten dollars in Ruby, which told me that I had to catch quite a few of those animals yet before we would be out of debts.

When I told Neal that on that very day that I also had seen a raven fly in the manner as Frank had described to me, Neal's sarcasm reappeared and he said, "Yeah, yeah, and tomorrow a moose will be standing in front of our door!"

That didn't dampen my spirit and I thought to myself, *Nonbeliever!* but kept my mouth shut.

Two days later, we had another nice sunny day, which beckoned even Neal to get back out on the trail with me again. While we enjoyed our walk, all my marten traps and the beaver set was empty. When we reached the very end of the trail and heard some branches break in the willow brush that surrounded that grass lake, we had no doubts that this noise was made by a moose. By the time we made our way through the willows and got a look at the situation, we saw two moose at quite a distance that made them look about the size of a couple of German Shepherds. In spite of the unfavorable circumstances, I adjusted the sight of my Winchester accordingly and aimed at the animal nearest to us.

Raven

"You'll never hit them from this distance," Neal argued.

"What do we have to lose?" I asked, and then held my sights about a hand wide over the moose and pulled the trigger. My shot thundered over the quiet winter landscape and the moose I had shot at ran in a tight circle before entering a small patch of brush and vanished from sight, while the second moose kept on running in a different direction.

"I told you it was too far!" said Neal.

"The way that moose was running in a circle didn't look right to me," I answered, and started walking out to where the moose had been standing. When I got there, I saw the animal only about thirty yards into the brush, where it had bedded down in between some willows. A second shot through the neck ended the animal's suffering, before Neal had caught up with me. As we later found out, my first shot had missed the moose's heart by only two inches.

Neal now congratulated me on a job well done and then suggested that he would go back to Kokrines to let Frank and Josephine know about our success, and afterward to return with Frank's homemade toboggan.

I knew that the job of cutting up the animal was not for my friend and he wouldn't have been much help anyway; therefore, I was glad that he would be out of my way. I had never taken any big game animal apart either, but I certainly wasn't helpless when it came to things like that—it came natural to me.

By the time it was starting to get dark, my partner returned with the toboggan, an ax, and a saw. But except for the backbone, I had the moose all skinned out, gutted, and cut up.

After chopping the backbone into manageable pieces, we loaded the toboggan with a hindquarter, liver, heart, and the tongue and headed toward home. The homemade toboggan was awkward and hard to handle on that narrow trail through the woods. In other words, it was hard work pulling that first load home, but knowing that we now could eat to our hearts' desire certainly made it bearable.

I still have to smile when I think back to that night: It must have been a sight to equal a scene from a horror movie, as Neal and I, smeared with blood, dragged that meat over that trail in the moonlight, accompanied by the crunching sound of our footsteps on the frozen snow.

Totally exhausted, we arrived in Kokrines, where Frank greeted us outside his cabin to congratulate me.

"The raven has spoken!" I said, and Frank smiled, as he invited us to dinner. The old Indian couple was well acquainted with the hard work that followed a moose kill and they knew that we would be too tired to cook for ourselves.

After dinner, I had to give a detailed account of our hunt and then Frank declared me the hero of the day. Even though I felt physically drained, I was spiritually too fired up to just lie down and go to sleep. So Frank and I ended up talking till late into the night. Neal had withdrawn to our cabin soon after dinner, to write down his experiences of the day and go to sleep. Almost as excited as I was, Frank started telling about his own first moose hunt.

"I was already twenty years old before my father took me on my first moose hunt," said Frank, after he lit his hand-rolled cigarette. "Without any warning, he told me to get my snowshoes, we are going hunting. The snow had fallen early that year and I could hardly contain my anxiety when we came across a fresh moose track. Soon, there was the sound of breaking branches ahead of us in the willows and my father told me to go the left, while he went to the right. A few minutes later, I saw the moose walking toward me, but I didn't dare to shoot, because I didn't know if my father was somewhere in the direction behind the moose. Hurriedly, I retraced my steps, but when I turned around, the moose was still following me.

"I finally shot at it, but as nervous as I was, I probably would have missed a whole herd of moose. Anyway, the moose ran away and I thought the hunt was over. Returning to the point where my father and I had parted, I looked over my shoulder and there was that moose again, pawing the ground only twenty yards behind me. In the excitement, my rifle got hung up in the brush, while the moose was coming closer and closer and making fake attacks. By the time I had my rifle free from the brush, I stumbled over my snowshoes and fell."

The memory of this event made Frank laugh so hard, that he had to take a break to compose himself. After a couple of sips of his tea and the last puff on his cigarette, he continued.

"By now, I was sure that my end was near, and, at first, I didn't even want to look up. When I finally lifted my head slowly and saw that moose pawing the snow again, only ten yards in front of me, I got up on my knees, aimed, and shot. The moose fell where it had been standing, but I held my position until I heard my father's voice next to me. Then my father took a couple of cups out of his pack, cut the artery at the animal's throat, filled the cups with blood, and according to our custom, he demanded that I drink the blood with him."

When Frank asked me if I had drank the blood of my moose, I told him that I didn't and that I had no desire to do so. But the next day, I ate a piece of the raw moose liver just with salt and pepper on it, which almost caused my partner to leave the cabin. I wouldn't have cared if Neal would have left, I certainly enjoyed the feeling of the rush that went through my body, as the long missed vitamins replenished my system.

For the next load of meat, we took the old dogsled we had gotten from Johnny May and figured that it would make our work easier, since it was a lot lighter than Frank's toboggan. But because the sled was lighter, we loaded a little heavier, and our work to pull it home was about just as hard as before.

On our way to get the meat, we found another marten in one of my traps and a grouse in another. Then just as we were leaving the woods with our second load of meat, we saw a snowmobile coming toward us from across the river. The driver was Phillip Albert, a Native of Ruby and his offer to pull our sled with us standing on the runners' back to Kokrines was greatly appreciated.

Philip Albert also had brought another Indian with him, who had a cabin in Kokrines, and had moved in for the beaver trapping season; besides that, we also received some mail, but no supplies.

Phillip spent that night in Kokrines and during the evening, Neal got the bright idea that one of us should go back to Ruby with Phillip to buy a few necessities at the Ruby store.

The idea was great, but I also knew that Neal wanted me to go, which was not to my way of thinking, and since I finally had started catch some fur, I wanted to stay in Kokrines and make a little more money for us. Neal, after all, didn't know how to trap or how to skin the animals, and therefore he had no argument left and had to go himself.

Al Hardluck, the Native Phillip had brought from Ruby to trap beavers, was an original inhabitant of Kokrines, but he lived the greater part of the year in Ruby. In spite of the fact that I was only a guest here in the Indian country, I still could not help myself to feel like I was being invaded by his presence; not that I cared much about Al's beaver trapping, since I didn't know enough about it and wasn't planning to make any more sets to catch them, other than where we had set our snares already. To get to his beaver trapping location, Al had to use the same trail as I did and while Al always pulled his little toboggan along, I had to take some of my traps off the trail. In exchange, I had made sure that Al wouldn't set traps on what I considered my trapping grounds. My reaction or overreaction to the situation was probably due to my new lifestyle, which must have brought out the primitive territorial instinct in me. Anyway, our differences were not only quickly resolved, but we actually became friends.

Al also had laughed about the way I had set my marten traps, but apparently a little too premature. While I by now brought one or two martens home per day, Al didn't seem to catch any. It took me a while to convince Al to try it my way, and when he finally did, he started catching martens, too.

"That's all I needed," said Al, "a white man coming out here and teaching me how to catch martens."

In turn, I paid close attention to Al's advice about beaver trapping and gratefully accepted an extra ice chisel to replace my axe. But for this year, I didn't want to interfere with Al's trapping sites and left the beavers to him.

Neal returned from Ruby three days after he had left. He had not only brought some long-needed staples from the store, but also our long-expected packages and a stack of letters.

The hard times of the past were soon only memories, as we sat up till late by the bright light of our kerosene lamp with a cylinder, and nibbled on all kinds of goodies while reading our mail.

The bright light in our cabin also inspired a laundry day, since we were now able to see how gray our whites had turned from all the soot of our inefficient lighting.

Neal pointed at a small pile of laundry and said, "As soon as spring arrives, these are going to the funeral pyre."

"Don't be too much in a rush about it," I warned, "we might be able to pay our bill at the store, but won't get that rich enough for a whole new wardrobe!"

"Okay," replied my partner after he thought about it for a while, "then I'll sell them as Yukon artifacts when we get back to civilization."

"Good idea, but you better wash them first, before they walk off on you!"

From my next trip to the trapline, I brought back another marten and finally also a beaver from our set, even if it wasn't a very big one. With the fur we had at this point, I was sure to cover our expenses at the store, but there certainly wouldn't be too much money left for anything else. That the trapping season was coming to an end was highlighted by the arrival of two trappers from the Nowitna River. They came in with their dog teams and just before reaching Kokrines, they got into the overflow on the Yukon, which had accumulated under the snow during the warming weather. One of these trappers was Billy Dean, a Caucasian old-timer; the other was Sullivan Wright, a native; both of them were from Ruby. Billy went to Frank's house to get his feet dried, while we took care of Sullivan. We actually had to thaw the outside of Sullivan's mukluks before we could get them off his feet. Both of the trappers naturally knew Frank and Josephine well, and they were invited there to dinner. But Sullivan returned to our cabin afterwards and complained to us that Josephine had not put enough meat on the table. When I pointed to the stove and told him that there is a small beaver cooking on the stove, his eyes lit up and between the three of us, we polished every bone of that beaver carcass during the run of the evening, while we talked about life on the trapline.

Our guest and his partner had trapped eighty martens, sixty beavers, and two otters, which sounded a lot more like trapping than my meager attempts.

But first of all, they knew what they were doing and had done it for years. They also had started at the right time, about a month or more ahead of us, and besides that, they had a better trapping area plus about two-hundred traps and dog teams to check their long trails every other day.

Sullivan thought considering that I was totally new to the game and had only a dozen traps to begin with, while trapping on foot, I could consider myself very successful with my twelve martens and one beaver.

Shortly after the two trappers traveled on to Ruby, Phillip showed up in Kokrines again with his snowmobile and brought our mail. One of the letters to me was from Alice, in which she announced her arrival in Ruby in the near future. We never had made an arrangement like that, but it was once again typically Alice. That meant that it was my turn to take a trip with Phillip back to Ruby with my furs, while Neal and Minado stayed behind this time.

Chapter 17
Springtime in the Kokrine Hills

The young teacher couple, Jim and Betty Gunn in Ruby, offered me room and board at their apartment in the Ruby School Building while I was waiting for my wife. With a shower and an indoor bathroom to my disposal, I felt like I had checked into a hotel. In return for their hospitality, I demonstrated some glassblowing and self-defense to the children in the Ruby School.

At the Ruby trading post, I sold my furs, paid our debt, and had $ 17.35 left over.

Harold, too, was surprised, that I, as a beginner with so few traps, had been so successful.

And then he told me a story about another greenhorn who had come to Ruby a few years earlier to try his luck as a trapper.

"I can't remember the kid's name anymore," said Harold, "but, at that time, there was an old man living here who liked to play tricks on people. So, when he talked to that young greenhorn, he also gave him advice on beaver trapping and beaver skinning.

When that young man came off the trapline in spring, he had almost the same amount of pelts like you, a handful of martens and a beaver fur. The first thing I noticed about that beaver pelt was that he had left the skinned out tail attached to the fur. But there was something else wrong with the pelt, which did not seem quite right. On a closer inspection, it dawned on me that the boy had split the pelt along the back of the animal instead of along the belly. He had stretched the hide nice and round like it should be, only that the belly was now the center of the pelt."

Harold had to wipe the tears out of his eyes from laughing so hard, but then he said, "I bought that fur anyway, just to have it as a souvenir, but I'll be darned if I remember right now where I put it."

It was the beginning of April when Alice arrived in Ruby. Luckily, she also had brought some money. With the seventeen dollars I had left, we would have had to start a new line of credit right away. To avoid the higher cost of living, we also wanted to get out of Ruby as soon as possible and after agreeing on a price, Gilbert declared himself ready to bring us to Kokrines. During the daytime, the temperatures had already been high enough to melt the snow, which meant that we had to start our trip early in the morning, so the snowmobile would not overheat while pulling the heavy loaded sled in the softening snow. "Heavy loaded" was almost an understatement for that sled packed with supplies, Alice's luggage, and we two passengers. While Alice was sitting on top of the load, I was standing on the runners of the sled behind her. This arrangement promised to work out nicely, except for the still frozen ruts in the early morning. Through the town and down to the river we went; now and then, a frozen lump of ice or snow would kick one or the other of my feet off the runner, which was somewhat irritating until, suddenly, both of my feet got hit at the same time and I was lying in the snow. Gilbert and my wife were on their merry way and only Alice had noticed that I wasn't on the sled anymore. It took her quite a while before she managed to draw Gilbert's attention to the fact that he was minus one passenger.

Rather than taking a chance on repeating the incident, I, too, now rode on top of the sled with Alice instead on the runners. I was sitting behind Alice, holding her with one arm, while holding on to the rope that held down the freight with the other and Gilbert, believing that he had solved all the problems, now drove even faster.

For a little over an hour we had to endure this misery before we arrived in Kokrines. At this point, I felt that I deserved some kind of a certificate as an accomplished bronco rider.

For three days, all three of us, Neal, Alice, and I lived together in that little hut of ours, but we knew that something had to be done about the situation. My friend, Frank, must have read our minds, since he came and offered me a key to an old cabin, which was one of the few cabins still standing on the opposite end of the village.

"This cabin belongs to Gilbert's brother," said Frank. "It is not in very good shape anymore, but with springtime coming, I guess you and Alice will be all right there."

I knew that Neal was glad to see us move, just as glad as we were to leave the cramped conditions of that little cabin behind us. Neal and I, once partners in an adventure, were mere neighbors from then on. During the long winter nights, we had talked a lot about future adventurous undertakings, but by now I was certain that Neal had enough of the rough life in the wilderness, and most likely had already plans of his own. Whatever these plans were, they would by far be not as harsh as our last winter, and they most certainly would not include me, much less my wife, Alice. I, on the other hand, had as usual no real plans, other than that I was not ready to leave Kokrines just yet. My thinking was more along the line to see what happens next and let all problems solve themselves as they usually do.

As an answer to my way of thinking, a military type vehicle, called a weasel, came upriver on the ice and stopped in Kokrines. The weasel pulled a big freight sled with a heavy load. Leonard and Pat Veerhusen, the owners of the vehicle, lived at the Melozitna Hot Springs, about eighteen miles into the Kokrine Hills, as the crow flies.

Frank and Josephine had known the couple for a few years. It was Frank who had guided Leonard with his D-8 Caterpillar over the old reindeer-herder's trail to the hot springs. The actual length of the trail from Kokrines to the Melozitna Hot Springs, up and down and forth and back through the hills and tundra, naturally is a lot longer than eighteen miles. Opinions about that distance vary around the thirty-mile range. When the Veerhusens invited us to spend some time at the hot springs with them, we had no idea how well we would get to know this trail and the hot springs area.

The Melozitna Hot Springs

The old reindeer herders hut

While we loaded our gear on to that weasel and got ready to travel with Leonard and Pat to the hot springs, Minado befriended himself with Leonard's elkhound, even though both dogs were males; but just before the start of our journey, Minado must have known that he would be gone from Kokrines for a while. He jumped off the vehicle, ran into the woods, and reappeared with a leg bone of a moose, which he had buried there.

"What kind of dog do you have there," asked Leonard, "he thinks and plans ahead?"

The high spirits at the beginning of this trip were soon dampened. Right at the beginning of the first hill, the freight sled loaded with building materials, which the weasel was pulling, proved to be too much for the vehicle to pull through the deep wet snow. After Leonard decided to leave the loaded sled behind for this trip, we only got a couple miles farther before our transportation broke down, and the whole trip had to be postponed. We moved back into our respective cabins while Leonard and Pat took their snowmobile off the big freight sled and went down to Ruby. Then the Veerhusens flew from Ruby to Fairbanks to take care of some business, but they sent Gilbert Cleaver to Kokrines to work and repair the weasel.

By the time Leonard and Pat returned after a couple of days, the weasel had been fixed and we finally went on our trip to the hot springs. Neal drove Leonard's snowmobile ahead of the weasel in order to warn us about any potential obstacle or danger along the trail. Only once we had to clear a fallen birch tree out of the way and we made it without further incident about halfway to the springs, just a mile or so below the summit. There, the weasel suddenly jerked sideways and slipped a track. Leonard checked the situation and then informed us that the damage was a little greater than just a slipped track. The tools which Leonard had with him were not sufficient to repair the damage and we had to make a choice of either walking on ahead to the hot springs, or return once more to Kokrines on foot. The Veerhusens were convinced that the trail ahead would be the wiser choice, if not shorter.

After reaching the summit, we had an open tundra, with only scattered small stands of trees ahead of us. The snow of the high open country and especially the north slope of the mountain that lay before us was more packed and crusted, which meant we practically could walk on it without breaking through. Leonard, still in recovery from a broken leg, was driving the snowmobile now and he drove forth and back to give the women a break from walking. Somewhat lower down the slope, the snow crust was getting weaker again and we broke through more often, which made the walking quite arduous.

Taking his bearings from the landscape, Leonard assured us that we were headed in the right direction on the most direct way to their cabin, but then a snowstorm developed and the snow came down so thick that no more landmarks were to be seen. In a small grove of spruce trees we made a fire, ate something, and hoped that the storm would blow over before it got too dark.

Daylight was vanishing fast by the time we were able to travel on, but it was all downhill from there and according to our hosts, we almost had it made. We just had crossed the invisible, totally snowed over Hot Springs Creek at the bottom of a hillside. Only Leonard had to make one more trip back to get Alice, but when Leonard returned with his last passenger and crossed the frozen creek at the same spot for the second time, a big gaping hole appeared right behind the passing snowmobile. While I saw and heard the snow-covered ice crash into the turbulent current below, neither Leonard nor Alice had any idea how close they had come to disaster until I told them about it later. Had they or even one of our dogs fallen though that hole, there would have been nothing we could have done to save them.

On the other side of the creek, we were under tall trees, on a broad, easy to recognize trail toward the hot springs. Neal and I were the last to reach the point where we had to cross the creek once more to reach the end of a snowed over landing strip for small planes; but here the creek was broad, only knee-deep, and already ice free. The two women had already waded through the icy water and were heading toward the cabin on the far end of the strip. Leonard was waiting for Neal and me at the creek with his snowmobile for us to help him carry it to the other side. The wet feet and legs didn't matter much anymore by this time anyway, and a short time later, we all got our turn in a bathtub, filled with the hot water from the spring, while we sipped a hot grog.

During the next two weeks or so, we helped our hosts with the repair of their D-8 Caterpillar and the erection of a sawmill under a hot sunny sky. We also enjoyed the gorgeous scenery of our surrounding, but as soon as the D-8 was drivable, Leonard leveled the landing strip for the bush planes, so it would be useable in case of an emergency or for whatever other reason we might have to call for a plane by radio.

Eventually, because of the good, hot, weather we had, Leonard prepared a thirty-five pound backpack for each of us men with provisions and some tools and then we men marched back over the now almost snow-free tundra toward the abandoned weasel. The two women had their work cut out around the cabin, and while preparing the large green house for the growing season.

In spite of the heat of the day and the hard walking on that wet tundra, we had made good headway until we reached the northern slope of the summit. The snow on that hillside was still better than knee-deep at times, and the crust was too hard to just plow through it, but not strong enough to carry us. Snowshoes certainly would have been useful at that point, but neither of us had expected to find all this leftover snow.

To prevent Leonard from putting too much strain on his freshly healed leg, Neal and I took over the trail breaking. For the approximate two miles to the summit, it took us six hours to get up there, and my dog Minado, who would not stay behind at the springs, was the only one who could walk on top of that snow without any understanding why Neal and I were so exhausted after climbing up the hill side.

In the Kokrine hills

It was late in the evening by the time we got to the weasel, but since it still was fairly light this time of the year, Leonard started working on the vehicle without delay. By the following morning, the repairs were done as well as could be expected under the conditions, but not quite to Leonard's satisfaction. He doubted that his repair job would hold up during the ride through the tundra and while crossing the creeks along the way.

Minado

Plan number two was that Leonard and Neal would drive the weasel back to Kokrines for further repairs, after getting help from Ruby, while I should walk back to the hot springs in order to inform the women about the new developments.

The walk back to the springs with Minado was more to my liking, than another long, bumpy ride in the weasel toward an uncertain outcome anyway. So Minado and I had barely gotten off the first snowy slope, when Minado chased a porcupine up a tree. To my disappointment, this porcupine was the only wildlife we encountered along the way, but on the other hand, I was glad that we didn't encounter a grizzly bear so early in the spring, when these animals tend to be quite grumpy at times.

"Where are the other two guys?" asked Pat as we reached the cabin and I told her all about Leonard's new plan. Not much later, we started hearing motor noises and sure enough, Leonard had changed his mind once more.

190

The two guys in that weasel came rolling through the tundra, looking like one of Rommel's tanks gone astray.

Had the Veerhusens been richer, they would have hired us for the whole summer, but that not being the case, Pat had called a bush plane with supplies and we were offered a flight back. Even though it wasn't easy for me, I had decided to leave Minado at the hot springs with Leonard and Pat, since the dog only would have made things harder for us during our uncertain future. The pilot of our plane didn't feel confident enough to land on that overgrown landing strip in Kokrines and therefore he dropped us off in Ruby. Would we have been ready to travel on from there, it would have been to our advantage, but since we had to get some of our gear from Kokrines, we had to hire somebody with a boat to bring us upriver to get our belongings. With Neal moving out of that little cabin completely, it made a good storage place for Alice's and my stuff, with Frank watching over it. We actually left a lot of our things behind, knowing only too well that we would eventually return, even if it would be only for a visit and to pick up Minado from the hot springs.

Chapter 18
There and Back Again

After getting our belongings from Kokrines and returning to Ruby, we took the next plane to Anchorage, where we were met by a couple whom Neal had befriended.

That Neal indeed had already some kind of business arrangement with his friend, Bob, was obvious, especially since he moved right into their house. Alice and I were allowed to pitch our tent in their yard for a few days, with the understanding that we would move on as soon as possible. I certainly had no desire to hang around where I wasn't wanted and that went double for Alice, since she felt discriminated against, probably rightfully so.

Neal didn't need us anymore and our future obviously was none of his concern. The fact that we didn't have any transportation intensified our problem. Even though I hated to rely on our friend Jerry again, I contacted him and we moved to his place for a few days.

Being closer to the center of town, we were able to search for some work, but without result, at least in part due to the fact that I was not too sure that I wanted to find any long-term employment. In the back of my mind, I was already trying to figure out how to get back to Kokrines. Jerry had set no ultimatum for our stay at his place, like Neal's friends had done, but I still felt pressured to find a solution, since I didn't want to take advantage of Jerry's good nature.

From Fairbanks to Kokrines in this raft 1970

Eventually, we borrowed one-hundred dollars against some jewelry from a rich acquaintance and another acquaintance gave us a two-man rubber raft, which brought us one step closer to our independence. Some belongings that we also had stored with Jerry since the previous year, we sent by train and barge line ahead to Kokrines. The cost of the shipping at that time could be almost counted in pennies, which was certainly to our advantage. After thanking Jerry to let us stay with him, Alice and I took the train to Fairbanks again, as we had done the year before. In Fairbanks, while staying with our in-laws, we made another half-hearted attempt to generate some income. I also called a social worker, whom I had met in Ruby that spring while waiting for Alice to arrive there. The social worker, Carla Nyquist, invited us to dinner so we could meet her husband, David, a professor at the University of Alaska in Fairbanks. Dr. David Nyquist was in the process of building a house and I was given the opportunity to help out for a day, and so earned thirty-five dollars. But when it came to somewhat steadier work, professor Nyquist couldn't help us either; not that I really cared at this point; in my mind, I was ready back in the bush.

The following day, our brother in-law, Dale, drove us and our belongings to the boat landing at the Chena River, near the Fairbanks airport, but even before we could pump up our rubber raft, we had to scramble for cover from a short, but heavy downpour. It was almost like déjà vu, as I was reminded of the first time Alice and I were ready to head toward the Yukon when we were camped at the Eagle River campground near Anchorage.

Tanana bridge in Nenana

Our two-man rubber raft turned out to be smaller than we thought and by the time we had it loaded, we hardly found enough room on it for ourselves. But undeterred by the cramped conditions, we let the slow current of the Chena River drift us to where the Chena entered the Tanana River. The Tanana was at flood stage and the sight of the rushing current with a lot of drift floating in it was pretty scary one. But staying in civilization was no longer an option. Therefore, I pushed our little raft into the dizzyingly fast moving waters of that big river. Because of a strong headwind and the returning rain, we soon landed again and found shelter in a shack near the riverbank.

At 4 a.m. on the following morning, the wind had settled down and the showers were light as we traveled on. But by the time we reached the town of Nenana, we were soaking wet and had to pitch our tent so we could get dry again.

Nenana was established in 1907 as the St. Marks Indian Mission. In 1916, it became the headquarters for the construction of the Alaska Railroad. It was here where President Warren Harding drove the golden Spike into the north end of the 700-foot long bridge across the Tanana River on July 15,1923, thereby completing the railroad connection between Fairbanks and the west coast. At our time there, the population of the town was about 300 people. Nenana was also the home port for the barge lines and the freight depot between them and the railroad. We took advantage of that and sent a suitcase and a big box of our stuff by mail to the village of Ruby before we left Nenana.

Now with a little more room in our craft and the rain gone, we camped that evening across from the old Indian village Minto, whose inhabitants had recently moved to a new village site, to avoid the yearly floods. As we traveled on in the morning, Alice pointed ahead of us and said, "It looks like there is a raft in front of us." A short time later, we caught up with a man on a big raft made of oil barrels. Rafts of that sort had been constructed in previous years for the yearly spring raft races from Fairbanks to Nenana. Because of the partying that went on those rafts, and some occurring accidents, the races were discontinued.

The man on that raft we just caught up to was alone and outside of an old car seat and an axe, he didn't seem to have any other possessions. The first thing he asked was if we had anything to eat. We barely had enough for ourselves, but paddling within reach, I handed him a handful of pilot-bread crackers.

"Sorry," I said, "but that is all we can spare." And then I asked where he was headed.

"Manley Hot Springs!" he replied, whereupon I advised him that the landing for that place would be coming up soon and that he should hold to the right side of the river if he wanted to land there. We ourselves made sure to drift ahead and away from the raft, since this guy did not look very trust-worthy, and certainly was not the type we wanted for a traveling companion.

Our raft had drifted in between two small islands, where a cow moose with two calves drew our attention, as they climbed upon one of the islands. A short time later, we passed the landing for the Manley Hot Springs. The man on the big raft was nowhere in sight, but that was no concern of ours. We had no good reason to stop at this particular place and rather enjoyed the strong current that swept us past it. Soon after, we discovered dark, threatening clouds coming toward us and since we didn't look forward to getting soaked again, we hurriedly looked for a suitable landing. Taking our tent out of the raft, we covered it with a tarp and got busy setting up our shelter. By that time, the sky was as dark as it could be, and I expected a deluge at any moment.

Alice, on the other hand, seemed to be highly amused by my frantic action to find some willows strong enough to hold our tent up, because we once again had not taken the original tent poles along. The first heavy drops flopped into the dry sand all around us by the time we finally crawled into our barely standing shelter. The awaited downpour never materialized, and the sky started to lighten again. All my anxiety had been for nothing.

Stepping out of the tent, we thought we spotted the big raft on the far side of the river, but we couldn't be certain if the guy was still on it or not.

After all the pain of setting up the tent under duress, we decided to stay at this place for the night. The many hare tracks in the sand around us promised a good evening meal and I made sure to cash in on it by hunting one of those creatures down.

Manley would have been the last chance for us to change our minds and stay within road connection of Fairbanks and civilization. Any farther downriver from this point, only airplanes or motorboats could return us to any bigger town, but we wanted no part of it, and looked forward to get back to Kokrines.

Before we reached the confluence with the Yukon, we passed another deserted village, watched some otters catching fish, and had to endure a couple of more showers. At one point, we also believed to have that character on the raft ahead of us again, and in order to avoid a new encounter with him, we took an alternate river channel. It was not until sometime later that we found out that this guy had not only missed the Manley Hot Springs, but also floated past Tanana, Kokrines and Ruby, before finally landing in Galena, where he was seen to wander aimlessly through the streets. Nobody seemed to know whatever became of him eventually.

Flocks of ducks, geese, and cranes greeted us on the mud banks at the mouth of the Tanana River. On the far side across the Yukon, we could see the town of Tanana, but again we had no particular reason to stop there. With the water of the Yukon under our raft, I already felt at home again, but still was anxious to get to Kokrines.

Making camp at the mouth of Sunset Creek, it was almost like we had landed in the middle of a bird migration. Even though it was already the middle of July, we were totally surrounded by flocks of waxwings, crossbills, and chickadees, which, after my thinking, should have been nesting at that time. A pair of yellow legs must have done just that, since they fearlessly searched for food in a puddle right in front of our tent.

We, too, were in want of food, and I wanted to see if I could catch some grayling in the clear waters of the Sunset Creek. As I stood with my fishing pole in between the man-high willows at the edge of the winding creek, a kingfisher, obviously looking for fish as well, came flying around the bend, and almost crashed into my face. For a few seconds, the bird hung there in midair, a few inches from my face, like he couldn't find his reverse gear.

Shortly after this comical experience, a second incident, somewhat funny as well, could have had a more serious consequences. A black bear cub came along the edge of the brush along the riverbank toward our tent. By the time we noticed each other, the animal had come to about ten yards of us. The cub cried out in a human-like voice for fear and frantically scrambled up the cut bank into the willow brush. We couldn't keep ourselves from laughing about it, but, at the same time, I was fully aware how serious this situation could turn if the cub's mother was nearby. Therefore, I quickly armed myself, but to our relief, no mother bear showed up and we had to assume that this poor fellow must have been an orphan.

The following day, after waiting out another spell of strong headwinds on an island, we finally arrived in Kokrines. Our trunk and the footlocker, which we had sent off by train from Anchorage, were already standing, neatly covered with a tarp at the beach in front of the old village. Naturally, Frank and Josephine must have had an idea about our return but in spite of it, they still were surprised, especially since we arrived once again unnoticed, as I had done the first time I arrived in Kokrines.

It had taken us two weeks to drift from Fairbanks to Kokrines and the old folks were as happy to have us back as neighbors as we were to be back in what we considered our new home. While Alice cleaned and rearranged the little cabin in which Neal and I had spent the winter, I built a cache, collected some firewood, and caught some fish with a borrowed net from Frank and Josephine and life was beautiful again.

Chapter 19
Return to the Hot Springs

We had just sat down for dinner, when an airplane buzzed Kokrines and eventually landed at the old strip behind our cabin. We knew right away it only could be Harold, but wondered what brought him to Kokrines at this hour.

As it turned out, Harold came to pick us up and bring us to the Melozitna Hot Springs, where Leonard and Pat were in need of our help. How the Veerhusens even knew that we were in Kokrines was a puzzle to me. A few weeks ago, we ourselves didn't know that we would be back at the old village site. When I mentioned my thoughts to Harold, he said, "Never underestimate the bush telegraph!" Not that there really was a telegraph line, like there had been at one time in earlier days along the Yukon; instead, Harold was referring to the bush gossip and the speed at which it spread.

Anyway, we didn't ask any further questions, got a few things together, said good bye to Frank and Josephine again, and hopped into the plane.

Only minutes later, we landed at the hot springs, where Pat and Leonard greeted us happily, but my dog Minado hardly gave us time to climb out of the plane, before he was all over us.

"I can't pay you much," said Leonard as we walked toward his cabin, "but I really could use your help this summer." With these words, he showed the newly started cabin to me and explained that he would like to have it done before the winter starts. That cabin naturally wasn't the only thing that had to be done before winter; things all around their place needed attention and preparation before the snow started flying....

"I'm sure we could scrape a few bucks together for your winter supplies," Leonard added after he was finished showing me around.

Working at the Melozitna Hot Springs 1970

That new cabin Leonard was working on was supposed to be the first guest cabin for his business plans to turn the Melozitna Hot Springs into a vacation spot for retired people.

The old cabin the Veerhusens were living at the time had been built about 1920 as reindeer herder's housing. A man by the name of Hill, or Hills, had started the reindeer herding business at that time in this area to supply the gold miners along the river with a reliable source of meat. Some natives from Kokrines had been employed as herders to drive a part of the reindeer herd periodically down to Kokrines, where they were slaughtered.

I had found a big, old cast-iron kettle in the woods near the old village, which according to Frank once had been used to render reindeer fat.

In 1929, the reindeer herding in the Kokrines Hills was abandoned again, probably because most of the gold miners and prospectors had moved on to Nome. A small herd of these animals, which had escaped the butcher, inter-bred with the wild caribou population, and the offsprings of that group still live in the Kokrines hills.

While Alice helped Pat with the household and in the greenhouse, I worked with Leonard on his new cabin. During our work, we also kept an eye out for fresh meat, in the form of game, but more often we angled for grayling in the evening, which were very abundant and easily caught in the hot spring creek.

The only change from our fish diet was the stringy, corned meat of an old black bear, which Leonard had shot after we had left that spring.

"We were already in bed," Leonard started to tell us the story one evening after dinner, "when the dogs started barking. Since their barking was nothing unusual, we didn't pay too much attention to it at first. But when the barking wouldn't stop and came closer and closer to the cabin, I finally got up to take a look. As soon as I entered the front room, I saw the bear looking into the window at me. By the time I took my rifle off the wall and made sure that it was loaded before I went out the door, the bear was already entering our porch. I saw as our dog, Happy, barely managed to squeeze out of the porch past that bear, as I stuck my rifle through the crack in the door. But the bear was as fast as he was determined to get into the cabin. By that time the animal started pushing against the door, Pat had come to my help. Together, we pushed back against the door, with my rifle being jammed in between. It took all our strength to keep that bear from coming into the house and there was no way I could make use of the rifle under those conditions. Luckily, Pat was able to reach my pistol hanging near the door. She handed it to me, which finally enabled me to shoot through that crack and put a bullet into the bear's head."

After Leonard had lit his after-dinner cigarette, he added, "The bear dropped where it was and I had one hell of a job to get him out of the porch before gutting and cutting him up."

Pat added, chuckling, "It would have made a terrific photo opportunity, as we fought for our lives against that bear in our nightshirts."

How lucky our friends really were during this particular bear episode, we became aware of a few days later. But for now, it was back to work. We took that D-8 across the creek to fell a few more trees and pull the logs back to the sawmill. The women accompanied us to pick blueberries during that time. I never would have expected to drive heavy machinery out in the wilderness, especially with my dislike for machinery in general. But in spite of it, I learned to drive that Caterpillar, at least well enough to haul the logs across the creek and keep the runway graded.

About a couple of days later, after cutting some more boards at the sawmill, we were working on the roof of the cabin, when I spotted a yearling caribou at the other side of the creek. There were no other caribous to be seen anywhere, but the yearling caribou would be a welcome change in our diet. Climbing off the scaffolding, I got Leonard's rifle out of the cabin and sneaked down to the creek, looking forward to a quick and easy kill.

After my third shot, however, the caribou was still standing on a rock at the edge of the creek, apparently totally unconcerned about the noise from my shots. Since I'm a very good shot in general, I had the feeling that something was quite wrong with Leonard's rifle and when my next shot showed no result either, I was about to climb back up the creek bank to get my revolver. On the way, I met Leonard and handed him his rifle. From our house tent, where Alice and I were sleeping, I retrieved my revolver and was back at the creek before Leonard could take the first shot with his rifle.

"That's fifty yards across," said Leonard as he pointed at my handgun, "You'll never be able to hit the animal from here!" But before Leonard could get back into position to shoot, I had bagged my game and Leonard could hardly believe it. We certainly enjoyed the tasty, tender meat that night and for some days thereafter. The heavily bloodshot front quarters of the caribou showed me how much damage a .44 caliber can do, but it also told me that is the wrong caliber for hunting anything as small as a deer or young caribou. The main lesson of that day came when Leonard decided to clean his rifle after dinner and found that the bullet from my last shot never had left the barrel. Had I, or Leonard, shot that rifle just once more, it might have spelled disaster for one or the other of us and Leonard probably could call himself twice as lucky that he didn't get a chance to use that weapon on the bear he shot in his porch.

Leonard defended the accuracy of his rifle from the beginning, but certainly didn't have an excuse for his outdated ammunition. Being too casual with his guns and ammunition was by far not Leonard's only shortcoming when it came to safety. Several times, I had told Leonard to nail down his scaffolding, since the planks were barely long enough to reach from end to end and that they were in danger of slipping off the supports. But it was Leonard's project, and he was not only the elder between us, but also the boss.

Leonard was using the chainsaw to cut the angle on the gable of the cabin, when I suddenly heard an awful crash, followed by some painful sounding moans. Sure enough, the scaffolding had given away. Leonard had been able to throw the chainsaw away before he fell, but he landed with his back across a two by four. I knew he was hurt pretty good, and I was afraid to help him to his feet until he made the first move to get up. By then, the women, who also had heard the commotion, had arrived at the scene and together we walked Leonard to his bed.

"It looks worse than it is," said Leonard with a pain-distorted face. "A couple days of rest and I'll be back on the job with you!"

Sure, dream on, Lenny! Two days later, Pat called for a plane over the radio. Leaving us in charge of their whole hacienda, the Veerhusens flew to Fairbanks to see a doctor.

For one whole week, we were in the dark, as far as Leonard's condition was concerned, but when Pat and Leonard finally returned from Fairbanks, my suspicion that Leonard might have cracked vertebrae was confirmed.

In spite of his injury, it was impossible to keep Leonard in his bed. At first, he came on crutches to supervise my work and a short time later, he was back on the roof of the cabin with me.

On that day, our dogs barked like crazy somewhere out of our sight, behind a stand of trees. Right away, our thoughts turned to caribou or moose and as I started to get off the cabin in order to check on the situation, Leonard handed me his pistol. I gave him a questioning look, but he assured me that he had bought fresh ammunition in Fairbanks for all his weapons. So down I went, running through the woods until I reached a small, rushing creek. While I was trying to find a crossing, the barking of the dogs stopped and through the trees, toward the main trail, I could see something yellow rushing along in the direction of the cabins.

There wasn't much time to reflect on the situation. I heard and saw Leonard on the cabin roof hollering and waving his arms. I had no doubts that we had a bear in camp and, at that moment, I heard branches breaking, coming in my direction. Before I could decide on what to do next, a young grizzly, coming from the direction of the cabins, ran past me at a distance of only about fifteen feet. Then a second bear cub appeared, followed by a big mama grizzly. Right behind her came my dog Minado, snapping at the grizzly's haunches. I stood there in a frozen position, hoping to be taken for a tree. I witnessed at close range as the grizzly turned around and swiped at my dog. Thanks to Minado's quick reaction, the chase did not come to an end right then and there. The grizzly sow ran on after her cubs, my dog after the bear, and Leonard's panting elkhound passing me a short time later. A half hour later, both dogs lay panting in the shade of the cabin as if it all had been just a part of an ordinary day, and I felt lucky that I had not been any closer to the path of the animals.

Minado was not only a fast dog, but his sense of play and humor didn't seem to have any bounds. One day, as Happy was lying in the shade, we observed as Minado came with a big box in his mouth and set it at some distance in front of Happy. Minado looked at Happy and wagged his tail, but when Happy didn't react, Minado moved the box a little closer to him, and Happy finally got up to go and inspect the box. But Minado grabbed the box again and ran off with it, with Happy in hot pursuit. Minado ran zigzag through the woods with the box in front of his face. How he managed to do that without running into any tree remained a mystery, until we discovered afterwards that the bottom of the box had a half inch gap, through which my dog must have navigated.

There also had been incident earlier during our first trip down the Yukon which showed us that Minado had a sense of humor. We had made camp and the fold boat was lying totally empty on land next to the tent. Normally, when during our little trips we returned to our boat, we just called to the dog—"Minado, hop!" and he would jump onto his rightful place on the boat. Now, with the boat lying on land, I wanted to play a trick on the dog and said, "Minado, hop!" The dog raced toward the boat, stopped a few feet short of it, and then returned to us, happily wagging his tail. It was obvious that he understood that I had been teasing him.

The day arrived when Leonard's new cabin was done, and we had to think about our own preparation for the coming winter in Kokrines. Harold was supposed to arrive with a planeload of supplies for Pat and Leonard, and pick us up at the same time to take us back to Kokrines.

I, however, had slightly different plans. Alice and all our gear could fly back to Kokrines with Harold, but I needed some time for myself to spend with Mother Nature; therefore, I opted to walk back home with Minado.

Without waiting for Harold to arrive, I drank my coffee, buckled my revolver, took my hunting pouch, my single-shot small caliber rifle, and whistled for my dog.

Pat wanted me to eat breakfast first, but I didn't want to waste the precious morning hours. I had a long walk ahead of me and no idea how long it would take me to walk back to Kokrines. I wasn't planning to spend a night on the trail, and did not prepare for that. After thanking Pat one more time for the nice time we had at their place and wishing her the best with Leonard's recuperation, I was on my way.

Minado's friend, Happy, followed us to the end of the runway, until we started climbing the first hill. Somehow, Happy must have known that Minado was leaving for good and, from the top of the hill, I still could see Leonard's dog sitting at the same spot at the runway, where we had left him behind.

Quietly, we followed a game trail along a small creek toward the high tundra. The sky above was clear and blue, promising another hot day, but along the trail, tatters of fog were still hanging in the brush like ghosts. Suddenly, the flapping of wings stopped us in our tracks. A flock of grouse noisily took to the air and then glided like paper airplanes ahead of us, until they vanished into the fog-webbed brush once more.

After reaching the open tundra and the sun rising higher, the air became hotter. Now and then, I would stop to pick a handful or two of blueberries, while Minado would quench his thirst at a water-filled moose track in the tundra. It was around noon when we reached the summit. From there, the trail would lead through woods, all the way down to the Yukon, but for now it was lunchtime. I sat down on the moss and lichen-covered ground and shared my bread and cheese with Minado.

From where I was sitting, I could look in all directions and see nothing but tundra and mountains to the north, and looking south, I had a view over an ocean of trees, only broken now and then by a glimpse of the Yukon River in the distance below me. I couldn't help to think back about something I had read as a boy about Daniel Boone. When he first went into what is now Kentucky, he, too, had sat there admiring nature in its full glory, but that night he was plagued by nightmares, in which he saw that beautiful place before him filled with the smoking chimneys of factories.

At that moment, I certainly felt fortunate to be able to be where I was and to be able to live the way I was living; but I also had to wonder how long it would be before things would change here as well.

Like an answer to my thoughts, I became aware of the dark clouds that had gathered to the west of me. "Come on!" I called to Minado as I got up. "We better get going, we have a long ways to go yet!"

The trail was easily recognizable from the summit to the Yukon, and there were no more water-filled potholes to watch out for. The woods were filled with the twittering of warblers, chickadees, and thrushes, only interrupted now and then by the chatter of a squirrel or the distant cawing of a raven. A somewhat rarer sound was the occasional hammering of a woodpecker.

Several times, we scared up a flock of grouse, an occurrence that became more frequent as the flocks got larger with the lower altitude. Soon, there were so many of these birds that I decided to take dinner home with me. I only had to decide on how many birds I wanted to carry.

Learning how to operate a bulldozer

Suddenly, the songbirds had stopped singing, the sky was covered with dark clouds, and the first heavy raindrops flopped noisily onto the brim of my hat, but we were almost home. Whatever the true mileage of this trail may be, we had walked it in ten and a half hours and even Minado was so tired that he curled up to sleep without eating. I told Alice how much I had enjoyed the trip while I ate a few bites, but then it was time for me to turn in for the night as well.

Chapter 20
Preparing for Winter

Repairs on our roof, the construction of a doghouse, and getting firewood for the winter kept me pretty busy after our return to Kokrines. During spare time, I took Alice berry picking, while I hunted grouse at the same time. But Alice had been pretty quiet lately and I wondered what was wrong, until one evening while we were making jam, she let the cat out of the bag. "You want to know something?" she asked.

"Well, what?"

"I'm sure that I'm pregnant!"

Well, when and where had I heard that before? Just like some years ago, during my previous marriage, I knew that my reaction to this announcement was closely observed. Searching for the right answer, I finally said, "It looks like we'll have to add one more room on to our castle!"

That was not a satisfying answer for Alice and I knew it. In spite that, Alice was fully aware about how happy I was out there in that old village and with our present lifestyle, she was afraid to have the baby out here in the old fashioned way and I couldn't really blame her. "I'll try to get a job in Fairbanks," I said, "but moving there will have to wait till spring. Right now, we have to make sure that we make it through the winter out here."

If that answer was satisfactory to my wife or not, I had no idea since she did not offer a reply. So our lives continued for the time being as if nothing had changed.

Frank had been restless for a few days and I knew him well enough by now to know that he had hunting on his mind. Meat and fish in the larder always was for Frank more important than money in the bank. As soon as I suggested a hunting trip, his eyes lit up and preparations were made.

Our first trip took us only a little ways upriver to the Hardluck Slough, where I had seen moose before around the grass lakes in that area. The water in the slough was too shallow for us to drive the boat very far into it, so we tied up the boat and walked the rest of the way. Frank walked along the bank of the slough, while I followed a game trail a few feet inside the woods. In the hope to at least shoot some grouse, besides my Winchester, I also had taken my four-ten shotgun along. Only a short way along the trail, I heard a noise, which seemed to come from high up in the trees, but I had no idea what might cause such a sound. Then I saw a black bear coming down a tree trunk, which would supply a lot more meat for us than a few grouse could. So I leaned my bird gun against a tree, I took aim with my Winchester, and fired.

As the bear fell off that tree, he certainly didn't look too big, but before I could think too much about it, a second bear came down from another tree and I shot him as well. The second bear wasn't any bigger than the first. At that point, it dawned on me that I might have put myself into a very peculiar situation. If the mother of those cubs was near, an understandably angry sow could enter the scene at any moment and I better be ready. With my back against a tree, I reloaded to full capacity, waited, and listened, but when no adult bear materialized after what seemed a long time, I carefully approached the cubs. Both of them were dead and neither one of them could be considered fully grown. After I had gutted and packed my prey to the edge of the woods, I estimated the weight of the gutted bears at about hundred pounds apiece. The young bears certainly would be good eating and the fresh meat was more than welcome, but where in the heck was Frank? Didn't he hear my shots?

After hunting with Frank

"Frank!" I hollered several times as loud as I could, but there was no answer. Then I wondered if Frank might be stalking a moose and therefore didn't answer my calls. I decided to follow Frank's tracks along the bank, but had not gone far when I heard noises in the brush behind me. Still thinking about the mother of those cubs I had shot, I turned ready to shoot and saw my hunting companion stepping out of the woods right next to where I had put the skinned out bears. Frank did not notice the dead cubs nor did he see me until I called out to him. He never heard my shots or my calls either, which made me ask myself if it was safe to take the old man on any further hunting trips.

According to Frank, there had been no moose at the grass lake. The sight of the two young bears, however lifted Frank's spirits and he helped me carry them to our boat and we headed home.

A hunting success, no matter how small, always put my old Indian friend in a festive mood and sooner or later, he would have a story to tell that related to our hunt. Already, on the way home, Frank told me that the cubs I had shot were most likely orphans, since he had heard that somebody from Ruby had shot the mother of three cubs this spring. He had reached that conclusion because one of the cubs of that mother bear supposedly had been a cinnamon colored animal, just like one of the cubs I had shot. As for the third cub of the family, Frank assumed that it probably had already fallen prey to wolves or to another adult bear, which would be a common occurrence.

Later that night, as we sat over tea and cigarettes in Frank's cabin planning our next hunting trip, Frank told me the story of his most memorable bear hunt. Then, he said, "Even today, I'm still not sure if it was a very big black bear or a black grizzly bear." I was surprised, because if I was able to tell the difference between those two bears by the tracks alone, I would have expected that my Indian friend would be able to do so. But I didn't want to interrupt Frank and kept my mouth shut.

"It was early in the winter and I was trapping at the Nowitna River, but to be honest about it, I had lost my direction in a heavy fog. Even though I had my dogs and a toboggan, I started to worry about freezing out there. You can imagine how glad I was when I saw a cabin appear in the fog ahead of me. Not only had I found shelter, but I also recognized the cabin and knew now where I was. With split wood still in the porch, it wasn't long before I was sitting comfortably in my shelter with a cup of hot tea. But once again, I had nothing but dry fish to eat. The following morning, I left my dogs behind and went across the river, hoping to find some grouse to shoot. As I approached the opposite shore, I saw what I believed to be a fresh moose track in the snow, but a closer inspection told me that a bear had passed there not too long ago. With my thoughts on fresh meat, I followed the track and hoped to find the bear in a den. When the track led me into some thick brush, I decided to walk around it and pick the track back up on the other side. But I couldn't find any track on the other side of the brush and assumed that the bear must be somewhere in that brush. Then I noticed a little hill at the slope and tracks leading right to that hill. Now I knew I had found the den and wanted to make sure that the bear was home. I got myself a long pole, approached the den from the top. As soon as I pushed that pole into the den, I felt it being pushed back, which gave me the assurance that the bear was in there. But it was getting too late to do anything about it and I went back to the cabin.

The next day, I took two of my dogs and the toboggan with me, but left them at some distance from the bear den. Then I circled the den on my snowshoes, to see if I could find an angle from where I could look into the den, but no such luck. Next, I approached the den like the day before, from the top. Carefully, I leaned over the edge of the entrance to take a peek and was shocked to find myself face to face with the biggest bear I ever seen. Lucky for me, the bear was sleeping with his head resting on his front paws. I carefully withdrew and tried to find a solution to my problem. The only way I could achieve that was to climb a tree. So I took off my snowshoes and climbed up a spruce tree below the den. By the time I could see the bear's head in the den, aiming at it from my position was still a problem. With one leg wrapped around the tree trunk, I still had to get on the toes with the other foot to get the gun leveled at the bear. The recoil from the shot almost threw me out of the tree, but I was sure that I had hit my target. To make sure, but mainly to calm myself after my acrobatics in that tree, I went back to my dogs and poured myself a cup of tea from my thermos. That's when I noticed my dogs looking excited into the direction of the den. I turned and saw the bear standing in front of his den. In my own excitement, my first shot missed, but the second shot killed him and finally put an end to this hunt."

Frank never claimed to be the greatest hunter or an all-around woodsman. Even after reliving this bear hunt, Frank's hands were shaking as he lit his cigarette, but once Frank was telling stories, he was hard to stop. It didn't take him long to get around to his favored category of stories—stories about his ancestors.

"The young men a long time ago," said Frank, "sometimes proved their manhood by making a sport out of waking up black bears in their dens. Once a den with a sleeping bear was found, the young men installed a couple of birch tree trunks in front of the den, in a scissor or nutcracker fashion. Then the bear inside would be teased with long poles until it finally appeared, still half sleepy in the entrance of the den. A strong youngster who wanted to prove himself would then push down on the upper log of the scissor contraption and pin the animal down by its neck. If the young man was able to hold the bear that way for quite a while, it would foretell that he would have a long and healthy life. If, on the other hand, the bear would free himself right away, it was said that the youngster would not live to a ripe old age."

Well, I could see where a young man's life might not have much of a future if a foul-tempered bear so near to him freed himself from a trap, but Frank mentioned that there were most likely enough armed warriors present to take care of any eventuality.

It also was said that under no circumstances should a hunter ever crawl into a bear's den while it was occupied, or he would fall asleep and never wake up again. While I thought that it was good advice not to climb into a den while the bear was inside, I still don't believe that falling asleep was the greatest danger in such undertaking.

In those days much more than now, there was a lot more respect given to the animals in general, but by Frank's ancestors, the respect was greatest toward the grizzly bear. While there seems to be an unreasonable hatred toward all bears nowadays by many people, Native or Whites, a hunt for a grizzly in the old days was never looked upon as a game for the inexperienced. The den of a grizzly is usually located higher in the mountains, on a steep slope, and can be found by a mound of dirt in front of it. The hunters, and there always were more than one, would place themselves at some distance above the den.

A ball made from twigs would then be rolled down the slope toward the den, so that it would hit the dirt mount in front of the entrance and repelled into the bear's den. If the bear was in the den, the twig ball would soon be flying back out of the den, followed by a sleepy bear. After the bear looked around, he usually would return to his den, but his anger over the disturbance would grow as he fully awakes. When he appeared for a second time in front of his den, he would charge straight up the hill toward the hunters and consequently be shot by them.

Two days after our bear episode, we drove in Frank's boat up a slough across from Kokrines. There we were hoping to find a moose, but not to get totally skunked, we also shot a few ducks along the way. As it turned out, the only moose we got to see was a cow with a calf. By the time the slough got too shallow and we turned around, it also was starting to get dark. This would have been the right time to see a bull moose on the move, but that hope faded as we neared the end of the slough. Not expecting to encounter a moose anymore, we drove faster now, in order to get out of this stagnant ditch with all kinds of obstacles in the water. The waterfowl that constantly had taken flight in front of us now collected into thicker and thicker flocks. At the opening of the slough to the river, we drove directly toward the setting sun at the horizon. The flocks of flying water fowl in front of us were so thick, that it almost looked like a swarm of mosquitoes from the distance against the blood red sky. The sight of it was like a picture from an earlier age on earth, something I had never experienced before, nor seen since.

In the June Slough across from Kokrines

Our third hunting trip that fall took us upriver again, just past the slough where I had shot the bears on our first hunt. There, we had barely turned into the Victor slough, one of the larger river arms of the Yukon, when Frank spotted a nice, big bull moose. I steered the boat toward shore, tied up, and then followed the moose on foot under the cover of the willows along the bank. When the animal crossed a dry slough toward an island, I suggested that I would circle the island, while Frank should wait where we were at the moment. That way, the moose would get my scent and walk back toward Frank. After all, it was Frank who spotted the animal and, at his age, he probably wouldn't get a chance to hunt a moose that often anymore.

By the time I almost had reached the upper end of the island, I heard Frank's first shot, then a second, and a third. Before I could continue around the tip of the island, the shooting started again. After the firing stopped, I carefully walked around the last bend and saw the moose still standing, about fifty yards in front of Frank, who was not making any further attempts to shoot at it.

With a shot through the neck, I put the animal down and then walked toward my partner to congratulate him on a successful hunt. But Frank was shaking like a leaf in the wind as he said, "I only have one shot left in my rifle and I was saving that one for myself, just in case the moose would attack me."

While Frank probably meant what he said, I thought to myself that he would have made a good drama teacher. However, Frank was convinced that I had saved his life that day, but what was more important for the moment, we had our moose and it was time to get to work. Even though Frank made sure that his long time ritual to cut the head off the animal first of all was observed, he did not insist on drinking the blood of our prey. By the time we had the moose gutted, it was getting too dark to do much more and since we only were a few miles from home, we used some willow sticks to hold the carcass open to let it cool out properly and then left for home.

To our chagrin, it was raining on the following morning, but that was no excuse to leave our game out there on the riverbank. Al Hardluck, the Native from Ruby, who had come to Kokrines for beaver trapping the previous year, happened to be back at the old village at the time and offered to lend us a hand in getting our meat home. Between us, it didn't take us long to cut up the moose and load it into Frank's boat. Since Al and I had done most of that work, Frank appointed himself as the driver of his own boat.

The rain had gotten heavier by then and the boat with all the meat and us three guys was loaded to capacity. But there was no wind and the river surface was smooth, aside from the spattering of the heavy raindrops. In spite of it, our self-appointed captain not only drove the boat at a snail's pace, but he also followed the contour of the shoreline instead of steering straight for Kokrines. Even Al's cynical remarks about Frank's overly caution could not bring him to speed up a little. We had no choice but sit there and endure until we reached Kokrines and as soon as the meat was hanging in the smokehouse, we sat in our warm cabins with feelings of accomplishment.

With meat for the winter in our cache and smokehouse, we still had to undertake one more trip to Ruby before the ice started running, in order to do some shopping.

A few days after our successful moose hunt, the rain had stopped and we were on our way. Al Hardluck took advantage of the free ride back to Ruby and Alice came along for a last chance to socialize with other people and have a checkup at the Ruby clinic on her pregnancy. Only Josephine decided that she had no reason to go to town.

With the two-hundred dollars that we had gotten from Leonard at our departure from the hot springs, we bought our necessities and then visited some friends.

When all the supplies for Frank and for us were in the boat and we were ready to leave, Frank was nowhere to be found. Eventually, we hunted him down in a friend's cabin, with some additional people and a bottle of whiskey. It was not easy to stop Frank from telling slightly enlarged stories about my woodsmanship during our hunts and convince him that it was time to return to Kokrines. I had to help finish that bottle before I was able to persuade Frank to come down to the river with us. There, he stumbled into the boat, fell in the middle of our bags and boxes, and went to sleep.

Alice took her place at the bow of the boat, holding on to a sled dog pup, which somebody had given to her. After pushing off, I had difficulty getting the motor started. Most likely, the whiskey was partly responsible for not finding the problem and so I cussed a blue streak until Gilbert Cleaver came with his boat to our rescue and started the motor for me.

In spite of the fact that it was quite dark by then, we made good time. The fresh air and a cold, cooked pork chop I was chewing on soon cleared my head. In spite of it, I still managed to find a submerged sand bank in the dark and got the boat stuck. It took me only a few minutes to solve our problem and we were on our way again as the sky was suddenly lit up with the greatest, multicolored display of northern lights Alice or I had ever seen.

As for Frank, he had slept through the whole trip and awoke as we pulled ashore in Kokrines. Almost sober by then, Frank was as happy as we were to be home again.

Chapter 21
Winter and Old Time Stories

The magical atmosphere I experienced during the arrival of fall may have been rooted to memories of my childhood, as we played cowboys and Indians and built grass huts in the near woods while the first frost was on the ground. But more likely, it were the last geese and cranes that were now flying south that made me restless at this time of the year. Not that I necessarily wanted to follow the migrating waterfowl, it was just a general urge to roam. The golden foliage of the trees under the blue Indian summer sky over the Kokrine Hills was beckoning me.

At first, I took Alice along with me into the near vicinity of the old village, so she would feel safe while she picked more berries and I looked for mushrooms and hunted more grouse. But soon, I would leave my wife at home and head farther upriver, downriver, or straight back into the hills toward the hot springs. It really didn't matter to me in which direction I was heading, nor did I have a particular destination or purpose for these trips. The main thing for me was to be out there with Mother Nature and feel totally free and unrestrained by man-made rules or laws. I truly felt like a king of my domain, while in the back of my mind the gnawing question remained for how much longer it would be possible for me to live this lifestyle. First of all, there would be the arrival of our child, which most likely would force me back to civilization, at least for a while. Then I had to ask myself how long was a while and what would the developments in Alaska bring with it? Would I be still allowed to return to Kokrines and keep on living this way after a year or two? Or would the encroaching civilization take all this away from me?

Frosty Morning

Well, there would be enough time to worry about that in the following spring; for now, I was determined to enjoy my life the way it was.

The abilities and habits I had developed to live the life I was living were the same which we as children had attributed only to Indians and mountain men.

Things that long since had become second nature to me, like to walk quietly in the woods and sneak up on animals, to smell scents of wildlife or smoke long before I could detect the source—all these senses had been sharpened to a height I never would have imagined possible, but most of all, I had learned to listen to nature, to my inner voice, and my feelings. The slightest rustle in the leaves would cause me to stop in my tracks until I was able to place its source. Usually, it would lead to the discovery of wildlife, like the time when a marten came bouncing toward me totally unaware of my presence until I made a squeaking sound. Then, instead of running away, the animal came within a couple feet of me, sat up and looked at me while I talked to it, before it calmly continued on its way.

Another time, I had the feeling of being followed during a grouse hunt. As it turned out, a fox seemed to have taken an interest in my doings. When I cut off a wing from one of the grouse I had shot and threw it toward my stalker, he promptly started to play with it and put on quite a show for me. As I traveled on, the fox sat down, seemingly disappointed in my leaving him, like he said to himself, "What did I do wrong now?"

Alice, in her condition, spending most of her time around the cabin in the meantime, had her own wildlife encounters of sorts, with voles and shrews who now wanted to move into our home for the winter, a situation that I was expected to remedy.

The days were getting shorter, the nights were getting colder. The fishnet that had supplied us with a variety of fish until recently was now hanging in Frank's cache again to wait for springtime. Ice flows started to drift on the river and a cool wind had stripped most of the golden color from the trees. Frost glistened on the brown, dry grass like diamonds in the morning sun and outside of the distant calls of ravens, the woods were quiet. A couple of gray jays would show up now and then to search noiselessly for food scraps around the cabins and the dog houses. Winter was coming on fast, but this time we were ready.

I didn't have any more traps than I had the year before, but at least I was on my trapline at the right time and had a better idea of what I was doing....

To break the trail on the ice across the river would have to wait another month or so, but I had enough terrain on our side of the river to trap on. Right after the first snow had fallen, I went out to set some traps and after the first time checking them, I came home with two martens and two snow-shoe hares.

219

Snow shoe hare

To give myself an excuse to go for a stroll after dinner in the evenings, I had put a couple of traps out on a trail surrounding the old village site. On one of those evening strolls, I suddenly was jarred out of my deep thoughts by a sound that went through my bones. For a moment, I was in total confusion over the unexpected sound. It almost sounded like the whistle of a train, but then it dawned on me that I just had been greeted by a pack of wolves at a very short distance. The following day, the tracks revealed that the pack had been within fifty yards of where I had been standing at that time. I knew enough about wolves to know that I had been in no danger, and in spite of my moment of confusion, this true sound of the wilderness was like music to my ears. But most of all, I felt honored to be greeted like that, which also reminded me of my rash action two years earlier, when I shot my only wolf. I felt like I had something to apologize for and hoped to be forgiven for the deed, which I probably was, but it was I who had to make peace with over the incident. I also had to chuckle to myself, because here I was trying to make a living as a trapper, but I had not set a snare or a trap for wolves, nor shot at a wolf since. Well, nothing is perfect, and the harsh and sometimes seemingly senseless laws of Mother Nature are hard to understand. I was walking along my trail that followed the river. The ice had stopped flowing since a few days and the snow wasn't deep enough yet that snowshoes would not have been necessary, but I had gotten used to wearing them, even if just to keep my trapping trails in good condition. While trotting along, I became aware of something moving out on the ice, or it might have been the unusual sound that drew my attention to the movement. What I saw way out on the river seemed to be antlers in between the rough ice and I thought that wolves might have downed a moose. A closer look with my binoculars revealed instead that two moose had broken through the ice and where now frantically fighting to keep from drowning. While the animals were trying to get out of the icy current, the ice around them kept on breaking, or their hoofs could not establish a hold on the slippery surface. The situation of those animals was hopeless and there was nothing I could do to help them. A timeless drama was repeating itself in front of my eyes and it was a hard thing to witness. Sure, I felt sorry for the animals, but I was not about to risk my own life and walk out there just to get close enough to put an end to their fears and anxiety with my revolver, or with my small caliber rifle. Feeling totally helpless about the situation, I kept on trotting along my trail in the hope that one or the other of the two moose might manage to escape its fate yet. On my return trip, I found only one of the animals still making a feeble attempt to escape the inevitable and had to assume that the other most likely was already at peace somewhere under the ice.

The way these animals had to die seems cruel and wasteful. Sure, wolves kill moose and so do I, but in either case it is done out of necessity, but what is the purpose of moose drowning in the river? If the incident had no other purpose, it brought me to the realization how unimportant any individual life in the greater scheme of nature is, be it animal or man.

Only two days later, I witnessed, right from Kokrines, how another moose vanished at about the same spot of the river and when I mentioned my observations to Frank, he assured me that these dramas had been common occurrences during his lifetime. We thought about the numbers of moose that might find an early death in this way every winter, but we were not able to make any sense of it.

According to the Indian lore, that the game gives itself to the deserving hunter is easy to understand if one is talking about hunting for subsistence. Why a so-called sport hunter deserves a trophy is harder to digest, but why the river has to take his share of moose every winter as well is something only Mother Nature can answer....

Our conversation turned from the drowning moose to trapping and to the wolverines who often can be quite a nuisance on the trapping line by raiding and eating the trapped animals. Luckily, I did not have that problem yet, but since I had been collecting the skulls of my prey animals, I mentioned to Frank that I wouldn't mind adding the skull of a wolverine to my collection. Frank's facial expression turned somber and I knew that I had touched on another sensitive subject. Flailing his hands through the air, he protested my intentions and said, "You can't do that!"

"And why not?"

"The skull is where the evil spirit of that animal lives," answered Frank while he lit his cigarette; then in a somewhat calmer voice, he explained how I should avoid the revenge of that animal at all costs. According to Frank, there were only two ways to do that: after catching a wolverine, collecting the skull of that animal was not one of them. One way to appease the spirit of a wolverine: a trapper, after killing one of those animals, should burn the entire carcass after skinning it and if that was not feasible, the whole carcass should be disposed of on a full moon night by putting it through the ice into the river.

I was sure that Frank knew that I wouldn't grow gray hairs over the revenge of a dead wolverine, especially since in my book a wolverine was neither evil nor revengeful.

Therefore, I couldn't be sure that Frank wasn't pulling my leg just a little this time, but I also knew that my friend, in spite of his worldly understanding, harbored a lot of ancient beliefs and superstitions. This was made clear to me the day Frank asked me to shoot his favorite dog and bury it in the ice on the river, because it was hopelessly sick.

After I returned from this unpleasant task, Frank asked for the dog's collar.

"The buckle of that collar was so rusted that I couldn't get it off," I explained.

"The soul of that dog can't run free that way," replied Frank, and I offered to go back and cut the collar off the animal.

"No, no, it's okay!" Frank interrupted, smiling, as if he had been pulling my leg this time.

On the following day, I found Frank's footprints, where he had gone to the dead dog himself to retrieve its collar.

The meat of our fall moose was almost gone. Frank had dropped another subtle hint that it might be a good idea for me to keep my eyes open for some fresh meat. I was still in my long johns the following morning when our dogs barked wildly. Hurriedly slipping in to my boots without bothering to put on my pants, I took my Winchester and went outside to see what the barking was all about. Right away, I caught sight of a cow moose with a calf on the opposite side of the river, but since the wind wasn't right for the dogs to have smelled them, I looked in all directions while walking toward the riverbank. As soon as I got there, I heard branches breaking below me and then saw a bull moose running straight out onto the Yukon. From my position, the animal made a lousy target, but I took aim anyway even though I wasn't sure if I wanted to risk the shot. By that time, the moose was at least quarter of the way across the river toward the other side, but he made the mistake of turning his head to look back while he was running and I pulled the trigger. The sound of my shot mixed with the barking of the dogs, the moose went straight up on his hind legs, fell on the spot. I went back to my cabin to put on my pants, then went to check on the moose. Assured that the animal was dead with a bullet hole behind the ear, I returned to stop at Frank's cabin. Frank still was occupied with his stack of breakfast pancakes, but he looked up at me and asked real nonchalantly, "Did you just shoot?"

"Yeah," I answered, "and as soon as you're done there, you are invited to help me cut up the moose."

While Frank's eyes lit up as he stared at me in disbelief, he said; "You must be some kind of wizard! We just talked about fresh meat last night and you shoot the moose this morning practically in front of our door!"

Got him with one shot, Kokrines 1970

I didn't have to guess what Frank had said next to Josephine in Athapaskan. She, too, looked at me as if I was a ghost and then started sharpening Frank's knife.

On the way out the door, Frank mentioned that he had only heard one shot.

"That's all it took!" I replied proudly and Frank just shook his head.

With all the work behind us and the meat hanging in the smokehouse by the evening, it naturally was story time again. But since we had talked a lot about hunting and trapping lately, Frank chose stories about his ancestors.

"Athapaskan, or Athabaskan," said Frank (the correct spelling was never decided on) "actually means westerly people, since it was the west where they had come from during the time when there still was a land bridge between Siberia and Alaska. According to the beliefs of our people, the raven made the world and the raven also led our people into the interior of this country. Part of the trail by which my ancestors arrived is still in use today. You might have heard of the serum run to Nome and that stretch of winter trail between Kaltag on the Yukon River and Unalakleet on the coast. This is part of that ancient trail the raven had lead the people and named many places along the way. Some settlements and places all over this country still have their original names, while others have been changed in time.

"Until the Russians came, our people had lived in some kind of tents in the summer and in underground houses in the winter. They hunted with spears and with bow and arrow, built canoes in the summer, and toboggans for the winter."

Frank only had a faint recollection about fishnets made from willow bark or spruce roots, but mostly his people built fish traps, which sometimes are still in use today, especially to catch blackfish in the lakes.

When I asked him about the battles around Nulato, he acknowledged that he had heard about them, but he had no further information or details about it.

Next, I asked what Frank's ancestors did to keep the swarms of mosquitoes off themselves besides burning the dried tree sponges of which I already knew, because I had seen them still being used in the fish camps today along the river. Frank thought that there also might have been certain plant juices for that purpose, but he did not remember any specifics. From Frank's brother, Henry, I later heard that the Athapaskans, sometimes when traveling, made tents out of fresh birch bark, which supposedly keeps the mosquitoes from biting as long as the bark stayed fresh enough.

"In the old days," Frank continued, "people were a lot tougher than nowadays." With that remark, I was assured to hear at least one more story that evening;

"A long time ago, even before my father was born, a very strong man used to live here. He never used a bow and arrow for hunting and even a spear only seldom. This man went bear hunting one time, leaving the village with nothing but his stone knife. After he had located a den with a black bear in it, he went to look for the right size birch tree and made a fire at its base. After the base of the tree had burned enough so the man could push it over, he then burned a piece of the trunk to the desired length. By burning and scratching with his stone knife, the man fashioned himself a club of just the right proportions. Then he went back to the den, teased the bear until it came out of the den. As soon as the animal's head showed itself in the entrance of the den, he would club the animal to death."

After that night of storytelling, the temperatures had fallen drastically. Minus fifty or even minus sixty was nothing unusual during the days to follow. Staying out of the cold while worrying about our wood supply was my main occupation during this cold spell. For a short time each day, I would go outside, dig up, cut, and pack home a log or two from a fallen-in cabin. At the same time, flocks of ptarmigans would land in the willows around the old village site to feed on their buds. I didn't want to pass up the chance to supply us with a change in our moose meat diet, and so I took my small caliber bolt action along on my wood foraging trips. Shooting with that rifle at such an extreme cold was easier said than done. The bolt action would get so cold that the bolt, after pulling the trigger, moved so slow that it did not set off the cartridge. Therefore, I kept the lock of the rifle in my pants pocket to keep it warm until I was ready to use it and that solved that problem. I also learned a lot about the behavior of these birds and how to hunt them successfully. The flocks of feeding ptarmigan would always have a watch-bird sitting at some higher position in a birch tree or taller willow. If I shoot this particular bird first, he would instantly be replaced by another bird to watch out for the flock, while the sound of my twenty-two caliber rifle seemed to have little impact, as long as I stayed under cover. In that way, I was able to shoot three or more birds before my deceit was discovered and the whole flock took off.

Especially on those cold, frosty mornings, the sounds of the feeding birds could be heard for a great distance and therefore they were easy to find. Ptarmigans, more than all the other grouse, like to sleep under the snow and often let themselves be snowed in during a storm. On one of my evening rounds, I once was startled by a large flock of ptarmigan as they dove out of the night sky and vanished without interruption under the deep snow, like diving birds in front of me. Toward springtime, when these birds feed heavy on the budding pussy willows, their feathers take on a pink hue, which gives them almost the appearance of a tropical bird.

After that cold spell ended, we were still a long way from springtime and I had to get back out to my traps. Just before the cold spell, it had snowed heavily and now it snowed again. It was not only that I wouldn't catch anything while my traps were deep under the snow, but whatever I might have caught earlier was now in danger of being chewed up by mice and shrews.

Another effect of the deep snow on animals I discovered on the trail just around the old village, when I encountered a cow moose with a calf. I assumed that the animals would run away as I moved closer, but by the time I was within ten yards of the animals, they still did not move; instead, the cow's ears went down, the neck hairs came up, and she lowered her head. This was a clear sign for me that it was high time to break a fresh trail and leave the old trail to the moose. All the moose I encountered after the heavy snowfall on my trips seemed irritated and not too willing to move. Even though I tried to keep my distance, I still was greeted by deep grunts and threatening gestures. Frank was convinced that for some reason or another, the moose people were angry with me and urged me to be cautious.

During our conversation about these encounters, Frank started laughing because I had said "moose cow" instead of "cow moose."

"What the heck is the difference?" I asked.

"No difference to me," Frank answered smiling, and lit a cigarette, "it just reminded me of another story."

"Some years ago," Frank said, "a white man came here and he had his own idea about a cow moose. Al Hardluck had just shot a cow moose, and we wondered why the white guy was so anxious to go with Al and help him pack in the moose. Al was happy to have the help, but when they got to the killing site, that greenhorn kept walking around the dead animal, looking at it from all sides and finally declared that this was not a cow moose. When Al asked him how he came to that conclusion, he found out that this greenhorn had talked to an old prankster in Ruby, who had told him that a cow moose would have horns and a tail like a regular cow."

Frank wiped the tears out of his eyes after finishing his story. And while I laughed with him, I then said, "Now, I'm starting to wonder how many funny stories you guys will have to tell about me by now?"

"You're not funny!" answered Frank with a stern face.

"I'll take that as a compliment." I answered smiling, before I bid my friend good night and went to my own cabin.

Chapter 22
Ghosts, Legends, and Angry Moose People

The holidays had passed and 1971 started with the usual darkness and boredom, the precursor to cabin fever. The months of January and February are known for this phenomenon, unless a person finds ways to keep him or herself busy. Activity on the trapline is at its lowest point in January and with little else to do besides keeping our cabin warm, we played a lot of Yahtzee. But Alice often went to bed early and I would usually visit my friend Frank to listen to more stories. On one night, when Alice was getting ready for bed and was taking out her contact lenses, she suddenly called out, "Darn it!"

"What is it?"

"I dropped my contact lens!"

Since the time my wife started wearing contact lenses, she had dropped one of them now and then and usually I found it for her. Alice had been especially careful since we lived in Kokrines, but this was not her luckiest days along that line. Now the search for her lens was on, but it was not a successful one. We searched on the table, under it, and looked all over her clothes, just in case it had gotten stuck there. After a second extensive search with the same results, we finally gave up and went to bed. For me, however, the search for that lens did not end there; it followed me right into my dreams.

I dreamed about my father as he sat there smiling in his home in Germany and was plucking feathers out of colorful birds. For some reason, I had the feeling that he knew where Alice's contact lens was, but he just didn't want to tell me. So, why was he plucking feathers out of those birds?

After I awoke from that dream, it stayed vividly in my mind and I sat there trying to make sense out of it. On the wall over our bed, I had pinned up a poster of American songbirds and for a moment I thought that I might have solved the riddle. When I moved our bed and looked behind it in all directions, wherever the tail of one of these birds was pointed, Alice thought I had lost my mind. My efforts had been to no avail.

But when I had the same exact dream during the following night, even Alice thought that there must be something to it. Before we started turning the place upside down again, I once more sat there trying to make sense out of my dream.

To the right of that poster over the bed, I had hung up some old eagle feathers, which I had worn when I was playing Indian in Germany. My father had saved those feathers and had given them back to me on my visit to Germany in 1968-1969.

As soon as I had made that connection between my father and the feathers, I had no further doubts that I had found the missing contact lens. Sure enough, the lens was in a crack between the wall and the floor board, exactly where the feathers had pointed to. How that lens had gotten there remained just as much of a riddle to us as my dream, but the important thing was we had found the lens.

Knowing that Frank was a great believer in such strange happenings as my dreams about the lost contact lens, I knew he would enjoy hearing about it. As suspected, my friend did not doubt a word of what I told him and he didn't waste much time before he told me strange stories of his own. As soon as he had stopped stirring his tea and lit his cigarette, he leaned back into his chair and started talking.

"Ray Cleaver was trapping at the Nowitna River when, around midnight, his dogs started barking like crazy. Ray took his flashlight and went to check on his dogs, thinking that wolves or a moose might have come into his camp. He could not find anything that could have riled his dogs, so he told them to be quiet and went back inside. As he stepped back into his cabin, a cool breath of air greeted him from the inside of the cabin, which he thought to be very strange, but he didn't give it any further consideration. As soon as he had closed the door, his dogs started barking even wilder than before, so he took his gun and went right back out again. Again, he found nothing that could have caused his dogs to go that crazy, and it took a while before Ray managed to calm the animals down.

"The following morning, a trapper, unknown to Ray, stopped by his cabin and sat down without saying a word. Ray gave the man a cup of coffee and told him about the crazy behavior of his dogs during the night.

"'Was that about midnight?' the stranger asked. When Ray confirmed that, the man told him that it was also the exact time when he had entered the cabin of Ray's trapping partner across the river and found that the man had hung himself."

Frank's opinion was that it might have been the spirit of Ray's partner that got the dogs all riled as it came to say good bye to Ray. I certainly could not argue with that idea, but when I asked who the unknown trapper was, Frank had no idea and as far as he knew, neither did anybody else, or if this mysterious visitor even existed in reality. In Frank's view, there are too many things we can't even begin to understand, much less give an iron-clad explanation for.

Frank got up and poured a fresh cup of tea for us before he said,

"From what I know about you by now, you seem pretty well connected with the wildlife and nature in general, that's why I have to tell you a story, which happened when my father was a teenager. In those days, there were not so many trees on those hills here as there are now, and the caribous used to migrate through these hills every year. Moose, on the other hand, were rare and the killing of one even rarer. That particular year, the caribou didn't arrive either, and the people of Kokrines got pretty hungry. So, the men formed hunting parties to comb through the hills in the search of game. It was the first time that my father was allowed to join one of those parties of hunters and for two days, the men had traveled on their snowshoes without finding any caribou. Exhausted and tired, they headed back toward the village just as it started to get dark. That was when one of the men discovered a small herd of caribou on a distant hillside. The animals were already bedded down for the night, and the hunters wouldn't have been able to reach them before it would be too dark to hunt and kill the animals. Frustrated and not sure about what to do, the men started to argue between themselves. But one man, who was generally looked upon as being a little odd, told everybody to settle down. Then he took off his snowshoes, climbed onto a big boulder, and started singing while waving his arms in the air from side to side. The younger hunters just like my father, thought that this guy was really going nuts, but they couldn't believe their eyes when the caribou on that distant hill slowly got to their feet and one by one started running in circles until suddenly the whole herd came across the valley toward the hunters."

Frank looked at me and smiled while he said, "I know it sounds a little far-fetched, but maybe you should try that sometime."

I told Frank that I didn't really look at it as that far-fetched, because I knew that a herd of caribou makes noises and therefore the animals could have been tricked into believing that the singing and the arm-waving constituted another herd. And since it is natural for caribous to form bigger herds, the caribou were fooled and moved toward the hunters.

I had planned to answer Frank's challenge, but up to now I regrettably never got the chance to try it.

As the days were getting longer and the weather somewhat milder, the moose, in spite of the deep snow, started withdrawing from the riverbank, but just before that happened, I shot another bull to replenish our meat supply. Any outsider reading that might think that I'm killing too many moose for one year. It should be considered, however, that we were four people living in this old village. Legally, we could have shot four moose between us, but with no refrigerator, we shot a moose when we needed it instead of all of them at once and let the meat go to waste.

I was thankful that the game during this year was more plentiful and enabled me to be a good provider for our mini-community. My trapping season, too, had been more fruitful during my second year in Kokrines, and in spite that I didn't have any more traps than the previous year, I caught forty martens and two foxes. In my book, that is quite good for running a trapline on foot.

While these furs still wouldn't make us rich, they sure would have bought more than enough beans for the next winter, but the way things turned out, with our child on the way, we would have to use part of that money for our travel expense back to civilization instead.

Kokrines 1970

Although I had not heard anything back from my application for a job at the University of Alaska, Alice had enough faith in the situation to prepare for our departure from Kokrines by starting to pack certain things. It was not that she hated living there, but to have her first child without professional supervision was not something she looked forward to, and I guess I didn't really blame her. Therefore, I also had agreed that in the event the answer to my application should be negative, Alice still should travel to Fairbanks by herself if it had to be and have the baby in the hospital. Well, we still had time and whatever plans we would make were not clad in iron.

For now, we enjoyed the warmer weather of the approaching spring and I still had time for a few more evenings with my friend, Frank. On one of these nights, we somehow got on the subject of wolves again and the question of why so many people were afraid of them, when there wasn't even one documented case about wolves ever attacking a healthy human being.

231

In general, we both agreed that some human beings just needed something to hate and since the wolves are living off the same game animals as the humans, it makes them, along with the bears, the perfect candidate for a hate campaign.

"At the time when the raven led our people into Alaska," Frank said, and settled down to tell another story, "the wolf was actually a companion of man and he even hunted for the people. But in time, the game here in the new land got more and more wary of the wolf and the wolf had to travel farther and farther to get the game. Soon, the wolf was often gone for a week or more and when he returned after a particular long absence one day, he found that the dog had taken his place in the human camps. Instead of being welcomed home, dog and man drove him out of camp. And that is why the wolves nowadays howl so melancholic whenever they find a human camp."

Frank didn't seem to have too many significant personal encounters with wolves, other than that he watched six wolves at play some day, right through his cabin window.

"The animals were just having fun in the snow, right out there along the riverbank," said Frank, "when suddenly they stopped playing and looked intensely out onto the river. The wind was blowing the snow around so that it almost looked like the river was smoking, but even I could still see that there was a dog team coming toward Kokrines. I was not able to see anybody on the runners of the sled, but I knew that Al Hardluck was out and about with his team and so my first thought was that the dogs might have gotten away from him and now were coming home alone. The wolves in the meantime were running toward the sled and I felt that I had to interfere somehow. I took my rifle and went outside, but by the time I kneeled down at the riverbank and took a shot at one of the wolves, they were almost upon the team. I never hit the wolf I had been aiming at, but my shot brought a figure out from behind the sled and the wolves ran off across the river into the woods. The man behind the sled was Al, who had humped down behind it to shelter himself from the driving snow and icy wind."

That the wolves mistook the team either for another wolf pack, or assumed that the dogs were without a master, was obvious to Frank and me, especially since the wind had not been in their favor. When Al appeared behind that sled, the wolves recognized their mistake and left. In contrast to most modern people, Frank, just like his ancestors, held the wolf in high regard, instead of hating them for no good reason. To make that point, my friend told me the following legend:

"It was a long time ago, when a hunter returned to his hut and found his wife murdered.

"Luckily, his twin sons were still unharmed inside the hut. The hunter knew that he would have to find and kill the murderer to avenge his wife, but first, he would have to take care of his children and bury his slain wife. By that time, it had gotten too dark to pursue the killer, but he was still able to establish that there had actually been two murderers, which had left some very peculiar tracks behind. Even though the hunter had gotten an early start the next morning, he still had to break up his pursuit once more, return to his hut, and take care of the children. His young sons just took too much of his time, as he had to delay his plans for revenge again and again. He found it strange, however, that the children never seemed to be very hungry in the evening, until one night upon his return he overheard the baby talk of his children, which seemed as if the boys were talking about a big brother. Naturally, the man soon rejected this notion as a misunderstanding on his part and went back out to hunt. But the urge to find the murderers over-came him again and he followed the trail of the odd tracks. By the time he returned to his home this time, it really was late, so he moved very quietly while approaching his hut, so he would not wake the children. As he came close to his hut, he was surprised to hear the boys inside laughing and calling for a brother with beautiful fur and mixed in with the kids' voices were the deep growls of an animal. He quickly put an arrow on his bow and stepped into the entrance of his home.

At that moment, something brushed past his legs and vanished in the woods behind him. When he heard the children calling for the brother with the beautiful fur again, it became clear to the hunter that he almost had made a mistake. As he stood there in the door of his hut trying to sort out his emotions, he felt the presence of his wife, but as he turned, he saw a big wolf care-fully approaching from the woods. The hunter already had put his weapon down and now went to the cache to get a big chunk of meat, dipped it into a container of fat, and held it out to the wolf. While the animal was eating, the man trailed his fatty hand from nose to tail across the back of the wolf."

Frank had stopped talking for a moment and reaching for his tobacco, he smiled at me and then said, "That's why the fur of the wolf is often darker along the back!"

I was afraid that his story had ended right there, or that Frank could not remember the rest of it, as it sometimes was the case. But after Frank had lit his cigarette and sipped his tea, he finally continued.

"The hunter now knew that the wolf would be taking care of the children and he was free to follow the trail of the murderers. Even though a little fresh snow had fallen in the meantime, the man had no problem following the trail. For two full days, he followed the tracks, until they led straight up a sheer cliff, where he couldn't follow. The top of the cliff was so high that it vanished into the clouds. In his anger not to be able to catch up with the murderers, the hunter shot an arrow into those clouds above him and to his surprise, the arrow turned into a big tree. Distrusting the whole situation at first, the hunter tested the tree to see if it was real and then climbed up the tree, full of hope that he would get his revenge. When he emerged above the clouds, he seemed to be in a different world, where a trail led from the treetop toward a cave. Ready for action, the hunter put an arrow on his bow as he approached the cavern, but instead of meeting danger, he was greeted by two old crones who addressed him as grandson. After the two old women asked him where he came from and what he wanted, he told them all about the murder of his wife. The old women admitted that they knew who he was looking for, but they told him that these beings were called the duck people and that they were very dangerous. When the crones were not able to talk the man out of his plans for revenge, they agreed to help him as much as they could. While one of the old women gave the man some food, the other prepared some medicine for him. They also gave him a full description of the so-called Duck People, told him where he might find them and also made suggestions on how he could kill them. After all was said and done, the crones sent the hunter on his way and wished him good luck.

"Full of confidence, he trotted along a trail toward some distant mountains and reached a valley with a big village. In the middle of that village stood a big meeting hall of some sort and from that hall came the sounds of a celebration. The man entered the hall and was greeted by what seemed to be the chief of the village. This man invited the hunter to join in the celebration and asked him where he would like to sit. The hunter had discovered the two duck people, who were sitting high on a log above the other guests, so he too asked to be seated there and before anybody could give a reply to his request, he had jumped up there and seated himself right between the two duck people. The other guests were awed by his ability to do so, but thanks to the medicine the old women had prepared for him, he had accomplished the feat effortlessly. The festivities went on with drumming and dancing, delicious food was passed around, and everybody enjoyed themselves. The hunter's attempt to strike up a conversation with the duck people was unsuccessful, but he had to test the old women's theory about the sensitivity of the duck people's external organs, so he tugged slight on the organ of one of these men.

The duck man's reaction was a grunt and a vicious look toward the hunter, but it was enough to let the hunter know what his next move would have to be. At a chosen moment, the hunter grabbed both duck people by their outgrowths and then jumped off his perch. The screams of his victims pierced through the noise of the festivities, as the bodies of the duck people were ripped open and plunged to the ground. Before the onlookers could recover from their shock, the hunter was out the door and running for his life.

"Again, because of the medicine the crones had given him, his speed and his endurance was so great that he reached the cave of the old women without a pursuer in sight. While he was fed again by the old ones, he gave an account of his deed, but when the faint cries and angry calls of his pursuers could be heard in the distance, the old women urged him to climb back through the hole in the clouds. No sooner had the hunter felt solid ground under his feet again, when the hole in the clouds above him was filled with angry faces and shaking fists. The hunter took an arrow and shot it toward the hole, but the hole closed with a loud clap while at the same time the tree leading into the clouds crumbled into a pile of arrows. On his way home, the hunter only needed half the time it had taken him to get there, and soon he was greeted by his sons and the wolf."

This was one of the longest stories Frank had ever told to me and because of its unique contents, we had a long discussion afterwards about the possible origin of the story and the meaning of it, but we were unable to reach a feasible conclusion. As Frank had said before, "Not everything can be explained in human terms."

Then, Phillip Albert came to Kokrines again and brought supplies for Frank and Josephine, but he also had some letters for us and one of them was the long awaited answer from the University of Alaska in Fairbanks. The answer was positive.

As of April 1, I was employed by the Institute of Water Resources as an Aqua-Biological Technician and it was not an April joke. My happiness about the news was mostly for Alice. Now she didn't have to travel to Fairbanks alone, but I also think that she was ready to get back to civilization after a long winter in that little cabin we lived in. Right away, I wrote my answer to the letter, so that Phillip could take it back with him and put it in the mail. Since Alice in her condition could not be expected to go on another wild ride in a sled behind a snowmobile, I also sent a note to Harold Esmailka, for him to pick us up by bush plane, in time for us to fly on to Fairbanks before the first of April.

My own emotions about the whole situation were as mixed as before. I really was not looking forward to live in civilization again, and as usual, looked upon it as a temporary solution, hoping to move back out into the bush soon after the baby was old enough for it. Many of our belongings would have to stay in Kokrines for now anyway, to be picked up at some later date, and Minado we put in the care of a friend in Ruby.

While Alice kept on sorting and packing, I still had some traps to pick up from my trapline on the Hardluck slough, where I had hung them in a tree. Traps are often left in the woods by trappers and I could have left mine there, too, but first of all, I didn't know how soon I might return and, second, it gave me a good excuse for one more trip into the woods.

It was a nice spring day as I undertook this last trip with my dog, Minado, and Frank called out to me just to remind me to take my rifle, because of the angry moose people. I smiled over Frank's concern, but agreed to take a weapon. Not that I was that concerned about the moose, but rather because there was always the possibility of an encounter with a hungry, grouchy spring bear this time of the year.

Even though my trails were well packed from my many trips over them, the warm weather during the last days made it impossible to walk without snowshoes and almost as impossible with them, because of the melting snow. Minado seemed amused about my slow progress as he bounced along in front of me. But in the Hardluck Slough, Minado broke through the already rotting ice and almost took another bath, but got away with just wet feet, since the water wasn't that deep to begin with. Being alerted to the condition of the rotten ice and because I was wearing my snowshoes, I, too, was able to make it to shore, but with dry feet.

A short time later, I had collected my traps, but decided not to go back onto that slough and take a second chance to get wet this time. Instead, I went through the woods to a nearby creek bed, which we could follow back to the Yukon. Breaking out of the brush to get onto the ice of that creek, I just noticed the rear end of a moose, as he walked around the creek bend. Luckily, Minado had not seen or smelled the moose, which gave me a chance to let that moose put some distance between us. I held on to the dog, sat down on a snow-free log, and took a cigarette break. Assuming that the moose was long gone by the time we continued on our way, we made it to that bend in the creek. Coming around that bend on to a straight stretch toward the Yukon, there stood the moose on the ice, like he was waiting for us. Before I got fully aware of the situation, Minado was running full speed toward the moose. The moose, seemingly not impressed by the dog, ran right over him and came straight toward me.

With steep creek banks on both sides of me, standing in the middle of that creek on my snowshoes, I felt like I was standing on the train tracks while the train was approaching full speed. Up to that date, I had put down every moose with my first shot, but this time, the moose was still running toward me after my second shot, which just left me enough time to throw myself aside while loading through. Landing on my back in the snow, I shot toward the neck of the angry animal.

The hoof of that moose could not have missed me by more than two feet and the image of that animal's face was something I will never forget: blood-shot eyes, raised lips, laid back ears, and raised neck hair, all of that accompanied by a grunting noise that probably was pretty close to that of a camel's angry grunts. If it was my hasty shot at the animal's neck, or the fact that my dog was back on its heels again, which made the moose run past me, is hard to say. Moose and dog vanished into the brush up the creek and I got back on my feet, reloading my Winchester with very shaky hands.

Next, I inspected the streak of blood and hair on the ice and snow. Due to the long neck hairs, I came to the conclusion that my last shot could only have scratched the upper part of the animal's neck. Had I hit the neck bone, the moose would have fallen right then and there. Would my shot have gone below the neck bone, the moose would choke on his own blood. But as I followed the tracks of the animal, there was very little blood on the brush at first and soon there was none. After about a quarter of a mile, I could not see or hear neither the moose nor my dog and I headed toward home. Shortly after, Minado came up from behind me, without a moose in pursuit, wagging his tail as if he was saying, "We showed him, didn't we?"

Looking back on that last day in my beloved hunting grounds, it could easily have been my last day period, but then again, such is the life of adventure, and being alive after an incident like that made it even sweeter

Alice, on the other hand, didn't quite see it that way. "One of these days, your adventures will put you in your grave!" she said, slightly irritated by my attitude about the whole situation. But all Frank had to say was, "I told you so!"

The next day, March 15, Harold landed his Super Cub on the river in front of Kokrines to pick us up. Our good-byes from Frank and Josephine were a sad affair, but my promise to return to Kokrines eventually if not sooner, were without reservations. And as already mentioned, once more we had to leave Minado behind, this time with a friend in Ruby, while Alice and I flew to Fairbanks.

Chapter 23
An Exercise in Futility

According to my travel log, our arrival in Fairbanks on March 26, 1971, was quite the culture shock for us. I had noted that we ate cheeseburgers for $3.90 on which the dried-up meat patty had been hard to detect, not mentioning tasting it. This treat had been further complimented by lukewarm coffee, which was, however, included in the prize. Afterwards, we had rented a room at the Steel hotel for $10.50 the night, which had given us the chance to enjoy a long-missed hot bath.

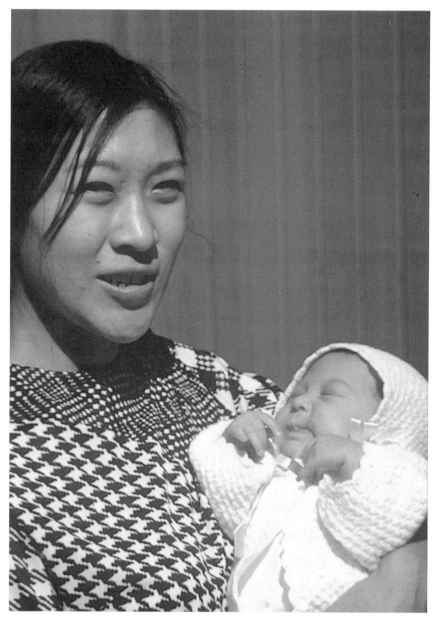

Alice with Diana, Fairbanks 1971

Since Alice's sister and her brother-in-law had moved to cheaper living accommodations themselves, they didn't have enough space for us to stay with them for even a few days. On the other hand, we couldn't afford to stay for much longer at the hotel, nor rent an apartment. Our whole situation almost struck me like a punishment for trying to assimilate. Getting used to living by the clock again and seeing all the people about us in a constant hurry looked to us more like a comedy.

Eventually, we decided that Alice would travel on to Anchorage to visit her brother and stay there, while I moved in with an older student from the institute, by which I was now employed. That would give me time to get settled and find a more or less permanent place for us to live.

Father and daughter

Starting out at my job at the institute, it seemed to have little to do with the work of a technician for water resources, but I wasn't complaining. I was sent out to accompany the students on their field trip to act as bodyguard, apparently to keep them out of harm's way from encounters with moose or bears. By the time I received my first paycheck, I rented a trailer home within walking distance of the university and my wife came back to join me in Fairbanks again. Our daughter, Diana, was born on May 13, and shortly thereafter, I was in negotiation to buy a small log house within walking distance to my workplace. All in all, we were well on our way to being ordinary, civilized people again. My work became somewhat more variable and interesting, but not to the point that I looked upon it as a permanent employment with the institute for the rest of my life.

Diana with sheefish in Kokrines on a vacation trip

Then I got to meet John Bradbury, a glassblower who had only recently come to Alaska to work for the Institute of Marine Science. Since both of our institutes were located in the same building and I too was a glassblower by profession, John and I became good friends. My new friend, also being a somewhat adventurous soul himself, agreed enthusiastically to accompany me on a trip to Ruby and Kokrines to pick up my dog and some of our belongings. After this short trip to the Yukon River, John, who had left his wife in Colorado, now almost became a member of our family. We spent many weekends together on picnics, on exploratory trips in the near out of doors, and while visiting old gold mines.

While I enjoyed John's friendship and our mutual excursions, it was a small consolation for the lifestyle I had left behind on the Yukon. My true feelings at that time are probably best explained by another entry in my log book.

April 25, 1972, the returning geese from the south are landing in the fields around the university. It is hard for me to keep my restlessness in check and to concentrate on my job. Our daughter, Diana, is already trying to walk by now.

Minado was by far not as patient as I with his love for adventure. Somehow, he had gotten off his chain and went on an exploration of our neighborhood. It might have been a bitch in heat, or just his urge to roam free. The fact remains Minado was gone and we never saw him again. Being as friendly as he was beautiful, he even might have been picked up by somebody and taken far away. We dearly missed our old travel companion, but only could hope that the rest of his life would be a happy one.

Finding some fresh moose tracks on our property in Fairbanks a few days later did not really help to calm my own urge to return to the wild. For the time being, however, I had to be satisfied with the approach of my vacation time. I already had bought another second-hand foldboat and had planned to paddle with my family down the Tanana and the Yukon Rivers to visit Korines and on to Ruby. That was the plan until our friend, John, announced that his son was coming for a visit from Colorado, and that he was expecting to see some Alaskan wilderness. John suggested that we all might travel downriver in his motorboat. The trip by motorboat would give us enough time for a visit to the Melozitna Hot Springs, which John had been anxious to get to see for himself. I liked John's idea, but Alice and Diana would take a plane to Ruby and fly from there by bush plane to the hot springs, while we three men would drive John's boat to Kokrines and hike from there to the hot springs.

Frank and Josephine naturally were pleasantly surprised to see me again, but they were a little disappointed that we stayed only one night in Kokrines before we started on our hike toward the Melozitna Hot Springs.

To make John's son's experience realistic, it started to rain right after we left Kokrines and it didn't stop all day. Therefore, progress was slow and we ended up spending a night in an old supply shack along the trail. A couple of short encounters with a black bear and a wolf along the way had been a welcome highlight for my guests in spite of the rain.

The second day on the trail, we were pleased that the rain finally stopped, and we safely arrived at the hot springs in good spirits.

Picking berries, looking for mushrooms, and angling for grayling in the hot spring creek was just the right thing for my friend John and his son. But they also enjoyed the evenings, as we reminisced with Pat and Leonard about the time we had spent with them. As the saying goes, when you're having fun, time flies and it was too soon for all of us that we had to return to our homes and to our jobs. Instead of walking back to Kokrines over the trail, we all flew from the hot springs to Ruby. Alice and Diana caught their plane from there back to Fairbanks, and we men hired someone to bring us by boat to Kokrines, where John's motorboat was waiting for us. When we continued our trip from there, I was tempted to almost stay behind. After saying our good-byes to Frank and Josephine, John steered the boat upriver. Turning around and looking back toward Kokrines, I could see Frank sitting on his old, wooden bench by the riverbank, sadly waving after us. That picture was a moment in my life I will never forget as long as I live.

In the following year, Alice had planned to visit her relatives in Nome with our daughter, and since John too had bought himself a foldboat by then, we planned a more adventurous undertaking by paddling down the Koyukuk River.

As soon as the plane had dropped us off at Bettles Field, which was right next to the upper part of that river, we put our boats together, loaded up, and took off. Less than an hour had passed before we got caught in a heavy rainstorm and had to seek shelter by erecting John's pop-up tent in a hurry. With most of that day gone by the time the rain had slowed down enough for us to travel on, we decided to camp for that night in the nearby old village of Bettles. Many of the buildings of what looked like a ghost town seemed still to be in use as fishing or trapping camps, but not a soul was to be found at that time. We pitched our tent inside a door and windowless skeleton of a cabin in order to save ourselves the search for a level spot and to keep our tent dry in case of more rain.

The town of Koyukuk

On the Koyukuk River

About seventy natives lived at this settlement at one time, but when in 1945 the airport of Bettles Field was constructed a few miles farther upriver, where our plane had landed, the people from the village of Bettles started relocating closer to the airstrip because of the trading post and the occasional employment opportunities.

The land around the upper Koyukuk was generally a little more open than the land along the Yukon, but therefore it seemed to be windier, which helped to keep the mosquitoes in check. The river was still relatively narrow at this point, and a fast current allowed us to make good time even if the wind was head on. Contrary to my first river trip on the Yukon, mileage was of some importance to us, since we were limited to our vacation time for the duration of our trip. But we refused to let that interfere with our goal and purpose to enjoy nature and getting to know another part of the Alaskan landscape. Hoping to see some wildlife and find a few good angling spots was of more importance to us.

In between the rain showers and our initial haste in getting out onto the river, hygiene had taken a back seat for the first couple of days, but as soon as we had our first real sunny day and found an inviting gravel bar, we stopped for a major cleaning. In no time at all, we had a nice fire going, and heated some water for bathing and a shaving.

"My underwear will have to stay here," I announced to my friend, "I just haven't decided yet if I should just bury it or shoot it first!"

John chuckled about my remark and pointed toward the fire, where his underpants were already in flames!

The next day was not quite so humorous, as we reached the village of Allakaket under a dark and threatening sky. At our arrival, it was so quiet in this village of about 115 Indians, that it almost gave the impression to be deserted. While I stayed with the boats, John went to find a store, in the hope to be able to buy something a little special for our dinner, since it was my birthday. No people, not even children or even a dog, was to be seen. As I stood there waiting for John's return, the only sign of life I could discover was a moving curtain at a cabin window. When John finally returned, he had a couple cans of peaches, a box of pilot bread crackers in his arm, and a very angry expression on his face.

"Let's get out of this dump!" he grumbled and then explained how he practically had the door slammed into his face when trying to enter the first store and at a second store he found there was not much else on the shelves, than the items John was carrying.

I thought to myself that we should have landed on the opposite side of the river, at an even smaller settlement called Alatna. This village consisted only of a few huts, and was populated by Eskimos, who might have given us a friendlier reception. But even if that village had their own store, they certainly wouldn't have had their own post office, which was the main reason we had chosen to land at the larger of the two villages.

Since John didn't want to go to the post office by himself to send out some mail, I strapped on my handgun and we secured our boats as well as we could. Then we went down the street in an atmosphere that would have reminded anyone, of the movie *High Noon*. Again, a moving curtain in a window was about the only evidence of life along the way, but our transaction at the post office and the return to our boat passed without incident. About a couple of years later, I heard that a white teacher had been shot in that village just because somebody did not like him.

Anyway, we stepped back into our boats and got the heck away from this unfriendly settlement. It had started to drizzle again and under a dreary, gray sky, we traveled a little farther downriver to pitch our tent at the mouth of the Kanuti River. We would have liked to travel a little longer that day, but the dreary weather and the depressing experience at the last village had taken the fun out of it; nor did we see any sense in getting all wet just to make a couple more miles of progress. The tent was quickly set up and we ate our meager meal, topping it with the canned peaches for dessert. Afterwards, John more or less settled in for the night, but I wasn't tired enough to just crawl into my sleeping back and call it a day. In spite of some the light rain, I walked the gravel beach, picking up flat stones now and then to skip them on the smooth surface of the Kanuti River.

When I saw what looked like a piece of broken beer bottle, I bent down in anger to pick it up. I was just about to skip it into the river when at the last minute I noticed something about that shard that didn't look quite right to me. It was a streak of a different color which caused me to take a second look, and that was when it dawned on me that I actually was holding an obsidian arrowhead in my hand.

"Mother Nature just gave me a birthday present!" I hollered toward the tent, knowing that John was a lover of artifact. My friend came out of the tent faster than I had expected and together we combed over every inch of that gravel bar, but couldn't find anything else of interest.

Below the merging of the Kanuti River, the Koyukuk became noticeably wider and the current seemingly slower. If we wanted to stay on schedule, we had to paddle a little harder or put in longer hours. But as mentioned before, whenever we found an interesting campsite with a promising angling spot for grayling, we called it a day; picked berries for breakfast and mushrooms for lunch or dinner along with the fresh grayling we caught. Before we reached the village of Hughes, I also managed to bag a fat goose, which was a nice change from our standard diet.

The village of Hughes had started as a riverboat landing for the prospectors and gold miners in 1910, but when the gold ran out in 1915, the settlement was taken over by the natives and it turned into an Indian village. We were pleasantly surprised that the Indians of this settlement were a lot friendlier toward us than they had been in Allakaket. But feeling more and more pressed for time, especially with the unstable weather, we soon traveled on. The gravel beaches along the river were now replaced by sandy beaches, which, combined with the rain, made this a perfect breeding ground for a particular species of gnats. These little pests soon got so thick that if we stopped paddling even in the middle of the river, we were instantly engulfed by swarms of these little critters. After landing our boats, we were left with two choices: either we made a quick fire and stand or sit in the smoke, or we could set up the pup tent, spray the inside with mosquito dope and zip up the screen door. Otherwise, these little flies would crawl into our hair, ears, eyes, and nostrils. Eating or talking became impossible without consuming gnats at the same time. In other words, the fun was over, and by the time we saw the first buildings of the village of Huslia, we knew that this village would be the final stop of our paddle tour.

This Koyukan Indian village had been built around a trading post in 1940. It also is the home of the well-known dog musher, George Attla, an Indian who had been portrayed in the movie, *Spirit of the Wind*.

George Attla himself was not home at the time of our visit, but as we made arrangements to fly out from Huslia, we met George's brothers, and were invited for tea.

The bad part was that this afternoon in the company with the Attla brothers turned out to be the only pleasant part of our stay in Huslia. Again, it had started to rain, and in spite of it, some older teenagers or younger men visited us at our tent. Not wanting to appear unfriendly, we talked with our beer-drinking visitors while we cooked and ate our dinner. Everything went well, until it got quite late and we wanted to turn in for the night. All our hints were either ignored, or went unnoticed; our uninvited guests just did not want to leave the campfire, even after we let it burn down. Hoping that our last two guests would finally get the point and leave as well, we withdrew into our tent. Eventually, they did just that, but then I heard the familiar rattling of clattering dishes and stormed out of the tent, to see one of the guys trying to run off with our kitchen box. He dropped the box when I came out of the tent and I put the box back under the entrance of our tent before climbing into my sleeping bag in the hope to have seen the last of those two young warriors.

It wasn't long before I heard footsteps behind our tent and I was not in the mood to play anymore games. So I took my Winchester and loaded through to put a cartridge into the chamber. The sound of that rifle's action had the desired effect.

"Come on, that son of a bitch is going to shoot you!" I heard somebody whisper, which was followed by hastily retreating footsteps.

"Now they understood you!" mumbled John from inside his sleeping bag and then we finally had peace and quiet.

In spite of the rain, our plane arrived the following day on time and we were happy to get out of there. Back in Fairbanks, our lives soon turned back to our daily routine. Alice and Diana returned from Nome and I settled back into my work at the university. Whatever little glassblowing had to be done for our institute I had taken over, since it also gave me a chance to be in company of John during the working hours. Besides, it was hard for me to look fully occupied in general during the whole day, since there just wasn't that much to do. In 1974, the Institute of Water Resources was in the process of being at least partly absorbed by the Institute of Marine Science. While I was assured that my position would be safe for the time being, I didn't feel that safe at all. To justify my employment, I also was passed around to different departments as a shopping or delivery boy, which was not exactly the way I imagined my future.

The main topic in those days was the Alaska oil pipeline and money for any kind of project didn't seem to be a problem. Many people came to Alaska to get a job working for the pipeline or related projects to make a fast buck and then go home again. Land settlements were in progress with the natives and the politicians promised everybody to turn Alaska into a state of milk and honey.

But my own view about the whole situation was once more a little different, because I knew that everything has a price. The first rumbles about dissatisfaction and suspicion we had experienced during our family vacation that year, during our foldboat trip to Ruby. While we enjoyed visiting our friends along the river and reminisced about the happy times we had spent with them, we also could feel the nervousness when we were talking about land ownership and the rights to the resources, such as fish and game. The general fear of the people to lose control of their lifestyle was not unfounded; stricter control of hunting, fishing, and trapping laws came along with the general restrictions on land use, which certainly was not in favor of the indigenous population.

I always knew that there was a much darker side to the so-called progress, for which I never had much enthusiasm. As is obvious from another of my travel log entries in September, 1974:

If our glorious civilization is supposed to be a blessing, I would gladly do without.

While the human race dreams about creating heaven on earth, it is destroying it to make rich people richer and make the rest of the population dependent on a self-destructive society.

Chapter 24
Becoming a Ruby Resident

At the return from our vacation, we already had made up our minds to move back out into the bush. We would have liked to return to Kokrines, but thanks to the economic progress brought on by the pipeline construction and the land settlement with the natives of Alaska, we didn't have a chance of ever owning any land in or around Kokrines. Not that it was impossible to claim land as a homesteader at all in Alaska anymore, but the land available for that purpose was wisely selected so that it was either along the road system, where civilization would soon catch up with us, or it was so far from the river that one would have to have enough money to own an airplane in order to get supplies and equipment into these places. If we wanted to stay in the general area along the Yukon that we were familiar with, we had to be content to make our home under the squatter's right within the township of Ruby.

Moving to Ruby 1974

I already had given notice at the university and as soon as the holidays were over, we started sorting and packing to get our belongings ready for shipping. A short time later, we had the first potential buyer for our house and Alice moved with our daughter Diana temporarily to Nome. I made preparations to travel by boat from Fairbanks to Ruby.

The fruits of our economic growth in Alaska were already noticeable through higher shipping and traveling cost. Progress in action!

On June 12, my friend John Bradbury brought me and a befriended student from the university, and all my pets and some belongings to the Chena River. There, we had a prearranged meeting with a man from whom I was planning to buy a used, wooden boat with two used outboard motors for eight-hundred dollars.

After trying out both motors and checking out the boat, I closed the deal and we started loading up. Even though the boat was 18 feet long and I was planning to pull my foldboat alongside it, against my better judgment, we had a hard time to fit all the stuff, plus my pets in and on to it. My new dog, Bozo, being a half Newfoundlander, was about the size of a small pony and outside of him, I had a few reptiles in cages, a cage with my daughter's rabbit, and a cage with our pet raccoon. There also should have been a cat, but Morris was on one of his several day excursions and didn't make it home before I left. John promised to be on the lookout for him, but neither he, nor our neighbors ever saw Morris again.

My student friend, Richard, had not seen much of Alaska outside of the city life, which was the reason he wanted to accompany me on my river trip, at least to the village of Tanana on the Yukon and then fly back home from there. John, too, would have liked to come with me for the adventure and because he had gotten used to be around my family, but he had only a few years left till retirement and could not just go and start a new life in the bush without an income. Therefore, it was time for us to say good bye for now and get the show on the road.

As I steered the boat from the mouth of the Chena River into the Tanana, Richard's face displayed the same uneasiness I had seen in Alice's face a few years earlier, as we entered that river in our two-man rubber raft. I couldn't help wondering how Richard would have felt if we would have been traveling in a small raft like that. Even while going extra slow, pulling the loaded foldboat was, as suspected, a bad idea. The water splashing up between the boats got into the foldboat and pulling the foldboat behind might have been all right if it was empty, but as loaded, it surely would get swamped sooner or later. To prevent total disaster, we soon had to make camp, dry some things out, pile half of the cargo from the foldboat on to the motorboat, and tie a tarp over the foldboat. That way, we limped on downriver the following day at an extra slow pace.

When we reached the town of Nenana, I shipped the foldboat including its contents by barge on to Ruby. Figuring to have gotten rid of that problem, we should have been able to relax and make better time, but things don't always go as planned; otherwise, such undertakings would hardly be called adventures. On the way back from sending off the foldboat, it had started to rain again and when we talked to a local inhabitant along the way, we were told that only a few days earlier, a boat accident near the town had claimed the lives of two men. This little news item did not exactly improve my companion's confidence in our situation and to make things worse, our boat motor needed a change of spark plugs before we got started; but, finally, we were on our way again, at least for a few hundred yards.

"Puff!" said the motor, and once more, we were floating along without power. Just as if to rub my nose in it, while I had the pleasure of messing around with the motor, the rain started coming down harder.

Soaking wet by the time we were on our way again, we eventually decided to make camp for the night in some fish camp to dry out, and by the following morning, the rain had stopped, we were fully rested, and our clothes were dry. We were ready for a fresh start, but the boat motor was on strike again. Since Richard claimed to be more in tune with machinery than I, which is not hard to do, I let him take care of the spark plug troubles this time and in no time at all, we were on our way. Sometime later, when the motor started acting up again, I made some interesting discoveries; unless I hadn't noticed that the threads for one of the spark plugs had been stripped when I bought the outfit, my companion must have stripped it that morning. At that time, I also discovered a bad crack in the motor mount and we probably could call ourselves lucky that the motor was still attached to the boat. It was high time to put motor number two to work. This motor was ten horse powers weaker than the first motor, but it started right up and ran smoothly. As for motor number one, I certainly had my share of headaches with it and since I have little, or no interest in messing around with machines anyway, we left the darn thing sitting on an island, where some lucky person could find it and have his fun with it.

Shortly before we reached Manley Hot Springs, we ran into a shallow spot and during the process of freeing our boat from the muddy shallows, Richard broke one of my paddles. Even though I had given no indication that I suspected my companion of having stripped the thread for the spark plug or blamed him for breaking my paddle, Richard must have felt like he was a curse on my trip and he decided that he had enough of his first Alaska adventure. As soon as he had arranged his flight from Manley back to Fairbanks, I continued my trip alone and made camp that night at a point on the river called Squaw Crossing.

From there on downriver, the Tanana River spreads out into an expanse of shallow channels and since I didn't want to take a chance to get stuck on another mud bank, I planned to be ready in the morning to follow whatever boat or barge would come downriver.

The weather had already turned beautiful right after Richard had left the expedition and I hadn't even bothered with putting up my tent. Early in the morning, after tending to my zoo, I was sitting in the sun eating my breakfast, when a boat full of natives came downriver. Being certain that they would know the right channel to take, I put the last few items in my boat, extinguished the fire, and waited for the boat to pass me, which it did without anybody in the passing boat even noticing my presence. Then I pulled on the starter rope of my motor, once, twice, and once again, but my motor wouldn't start. After a few more tries and a lot of cussing, my boat had drifted into a narrow side channel, where I expected to be halted sooner or later by a beaver dam or by shallow water. So I lit a cigarette to calm my anger and planned to check on the motor out when the boat came to a halt. The awaited beaver dam or the shallows never materialized; instead, I soon found myself back in the main channel of the river, with all the suspected trouble spots behind me. A calmer check-up of the motor revealed a disconnected spark plug cable and as soon as I had reconnected it, the motor started at the first try.

By then, I was out of the Tanana River and happily on the Yukon again. After I puttered past the village of Tanana, I held to the north shore of the river, hoping to reach Kokrines long before nightfall. At a big bend in the river, a slough beckoned me to take a shortcut, so I steered my boat out on the river to reach the other side in time. About halfway across, I heard a big splash and my dog, Bozo, had rolled over in his sleep and fallen in to the river. Since he was on a chain, he was now being pulled along under water, next to the boat, looking like a torpedo. It took a bit before I got the whole picture of the situation and stopped the motor. Getting that big, waterlogged dog, which weighed about one-hundred and twenty pounds in dry condition, back onto the boat was no easy task, especially since the dog was so dazed by the incident that he was of no help at all during his rescue. Once back on board and on his feet, he shook the water out of his fur and gave me a shower, just to say thanks! But it was a warm day and I almost enjoyed being refreshed and overcame the temptation to push him back into the river, even though the S O B looked like he was smiling.

By that time, my boat had drifted long past my intended shortcut, but the motor started right back up and I stayed in the main channel of the river. Next, I heard a chainsaw and stopped to investigate, thinking that an acquaintance I had met a year earlier might be back on the river as he had planned. Instead, I found a land surveying crew at work and got into a lengthy conversation with the boss of that crew, Richard Skinner, who later became a permanent friend of mine. It was getting late by the time I continued my trip, but the quiet beauty of the evening atmosphere was highlighted twice by the observation of a black bear walking the shoreline before I reached Kokrines.

It was about midnight when I found my old friends, Frank and Josephine, still awake in their cabin and as usual it was a happy reunion. We had a lot to talk about and I would have stayed there overnight, or even another day, but I had to think of all my pets on the boat and therefore I traveled on toward Ruby in the early morning hours.

Just so I wouldn't get too spoiled by the nice weather, the rainy weather returned upon my arrival in Ruby. On a prior visit, I had already chosen a piece of the available land under the squatter's right in Ruby, but on this property, somebody had already undertaken some feeble attempts to build a cabin, and an alternate location also had been claimed by one of the locals. As a newcomer to this village, I wanted to be as polite as possible and tried to find out where there still might be some land available for me to build on, but the people I asked about it either didn't want to tell me or really didn't know. So I figured that I could play dumb as well; I chose a spot, pitched my tent, and considered it home. Lacking motorized transportation myself, I talked Billy Dean (the trapper I had met in Ruby a few years earlier) into driving all my belongings from the barge landing to the other side of town. From there, I had to carry or push my stuff in a wheelbarrow up a steep Caterpillar trail where Billy was worried that his old pickup might get stuck.

My building site was about fifty yards or so away from the Yukon, high enough to give me a good view across the river and out of danger from even the highest flood.

My reptile collection found a temporary home in the classroom of the local school and for the rest of my zoo, I constructed quick accommodations from my packing crates and some freshly cut poles. Even after I had put up a tool shed, I still had not gotten any complaints about my settling on this piece of land and so I started preparing my cabin site. Most people in Ruby probably didn't care if I built a house there or not, but I'm sure that there were some who thought that I would never be able to build a house all by myself anyway and that I would be gone from Ruby by the end of the summer.

Start for our cabin in Ruby 1974

It was in my favor that I was able to buy some cut and dried logs locally, and after discussing the situation with Billy Dean, he decided that his old truck might be able to pull those logs down that partly swampy cat trail to the front of my property. Now, construction of my future home could begin in earnest. After cutting the logs to the needed length, I pulled them one by one with a come-along to the building site. I still didn't have all the material I would need by far, but I was happy to be able to start on my construction.

Then the fourth of July came around and I joined in the local festivities. While I found renewed acceptance in the community, it also caused more interruptions by visitors while I was trying to get some work done. Most of my younger visitors were holding on to a beer can, which prevented me from even asking them to lend me a hand here or there, but I still got more advice on my project than I asked for.

For some of these young people, there was no need to have an excuse for a party and as long as there was money for the beer or booze on hand, a party always could be found. Wanting to fit in and for diplomatic reasons, I played along to a certain level, but I certainly wasn't about to forget that I had a house to build.

One of the older schoolboys accepted me to such an extent into his world, that when he came to visit me in the evenings and talked to me all about the bad things the white man had done to the Indians, he obviously had for-

257

gotten that he was talking to a white man, which amused me. I even agreed with some of his statements that, in most cases, however, did not apply to the Alaskan Indians, but I was fully aware that many of his viewpoints were trash talk fed to him by some older persons who thought they had an axe to grind.

Now and then, it even happened that one or the other of the more impetuous young men would offer me a physical challenge, which I usually avoided diplomatically.

Home sweet home

"I have heard that you know judo and karate," a young man called out to me, while passing my building site, "would you like to go a few rounds just for fun?"

"I don't fight for fun," I answered, "and when I fight, I win!"

Apparently, my answer was convincing enough, that I never was challenged by that boy again. But, on a couple occasions, I had to prove that I meant what I said, and in time I earned my respect. All in all, I found that living in Ruby was no more, or rather less problematic, than living in any other community, and my main problem remained my shortage of building material.

Since I didn't have enough logs to build a conventional log cabin of efficient size for my family, I erected a framework of logs in European style, in which I later filled the sections with woodblocks, chinked with insulation and moss. By the time Alice and our daughter came to Ruby in August, the house was far from being done, but we pitched our big tent inside the unfinished building, while I scrounged for wood to cut into blocks, to fill in the rest of the walls.

Diana with Bozo in Ruby 1974

Eventually, I had to take a trip to Fairbanks, not only to do some shopping for our house, but also to meet and pick up my brother from the airport. Peter came from Colorado on a visit, just in time to help me with the ridge pole. After that little chore, we covered the whole framework with plastic tarps, and then made sure that Peter would get to see a little more than just the village of Ruby on his Alaskan vacation.

The weather was certainly in our favor and a break from building was due to me. So, for the next few days, we moved to Kokrines to visit Frank and Josephine, and pick some berries and mushrooms. Pete and I visited the Horner Hot Springs while hunting grouse along the way. These hot springs near the Yukon are undeveloped and not to be mistaken for the Melozitna Hot Springs, where Alice and I had spent some time with the Veerhusens some years prior. Before we returned to Ruby, we also went on a duck hunt with Frank and on one of our outings, Peter even got to see his first moose in the wild.

Back in Ruby, we took my brother angling for grayling right across from Ruby at the mouth of the Melozitna River. A less enjoyable part of my brother's vacation were the mosquitoes and the many wasps we had that year. There were wasp nests everywhere, in the ground or in the trees, and before Peter returned to Colorado, he had been stung by a wasp three times.

"It sure feels lonely now," said Alice, after I had brought my brother to the airstrip. Well, she was right, we had a lot of fun during Peter's visit, but now it was time for us to face the facts of life in the bush again. The cranes and geese were heading south and we still lived in the tent. If I liked it or not, winter was coming and there was no chance in hell that our home could be finished this year, and for us to stay in Ruby, we had to rent a cabin for the winter.

By the end of September, I got an offer to take a job as a teacher's aide at the Ruby school. It was not exactly a job of my dreams, but it would provide us with some regular income for the season. Going to work in the morning at a place that had electricity and a heating system other than a woodstove felt almost like I was cheating on my family because of that luxury. The only other place in town that had its own generator at that time was the Ruby Trading Post. All other inhabitants of the village still lived by kerosene or white gas lamps, but after all, simplicity of life was one of the reasons we had moved back out and away from the big city.

After the first couple of weeks at my job as a teacher's aide, I was wondering how long I would be able to stand it. By German standards, discipline in the classroom was practically nonexistent, and to change that was at least part of the reason I was hired. As time went on, I was actually filling in as a staff member when the newly hired high- school teacher played sick or had to fly in his private plane to some teachers' meeting. Being in charge of the high school students was not only quite overwhelming, but also one heck of an experience for me. I just couldn't help but think about what my old teacher, Otto Schmidt, would have said if he could have seen me in that position.

Salmon for the winter

"You better learn your German first!" Herr Schmidt had said when I tried to sign up for the English class in Germany. Sure, I was no Einstein either during my time in school, but these students before me, who were supposed to graduate from high school the following school year, made me feel like a genius.

One of the smarter students I had in my class was Joseph. He belonged to a small group of students from Arctic Village, a Native community further north that did not have a high school. But Joseph had a tendency to get in trouble with alcohol or other drugs, to a point where he would march out the road toward the gold mines fully armed, as if he was going to war. To keep him from his vices, I often invited Joseph on weekends to play chess or cards at our house.

It was on a Friday or Saturday evening toward spring that Joseph didn't show and we finally went to bed. But at five a.m., knocks on our door interrupted my dreams.

"Who is there?" I asked.

"Joseph," he answered in a weak voice.

"Go home, it's too late now!"

"I can't."

"Cut out the bull, go home and sleep it off!" I said angrily.

"Please let me in!" Joseph pleaded and I got up to see what his problem was. As soon as I opened the door, Joseph fell into my arms, smelling of alcohol mixed with the sweet smell of blood. In his lower arm he had what looked like a stab wound, but Joseph was too weak and incoherent to answer any of my questions.

Alice, too, had gotten up by that time and together we bedded the boy down next to the stove. Then I went to get the village medic, with whom Joseph was officially living as a guest student. All I had to do was follow the trail of blood droplets, which lead straight to the medic's cabin. Instead of the medic, I found a bloody sleeping bag and a bloody knife inside the place on the floor.

I didn't really know what to make of it, or what to do next. The village at this hour, on a weekend, was as quiet as a ghost town and the only place I could think of to turn to was the preacher's house.

The preacher's wife opened the door and told me that her husband, George, just flew the medic to town, since he had a stab wound in the belly. I asked her to call the troopers over the radio and since she at times had functioned as a nurse, I also asked her to come down to my place to take care of Joseph's arm. Having a better picture of the whole situation at that point, I hurried back to our cabin, even though Joseph was in a too weak a state to be of any danger to my family. When I got there, Alice and Diana were already preparing breakfast outside in the morning sun, while Joseph was sleeping inside our by now quite smelly abode.

When the state trooper arrived, we led Joseph between us to the trading post, where a truck was waiting to take the trooper and Joseph to the airstrip. On the way to the trading post, we passed the medic's cabin and I gave the trooper an account of my findings from the trail of blood to the bloody sleeping bag and the knife, but it seemed that the trooper was not interested in any part of it. He did not look at the cabin or at any of the evidence at all, and he took no pictures either. Instead, he tried unsuccessfully and in my view, illegally, to get information out of Joseph. When he next started to put the handcuffs on Joseph, I just had to say something and remind the trooper that he had forgotten to read Joseph his rights. The trooper gave me a dirty look, but then followed my advice nevertheless. Needless to say, my confidence in the efficiency of our law enforcement officials suffered gravely on that day.

As for the medic, he was lucky, since his liver was only nicked by the knife. The stab wound in Joseph's arm turned out to be self-inflicted during his rage and I never saw or heard from Joseph for a long time. There were rumors that Joseph eventually might really have killed somebody and went to jail for it. It was not until I received a phone call from Arctic village some years later, but I'm still not sure if I was talking to Joseph, or to his brother, who also was in my class during the year of the incident.

As this school year came to an end, I wanted to make sure that nobody harbored any ideas to reinstall me for the next season, and I handed in my resignation. In spite of my strict ways, I actually was held in high respect by most of the students, but somebody at the school board must have had a different opinion about me because I received a note from that school board a few days after I had quit, that I was fired. Personally, I think that somebody we will not mention was trying to prove his authority and save his dignity.

Anyway, it was springtime now and the river ice had broken up in a noisy display of tumbling ice blocks rushing past our village. After a few days, when only a few dirty ice flows and a lot of driftwood were floating in the strong current, I put my foldboat into the river and went to work catching drift logs with a rope.

The more suitable logs were cut into eleven-inch long blocks, to be used to further fill some sections of my cabin walls and the rest gave us a good start on the firewood for the next winter.

Since the cabin we had rented was right next to the river, we also got to watch everything that floated downriver, including the occasional beaver in search of a suitable home site. Behind the cabin, a pair of redstarts had built their nest and an ermine had his young somewhere in the old cache in front of our temporary home. Spring had sprung!

Birds of a feather flock together, as the saying goes. And so I befriended some newcomers to this area. Like me, they had been seeking a way out of the everyday hum-drum life in civilization and like me, they were pretty independent characters.

Mark Freshwaters soon had established himself as a trapper on the Nowitna River and later build himself a cabin in Ruby. Neil Eklund, by his looks obviously coming from Scandinavian stock, and with his long blond hair looking like a true Viking, spent his first winter in the hills above Kokrines in a tepee and in spring, he came down the Melozitna River on a raft. This, however, was an adventure he would not forget and had no wish to repeat. As another unique character, Neil soon joined our circle of adventurers, dreamers, and friends. In time, we hunted, fished, or partied together, but for now it was time for me to finish our house before the next winter came around. Besides making new friends, we also lost some old ones: Leonard Veerhusen from the Melozitna Hot Springs had died of prostate cancer. His wife, Pat, would die a couple of years later of lung cancer and with them died their dream of turning the Melozitna Hot Springs into a spa for retired people.

As usual, life had to go on in spite of bad news, unexpected visitors, and some bad weather. In between fishing, we also finished our home that year and by the time the moose hunting season came around, we moved into our very own home.

Chapter 25
Bone Yard Fever

The first winter in our own house we undertook with a lot of enthusiasm, but it didn't exactly turn out to our satisfaction. The many mistakes I had made because of my lack of experience during the construction soon came to light. Some of my ideas, even though they were well meant, were not agreeable with the Alaskan winter. For instance, our cast-iron Franklin fireplace might have looked very romantic and blended well into my rustic interior of the building, but it certainly was not efficient or practical when it came to heating our home. For the coldest part of the season, our living space was restricted to our sleeping loft and a small room separated and insulated from the rest of the house by blankets. As the engineer and builder of our unconventional abode, I naturally had to take the full blame for all the shortcomings. That meant I had to get up earlier than the rest of the family and see to it that a blazing fire was going in the Franklin fireplace to bring the temperatures of our living space above freezing. Only then, and not before, could my wife be persuaded to start her day. But in spite of all the hardships, we survived that winter to make the necessary improvements to the building for the following year.

With the arrival of springtime, my outlook on our situation and even Alice's spirits were revived to a degree that she put a lot of effort into the cultivation of the greenhouse and the garden. In between making improvements on the house, I fished, hunted, or collected driftwood for the next winter.

Winter on the Yukon

When visitors came by, we often took time out from our chores and sometimes had a little party. At one of those parties, I got to meet a somewhat different character by the name of Kelly Painter. Kelly had retired from the military service and was living and working as Jack of all trades fifty miles farther downriver, in the community of Galena. Full of wild and somewhat farfetched ideas, Kelly usually was willing to try just about anything once. But he also liked his whiskey, his country music, and he knew almost every dirty joke ever told. If anybody asked Kelly how he ended up in Alaska, Kelly smiled and said, "I told my wife one morning that I was going out for milk and cigarettes and just kept on going."

Kelly's free and friendly spirit surely made him likable and he made friends easily, but my closer friendship with Kelly was actually started by a chunk of mammoth tusk, which he had hanging over the door of the little romantic-looking cabin in which he lived, whenever he came to Ruby.

But for now, another summer had passed and it was time to get ready for the cooler season. I had shot my moose already right across the river from Ruby and our firewood was stacked high in front of our house by the time the first snow fell. Outside of trying to make a little money by trapping within walking distance of Ruby, I also got an unexpected opportunity to work for the University of Alaska again, by teaching soapstone carving to the people of Ruby. Soapstone carving had been a hobby of mine already during the last few months in Fairbanks, and I had become fairly successful at it. All the material and tools were now supplied by a university program, which paid me for one day per week to teach this craft to the local population. Their interest in becoming an artist was greater than I had expected. I started my classes with ten students, from teenagers to adults, but soon none of them took it seriously enough to make it their hobby, and only one of my students survived through the tenth session. To be honest about it, it was no skin off my teeth. I did what I was paid for, besides having a lot of fun to boot, and I ended up with a lot of extra tools and material.

The winterization improvements and heating system for our house was still far from perfect, but the second winter in our home was a lot more pleasant. Like the previous year, with springtime arriving, any hardships or minor discomforts we might have experienced were soon forgotten.

That spring, I also found out that Kelly had sold that chunk of mammoth tusk hanging over his Ruby cabin door and he told me that he had gotten a pretty penny for it. I knew that Kelly had found the ivory at those cliffs we called the "Bone Yards," the very cliffs that had been such a mysterious puzzle to me at my first trip down the Yukon, and now I felt an urge to return to them to go hunting for fossil bones and ivory.

It didn't take me long to talk Mark Freshwaters into taking that eighty-mile trip up river with me, to see what we could find.

Our initial inspection of the so-called bone yard or palisades, as the place was officially called, was undertaken with a lot of anxiety and high expectations. Our dreams to stumble over whole tusks and bones, however, were quickly vanishing. The stretch of two to three miles of hundred to three-hundred foot high sandy cliffs with narrow canyon like gullies did not lose its fascination for us and it was only after a longer search in one of the canyons that we eventually found our first small fossil bones in a muddy creek bed. With fresh enthusiasm, we kept on searching and eventually we made a more promising discovery; on a steep wall, we discovered what obviously was the protruding end of a chunk of mammoth tusk. A short time later, we had dug up and collected a pile of broken and splintered portions of mammoth ivory out of the partially frozen sand. Splintered or not, at least we had found some useable and valuable ivory. A quick search through the other gullies brought us a few more interesting bones before we went home. The outcome of our venture had certainly fallen short of our expectations, but the income from our few pounds of mammoth ivory, as it later turned out, covered our expenses and then some. The fossil bones and the chunks of ivory also spurred my creativity, and I took an interest in the material for my artwork. For most of my friends, hunting the fossils was no more than a possible opportunity to make some easy money, but whatever reasons there were, the bone yard fever had more or less broken out.

Barry, the son of a gold miner in Ruby, was probably the youngest of our circle of friends and when it came to making money, Barry easily got stars in his eyes. Therefore, Mark and I were hardly surprised to find Barry and Kelly at the bone yards during our second trip. In spite, or maybe because of the competition, this second trip turned out more profitable than our first attempt. But if one was to figure it by the hour, counting traveling time and expenses plus searching and digging, we certainly were not on the road to riches, but like the prospectors in search of gold, we, too, kept on hoping for the big strike and find that big, whole mammoth tusk. For me personally, the money aspect of finding that big tusk for a quick turnover was not quite as interesting as finding strange-looking bones or pieces thereof, for my artwork. Besides that, it was the whole adventurous atmosphere of the search for the unknown. Wondering what one would find next and trying to figure out to what kind of animal a certain bone might have belonged to, the feeling to be first human to have seen and touched that particular bone, was more exciting to me than the purely monetary part of our venture.

After these first trips to the bone yards, I had been ready to go searching and digging for the fossils with whoever was willing to go with me, and, often, I also went alone. In time, after so many strenuous and dangerous climbs on those frozen sand cliffs and searches in the muddy creek beds, we had gathered some experience about where to look and how not to be fooled by pieces of wood sticking out of the cliff walls. We came up with all kinds of theories about the accumulations about these Pleistocene fossils in this area, which only held up until we found a bone or a splinter of ivory where it should not have been. One thing, however, was very clear: these remains were not lying where the animals had died, because we found a leg bone of a bison next to a splinter of mammoth ivory, or a horse's hoof next to a mammoth molar. Many bones and ivory pieces which had not fallen out of the cliff walls yet, were often bedded in a layer with small snail housings, which indicated to us that the bones, ivory, and wood, probably had been washed into small lakes, ponds, or depressions of some kind in the past.

At the Bone Yards

And, yes, we had heard about the antiquity law, but at that time it was an unwritten law in Alaska, that fossil found where they could be destroyed by the high water or were in danger of falling into the river could be legally collected. Since the cliffs in which we were searching were constantly eroding and eventually falling into the river, they were legal ground for our actions after our understanding. Once, I actually had made a personal effort to get some information at the University of Alaska, in order to better identify the fossils, in case we would find something of particular interest. At the time, I had taken some teeth with me to Fairbanks for identification. Right away, I was confronted in an unfriendly manner for having even picked up those fossils. After I explained the situation and the fact that most likely nobody ever would have found those teeth if I would not have picked them up, the person in charge calmed down. Recognizing my intent to be helpful, she suggested a forty-dollar book, which later turned out to be far too general and of little help to me. The teeth in question, which I had brought along for identifica-

Bone Yards

tion, I eventually identified with the help of a ninety-nine cent zoo book for children as big-cat teeth, such as the American lion.

During our bone-hunting expeditions, we also were exposed to physical dangers. The frozen sand and mud of these steep cliffs will thaw for about a foot or so at a time and then start sliding off the face of these walls under its own weight, especially when disturbed through digging at the base of them. The very fine sand and silt comes down like a waterfall, burying everything below and steering up big clouds of dust. At least twice, I had to help Barry dig himself out, after he was buried up to his armpits, and on one occasion a big chunk of thawing mud crashed down onto a the spot where I just had been standing a few seconds before.

With the advance of so called progress in Alaska, the laws were tightened and the bone yards eventually became part of the Nowitna Wildlife Refuge. From then on, the fossil collecting would be strongly frowned upon. But at our time, even state troopers who traveled the river for some reason or another would slow down their boats at the bone yards, in the hope of finding a worthwhile souvenir.

The summer was over and I had shot my moose early in the season right across from Ruby, at the Melozitna River. Neil, who had been planning to spend the winter in Kokrines and trap from there, had come to Ruby for a shopping trip. It was only natural that we, during our conversation, would also be talking about our fossil hunting, and before we knew it, we had talked ourselves into just one last trip to the bone yards for the season. The prospect of finding something worthwhile and make some money in the process had become of somewhat greater importance for me as well, since Alice had given me the unexpected news that she was pregnant again.

Our first attempt to start our trip the following morning was interrupted when we encountered a moose only a couple of miles upriver from Ruby. Since Neil still didn't have his winter meat yet, he welcomed the opportunity. So, we hunted down the moose, butchered the animal, and returned to Ruby for another night. During this unplanned delay, Kelly had arrived in Ruby and decided to accompany us on our bone hunting trip. That meant we had to wait an additional day for Kelly to prepare for the undertaking. But eventually, we got on our way and stopped in Kokrines, to unload and store the meat of Neil's moose in the old smokehouse. A strong wind had developed in the meantime, but since Neil's large freight canoe was an all-weather craft, the wind was of little concern to us at that point.

A few miles above Kokrines, we turned into the Victor Slough, but soon recognized our mistake. We would have liked to change our minds, but it was too late for that. The strong wind blowing straight against the fast current in that shallow slough resulted in waves high enough to break over the bow of the canoe. We couldn't turn around, because the waves would have rolled our boat. Neither could we pull to one side or the other, because contact with the rocky bottom of that slough would have resulted in a broken shear pin, which would have left us without control of our craft at the mercy of the waves as well.

Neil slowed down the motor to a point where we barely made headway against the current, and true to his Viking ancestry, he held the bow of that canoe stone-faced into the waves, while Kelly played bilge pump by scooping out the water behind Neil with a coffee can.

Finally, after many tense minutes, we entered the main channel of the Yukon again and Neil steered the canoe to the left against the main current. However, he took the turn somewhat too early, our prop hit a rock, and the shear pin broke. Neil and I grabbed the paddles and gave it all we had to keep the boat from drifting back into the slough, while Kelly worked feverishly to replace the shear pin. Our efforts paid off and we soon were on our way again, but if we thought that all our problems were behind us for that day, we should have considered that the day wasn't over yet.

Soon, the boat motor started to sputter and it took a couple of checkups to keep the darn thing running. Next, we were surprised by the first snowstorm of the season and we almost felt that a higher power tried to keep us from getting to the bone yards. By the time the snow slowed down again, it started getting dark. Kelly remembered an old shack somewhere nearby, where we decided to call it a day and make camp for the night.

Too early in the season for the snow to stick, it was gone by the morning. There was not a breath of wind and a layer of fog lay over the glass-smooth river surface. Not a sound was to be heard in this ghostlike landscape; it almost felt like a crime to start up the boat motor and disrupt the peaceful atmosphere. But our motor started without a problem and ran as smooth as it did in the beginning of the trip. Continuing upriver, we passed a fancy boat tied up to the riverbank, which probably belonged to a well-to-do visitor, who was out here to hunt moose. What was funny about it was that person or people in the boat still were asleep inside, while a bull moose was standing only yards away from the boat watching us drive by. Since we had our winter's meat, the moose was merely a pretty sight to us. Then we reached the old cabin on an island below the cliffs, where we often sheltered during our bone yard trips.

When motor noises drew our attention, we discovered a boatload of hunters, as they chased after a swimming moose, but our minds were rather set on finding ivory. We unloaded our gear at the cabin as usual and went on to the cliffs to see what we could find.

Neil guided the boat slowly through the sometimes very tricky currents near the cliffs, while our eyes searched the steep walls full of hope to discover a tusk or large bone protruding from them. We also had to watch out for landslides or chunks of real estate ready to fall down upon us. Not far into our search, we saw a suspicious something on a small ledge about twenty yards or more up a shear wall. Making a mental note of the location, we went on to search the full length of the cliffs, so we wouldn't miss out on any other fresh exposed pickings, but had no luck. So we returned to our initial discovery and as far as we could determine from our moving boat on the river, we agreed that it most likely was a fair chunk of mammoth ivory we were looking at and that it deserved a closer inspection. We landed the boat at the nearest crevasse, took some rope and tools, and climbed from there to the top of the cliff. Walking along the edge as much as we could, we had to judge by the contour of the landscape where to start our descent. On a rope tied to a tree, we let ourselves down into a deep, muddy pocket below. A melting ice lentil kept the muck on the bottom to a tarry consistency, which flowed almost imperceptibly toward the edge of the cliff. Carefully, we worked our way through the muck to the point where it dropped down to the river, sounding and looking like cattle manure in production. If we had figured it right, the suspected chunk of ivory should be somewhat to the left, right below us. But there still was no safe vantage point from where we could take a good look at it. Tied to another rope, I worked my way around a sandy outcrop on the cliff wall, and got close enough to see and confirm that we had possibly found a whole mammoth tusk, but to get to it in order to get it out of the wall was another story.

Eventually, we came to the conclusion that the only way to reach our prize was by going over the top of the cliff. The only one crazy enough to volunteer for a job like that was Neil. So we tied our companion on a robe, which in turn was tied to a fallen spruce tree behind us. Kelly and I controlled the slack of the rope while watching Neil, shovel in hand, as he vanished over the edge of the cliff.

"It feels like I have a fish on the line!" joked Kelly after Neil was out of sight.

"Yeah, it's a big sucker!" came Neil's reply from below.

But then we had to pay attention to Neil's requests to loosen or tighten the rope to bring our companion into the right position to scrape a foothold for himself. A few minutes later, we exchanged Neil's shovel for an axe by letting it down to him on a separate rope.

From then on, the dull thumping of our partner at work, as he chopped at the frozen sand, was all we heard. Since it didn't take two people to let out or tighten the rope, I started to explore the near surroundings for further bones or ivory, while Kelly stayed with the rope. When I couldn't find any further signs of fossils, I returned and kept Kelly company.

Neil had long since confirmed that we had found a complete tusk, the question was only if we were able to get the whole thing out of this frozen wall. The tip of the tusk was very deep in the frozen sand and muck, which can be as tough as concrete. At least two hours had passed since Neil had climbed over the edge, but he still was working away like a jackhammer. If I would have been hanging on that rope, I'm sure that by now the axe would have fallen out of my hand.

Sitting there with nothing to contribute made Kelly and me feel like lazy bums, but it also gave me time to visually examine every bump in that mud flow to our right. My eyes always went back to what seemed to be a mud-covered tree stump. After a while, I couldn't take the suspense anymore and had to make sure, but the muck was too soft and too deep to let me get close enough. When I thought that I saw a small branch on it, I was sure that it must be a tree stump and took my place next to Kelly again.

"You thought you found a second tusk, didn't you?" said Kelly with a cynical smile.

"Can't blame a man for hoping!" I answered, but Kelly's cynical remark had irked me, and I had nothing better to do. Therefore, I started breaking branches off that fallen spruce to which Neil's rope was tied and built myself a walkway over that muck, right up to the muddy stump. After scratching the stump with my knife, I had no more doubts as to what it consisted of.

"Are you satisfied now?" Kelly hollered out to me.

Without answering Kelly, I cleaned my knife and put it away. When Kelly saw the smile on my face, he asked, "Now you're trying to pull my leg, aren't you?"

"Tree stump, my ass!" I replied triumphantly, but before Kelly could say anything else, Neil was hollering for us from below and a few minutes later, we had pulled him and a one-hundred-fifty pound tusk to safety.

Neil had spent almost four hours on that rope while cutting that tusk out of the wall and his first words after reaching level ground were, "That's enough!"

"That's what you think!" Kelly replied smiling, "Hebel here already found the next one."

Neil's tired face lit up at once and full of new enthusiasm, he asked, "Where?"

Together, we went to inspect the discovery and shoveled the mud away from all around that protruding ivory, but we couldn't say for sure if we had found another full tusk or just a chunk of it. In either case it looked to us, if it was a whole tusk, it went straight down into the frozen ground. Even Neil had little hope of getting this thing out of there and he wanted to cut the exposed part off for us to take whatever poundage of ivory it would bring. I didn't see any reason to rush that decision and suggested that we wait till the next day before cutting it and my buddies agreed. The tusk which Neil had dug out we pulled up to the edge of the cliff, hid it in between the trees and brush, and then called it a day.

To our surprise, we found that the hunters we had seen chasing that swimming moose had moved in to our camp for the night. Our belongings were all nicely stacked in one corner. The cabin, after all, wasn't ours either and therefore we hardly could throw them out, but we made it clear that there had to be room in the cabin for everybody.

Our uninvited guests had gotten the moose they had been chasing and their women had already cooked up enough moose stew, so that we didn't even have to cook our own dinner.

As dirty as we were, there was no sense in denying what we had been doing, but our success we kept a secret. In the morning, we again had our breakfast served to us, for which we expressed our thanks before saying our goodbyes and headed back to the diggings. During that night, there had been a pretty healthy frost, but a blue and cloudless sky promised another warm day. The frost, as it turned out, was to our advantage, since it allowed us to walk on the frozen crust over the knee-deep muck flows. Working a little more by chopping some frozen ground away from around that stump of ivory, we discovered that we had indeed found another full tusk, which was curved in such a way that the whole thing was only a few inches under the frozen muck.

By about noon, we had the top side of the tusk exposed, but the tusk was still frozen into the ground and didn't want to budge. So, we took our lunch break and when we returned, the sun had done the rest of the work for us. The tusk popped out of the ground, like a casting out of a mold. The only work left for us was packing the tools and our tusks down to the boat and load up.

The Bone Yards with its fossils were not so secret that we were the only ones to make visits there and look for bones and ivory. Some fossil hunters even came from as far as the city of Fairbanks to try their luck, but this time we had gotten there at the right time and had found the right spot. Feeling like successful fortune hunters, we picked up our gear from the cabin and soon left the frozen cliffs behind us, as we headed back to Ruby.

Chapter 26
Following the Geese and Cranes

Our success at the bone yards was impossible to keep a secret, in Ruby and certainly not from the rest of our friends in the village. The excitement over our tusks caused some of our peers to make big plans for the following year, but for now, winter was coming and I was sure that all the hoopla about going to the bone yards would have died down by the following spring. Most of the natives in Ruby, as well as those from other villages, seemed to have a superstition about collecting these fossil bones anyway and that was just fine with us. Kelly had gone on to Galena from Ruby and right away, he had negotiated a deal with his part-time boss at the Galena Liquor Store. While the liquor store owner wanted to buy our tusks as an investment for his future, Neil and I wanted to get a higher return for our troubles than what we had been offered. So we rejected this first offer and flew with our tusks to Anchorage, where we made all kinds of contacts before we sold our ivory for a handsome prize. We might have been able to get even more for our tusks, but that would have meant holding them for an undetermined time, for which we were in no position.

I also had taken advantage of the trip to Anchorage and had brought some of my artwork along to sell. By the time we returned to Ruby, I had more money in my pocket than we had seen in a while.

Neil spent quite a bit of his money on supplies for his winter in Kokrines and moved up there right after our return from Anchorage, to get ready for the trapping season. Kelly, true to his nature, couldn't leave well enough alone and squandered his share of the bone yard money by hiring a diver to go and look for a bonanza on the bottom of the river, below the cliffs. This was a subject we often had discussed, but I personally never had taken it very seriously. As suspected, the idea turned out to be a total failure, in part because of the unsuspected depth of the river, the turbidity of the water, and the strong currents. Besides, Kelly had also chosen the wrong spot by searching at the beginning of the cliffs instead toward the end, where an accumulation of the fossils could have been more likely.

Anyway, Alice and I had no particular plans until we talked to our friend, Barry, who planned to visit his mother in California and also wanted to spend some time in Mexico during the winter. The more Barry talked about Mexico, the more appealing became the idea to me to revisit this country. I also knew that Alice in her condition was not exactly looking forward to the next winter in Ruby and before long, we found ourselves packing and closing down our home for the season. In Anchorage, Alaska, we stayed for a few days with some of Barry's friends, while I also sold some more of my artwork in the local nightclubs and bars to further fatten our travel account. Then we flew to Seattle, Washington, and while Barry traveled on to California, I went with my family by bus to Spokane, Washington, where we had been invited by acquaintances to spend Christmas with them. Right after Christmas, we went by plane to Los Angeles, California, where we were warmly greeted by my old friend, Horst Stumpf.

For a couple of weeks, we stayed with Horst and his family. Horst and I had a lot of catching up to do, while Alice and Horst's wife, Arlene, became fast friends and played a lot of scrabble together. Our daughter, Diana, had found a friend right next door to Horst and Arlene's place. But besides visiting, with my friend Horst, some of our watering holes and reminiscing about our mutual outings in the years past, I had to be fair to the rest of my family, and took them to Disneyland and to the nearby Knott's Berry Farm.

Afterwards, we moved for a week or two to Barry's mother's house. There, even Kelly showed up for a short stop and gave us the feeling that everybody had left Alaska for the winter.

On January 22, we headed in Barry's car, toward Baja California, Mexico. Along the way, we made arrangements for Alice, so she would be admitted in the San Diego hospital when her time came to have the baby. To the great delight of our daughter, Diana, we also visited the San Diego zoo.

The catch

It was 5 a.m. on the following day before we finally reached our destination and climbed out of Barry's little, cramped vehicle to fill our lungs with the fresh sea air at Campo Lopez in Baja California. At that time, Campo Lopez was a small collection of weekend houses, owned mostly by Americans, and was, or most likely still is, located right at the ocean, halfway between Tijuana and Encenada. Through Barry's friends, John and Janette Blasinski in Anchorage, Alaska, we had access to a combination trailer-cabana at the camp and had planned to spend the next two months there. A fireplace and a row of large windows with a view of the ocean made us feel like upper class vacationers.

While the ocean supplied us with fresh fish, clams, abalone and octopus, a nearby store enabled us to buy all our vegetables for very reasonable prices. Diana enjoyed the ocean so much that we practically had to force her to take time out to do her daily schoolwork. Other times, she liked to go on walks with me to explore our surroundings, where we caught frogs, lizards, and snakes to take pictures of. Barry, on the other hand, only had spent a couple of days with us before returning to California, but he would come back to visit us from time to time. On one of Barry's visits, he drove us down to Encenada, where we visited some stores and the open-air fish market, which made it kind of an interesting trip, especially if we took in consideration the danger of getting bombarded by the overly friendly pelicans at the fish market.

A more interesting situation occurred the following day, which could have turned into quite a serious adventure. Barry and I wandered along the shoreline at low tide to collect some abalones from under the rocks in the ocean. When we came to a sheer rock wall with a stone staircase leading to the top of the cliff, Barry suggested that we should go up there.

"What's up there?" I asked.

"If I remember right," replied Barry, "there is a neat little cantina up there and the way I see it, we have earned a beer."

"Sounds good!" I agreed and up we went. The first thing I noticed was that the stairs at some places were in dire need of repair, certainly not safe, and probably not meant to be used by the average tourist....

Arriving on top of the cliff, it was almost like entering a different world. We found ourselves in a very clean, European-style village, which looked like it was taken out of a fairy tale. The people we encountered greeted us in a very friendly and polite manner to the point that I started feeling a little uneasy.

Seeing that Barry wasn't too sure about his whereabouts anymore either at this point, I asked him, "Where is your damn cantina?"

"Must be right up there!" he answered, pointing at the narrow cobblestone road leading up a hill. That, however, was as close as we got to our glass of beer at the cantina. We were approached by two uniformed and heavily armed officials with the words,

"Dónde va ?"

Before I could put my limited Spanish to use and answer the man, Berry started to bubble in English about his cantina. To me it was obvious that we had wandered into an area where we were not wanted. But even after one of the armed men pointed with his rifle toward a big iron gate leading out to the main road, Barry didn't seem to get it and tried to explain his intentions to the guard in English. It was obvious that the man was getting increasingly irritated with Barry, and I felt that it was time for me to intervene.

"Shut up and get your ass over here!" I called out to Barry. A minute later, we found ourselves on the main road, while the Iron Gate crashed shut behind us.

My suspicion that we had accidentally entered some kind of sanatorium for the insane was later confirmed, and I turned toward my friend and said, "And you were trying so hard to be accepted there!"

After his next visit, I came to the conclusion that Mexico probably was not a safe place for our friend, Barry. He showed up with a carload of friends to spend a wild night in the bars of Encenada and my decision to stay with my family turned out to be the right move. In the morning, Barry was brought back to camp by a stranger, without his friends, or his car. Apparently, Barry had fallen asleep at the wheel on the way back from Encenada and had driven into a boundary marker along the highway.

Outside of the car, everybody had survived the accident unharmed. Barry's drinking buddies left the scene, like rats on a sinking ship, and hitchhiked home to the U.S., while the Mexican police impounded Barry's vehicle. That meant that Barry had a lot of running around to do between his home in California and the Encenada, Mexico Police Department, to get his car returned to him. Papers had to be filled out; officials had to be paid, and so on. By the time Barry was allowed to transport his heavily damaged car to the United States, he still needed his brother-in-law's help to have it hauled home.

Before I knew how small Barry's car actually was, the plan had been for all of us to ride back to Alaska in it. Now that it seemed the capacity of that vehicle wasn't even an issue anymore, I had to start thinking about alternate transportation. I have so little interest in such things as cars that I don't even remember what make Barry's car was, but it was clear to me that Barry's car was a goner. He, however, still claimed to be able to fix his car in time for our return trip to Alaska. I was in no mood to argue that point right then and there, for now we were still in Mexico at Campo Lopez, and enjoying it. I would solve our problem of transportation when the time arrived.

Barry had promised to return with his mother's car by March 18, to take us back to the U.S. On March 17, Alice and I quietly celebrated our anniversary, but Barry failed to show up on the following day.

"It doesn't matter to me," said Alice. "I like it here and I figure that I have at least another week before the baby arrives."

The baby, however, didn't know about Alice's plans. By 2 a.m. that night, Alice's labor pains had started, and by 5 a.m. the contractions were only seven minutes apart. Sure, we had made arrangements with our new friends in the camp for just such a more or less expected event. Our new acquaintances were to drive us back to San Diego, so Alice could be checked into the hospital there. Again, true to my nature, when under stress, all previous plans were ignored. Instead, I went to get one of our neighbors out of bed. Knowing that she had been a nurse, Susan's presence made me feel safe enough, even though she had never delivered a baby before. After bedding Alice on the blanket-covered old couch in the front room, she made pull-ups on my arms till 1:45 p.m. That was the time when Susan held our son, Logan, out to me for me to tie off the umbilical cord.

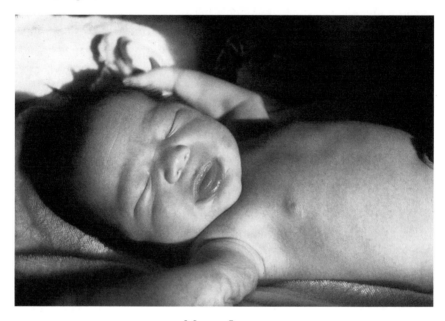

My son Logan

Later, we took mother and child to a hospital in the nearby town of Rosarito for a checkup. Alice was all right and we had a healthy, eight-pound, twenty-inch tall boy. The doctor also gave us a birth certificate for Logan, but as birthplace, the doctor had to write down Rosarito, since he would have to have been present at the child's birth, which he was not. In that way, Logan's life began with a lie.

Up to that point, the birth of our child had cost me exactly fifty dollars, but our problems were not quite over yet. The birth of our child was a big event at Campo Lopez and even people we hadn't met yet came by our bungalow to congratulate us and bring us presents.

Then Barry showed up two days late, and with a new, temporary girlfriend in a pickup. It was not only that our friend was surprised to see Alice with a baby in her arms, unless he figured that our son Logan could wait until he had time to come and get us, but what really puzzled me was that Barry must have assumed that we would just jump on the back of his pickup to ride back to his mother's home.

Instead, we sent the lovers back home with their pickup, and Barry promised to return a few days later with his mother's car as we had agreed upon to begin with.

Mexico in our rented cabin

On the day we actually were ready to leave Campo Lopez and Mexico, Easter had passed, and if we thought that everything from here on would be a piece of cake, we had another guess coming. As it had been suggested to us, we stopped at the American consulate in Tijuana to apply for Logan's U.S. citizenship, but were informed that we needed a somewhat more official birth certificate for Logan from the town of Rosarito. Back we went to Rosarito, where it was pointed out to us that our visitor visas had expired and we had to have them renewed before we could get the official birth certificate for our son.

To get the renewal of our visas, we had to cross back into the U S and reenter Mexico. In order to save ourselves more trouble, while crossing into the states, we lied by telling the border guard that Logan was a U S citizen.

With our visas renewed, after paying another small fee to the town of Rosarito, we also got an official birth certificate for Logan. By the time we were back at the U. S. consulate, it was already closed for the weekend and we had to come to terms with the idea that we had to return for Logan's citizenship at a later date.

So, after one more little lie about the nationality of our son, we crossed the border again and drove to Barry's mother's house. To get ahead of the pending game with the consulate, I wrote to Alaska for some more documentation and as soon as they arrived, we returned to the U.S. consulate in Tijuana, Mexico. It took only minutes for all the formalities, but we were told that Logan's certificate would be sent to us in Alaska, and therefore we still had no proof of Logan's U.S. nationality. Ahead lay more border crossings and more lies.

By that time, Barry still couldn't give us a date for the restoration of his car, not that I had expected it. It didn't matter to us anymore, because I was about to conclude my deal with an acquaintance from Campo Lopez to buy his car. Not knowing much about cars, I only could hope that this old Dodge for three-hundred and fifty dollars would get us safely back to Alaska. But I was willing to put more faith into my new acquisition, than into the reliability of Barry's car. In my book, there are only two kinds of cars: those that work, and those that don't.

Our newly acquired transportation certainly needed a good checkup and a newer set of tires, but that was something where Barry's connections came in handy. In return, we offered Barry a ride back to Alaska with us, but he was still set on repairing and driving his own car. Plan "B" was that we eventually would meet up with Barry at his grandparent's house in the state of Washington, after I and my family visited my brother and his family in Colorado.

After I managed to buy affordable six months of insurance for our transportation, we said our goodbyes to friends and acquaintances and happily went on our way. To be totally independent sitting in our very own vehicle with lots of room sure felt great. Along the way, we visited the Grand Canyon and then let my brother and his wife show us around in Colorado. By the time we arrived in the state of Washington, where we were warmly welcomed by Barry's grandparents, there still was no sign of Barry. When Barry made further excuses for time delays, we decided to continue without his company.

At the borders in to B.C. Canada and then again while entering Alaska, we told our little lie about Logan's citizenship once or twice more, while our son lay, seemingly very content, in his cardboard box cradle inside the car and couldn't care less. Our daughter, Diana, enjoyed the ride through

Canada, too, especially since her schoolwork was kept to a minimum during our traveling time. My so-wisely purchased old Dodge proved not only to be a smooth ride, it also got us all the way back to Fairbanks, Alaska, without any problems whatsoever. In Fairbanks, I sold the vehicle for fifty dollars more than I had bought it for and thereby had covered the cost of the short-term insurance as well.

Chapter 27
Winds of Change

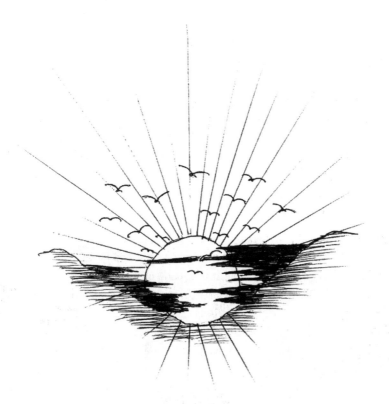

B ack in Ruby, everything seemed to be more or less the way it had been when we left. As soon as we were settled back into our home again, I found a partner here or there to continue my fossil hunts at the bone yards, and if I didn't find anybody willing to go with me, I went by myself. To find another full size mammoth tusk in order to make some quick money again, is something one always could hope for, but my main purpose was finding anything that could be used for creating some interesting artwork.

This summer turned out to be a pretty rainy one, which made it a fitting setting for all the tension and mishaps of that particular year. For me, it started out with the bad news that a befriended artist of mine, living in Fairbanks, had died in a car accident. Next, a young man who used to be one of my students and sometime chess partner, committed suicide in our community of Ruby. Besides that, there seemed to be a lot of arguments between the locals and the newcomers, which included most of my friends over the trapping rights in certain areas. These arguments usually flared up during parties, and parties were something Ruby had no shortage of at that time. The altercations and accusations usually were not exaggerated, nor were they limited to the disputes over the traplines. But the cause was usually the alcohol consumption, and more often between the natives over their women. In extreme cases, they could lead to fights or even gun play, but most likely because of the influence of the alcohol, or the lack of marksmanship, shootings generally had no serious consequences. An old Finlander and long-time resident of Ruby used to say, "If they could hit something, I would supply the ammunition." But that was typical for old Albert. If Alaska could be shaped to Albert's likings, all wolves and bears would be exterminated as well, and the moose would be bred like cattle. A hatred of wolves and bears seemed to be common among the gold miners, as well as for many natives in the villages along the Yukon. Many people across the racial line would shoot any wolf, black bear, or grizzly on sight, at any time of the year, just to get rid of them.

Black bear at the Melozitna

I'll never forget when the subject of wolves came up during a picnic and a visiting miner said to me, "What's wrong with getting rid of the wolves, do you miss the dinosaurs?"

I just shook my head and left the party, since I knew if I had to explain the difference between dinosaurs and wolves to him, he wouldn't understand it anyway. You can't fix stupid!

Since my early attempts to find good carving material at the bone yards had not been too fruitful that year, our friend Barry and I had made plans for a different adventure. Yes, Barry, too, had finally returned to Alaska, but without his car, as I always had expected it to turn out.

We knew that fossil remains also could be found in the Nowitna River and since Alice and our kids were headed for a visit to Nome again, Barry and I planned to take my foldboat and paddle down that river. Norm Yeager, a bush pilot from Galena, flew us way up that river, dropped us and our gear off on a sandbank, and wished us well.

In a short time, we had put our foldboat together and blown up a small rubber raft, which we hoped to fill with finds of fossil bone and ivory.

Right after we started floating down the river, the sunny weather changed into mostly cloudy with rain showers. By the time we floated through the Nowitna Canyon, it was clear to us that we would not make a killing on fossil bones and ivory either. In spite of it, we enjoyed seeing some interesting country. Toward the end of that canyon, we caught a big pike while floating in the boat and let him pull us downriver for a spell. Then we met Alex Tarnai near his trapping cabin. Alex, a resident of the Town of Tanana, was not only a trapper, but he also guided tourists. He invited us for dinner to his cabin, where we exchanged some of our experiences of our lives in Alaska. Our host also was well aware of the value of fossil ivory and had collected some ivory splinters at the sand and gravel bars along that river, which certainly left that much less for us to find, and the pieces we did find were generally of low quality, bleached and splintered by the weather.

I still hoped to find at least a few interesting and useable bones for my art-work and so we kept on searching along the way. At the river bends, we took turns searching the sandbars, while the other would paddle the boat around the bend. Besides the few low-grade ivory splinters, we also found a mammoth molar and a shoulder blade from one of these prehistoric elephants. While all in all our harvest had been meager, we had a relatively good time and had made a new friend in meeting Alex.

The weather had taken a turn for the worse and the river had gotten wider and slower, which meant more paddling and less promising sandbanks. It was the last sandbank I had planned to walk, and when I was just about to step back into the boat, a black bear stepped out of the willows, only a few feet behind me, which caused Barry to frantically urge me on to hurry.

"That bear almost bit you in the butt!" said Barry while hurriedly paddling us away from shore.

"Don't be so dramatic," I answered, "he only wanted to make sure I didn't take any of his belongings!"

A little humor like that always seemed to help in settling Barry's nerves when it came to bears. Soon after this incident, we had reached the mouth of the Nowitna River, where it enters the Yukon. It seemed to be a fitting conclusion when we were hailed by the howls of a lone wolf. Thinking back, the howls of that wolf felt rather like an ending of an era than a personal greeting, because at the landing in Ruby, we were confronted right away by the advancement of the so-called progress. Right below my property, a new gas station with big storage tanks was under construction. The Ruby Trading Post in our town now also had a public telephone, which was another thing I had not missed or longed for, but since it was there, I took advantage of it and called my wife in Nome at her parent's house to let her know that we had survived the trip.

Since Alice always had it in her head to get me to move to Nome sooner or later, she promptly tried to talk me into moving there at least for the coming winter. I had been in Nome for a short visit before and the town had not impressed me in the least. This old gold rush town was long past its frontier stage and had just about all the modern contraptions of civilization along with high living expenses. Situated right at the ocean and surrounded by open treeless tundra, it is a windy place most of the time, which contributed to my dislike of the place. Naturally, I did not agree to move to Nome for that winter or any time in the future. Knowing that my wife was not too thrilled about the idea of spending the approaching winter in Ruby, I compromised and suggested that I meet up with her in Anchorage instead.

As far as civilized living was concerned, the cost in Anchorage would be cheaper for us than in Nome, besides offering us a chance for an income. After packing all my carvings and some fossil bones and ivory to take and ship to Fairbanks, I closed down our house and flew to Fairbanks myself. My old friend John Bradbury had just bought himself a new car, which enabled me to borrow his old Dodge Van to drive to Anchorage with and have some transportation for the winter in town. The limited market for my artwork in Fairbanks was quickly exhausted, but in Anchorage, I knew more people in the right places, such as nightclubs, where I could catch a lot of the affluent pipeline workers as they traveled home to the states for the holidays.

As usual, I played things by ear, but had figured it right as far as spending the winter in town with my family. Staying with friends at first, I sold some of my work and touched bases with all my business contacts. When Alice and the children arrived from Nome, we rented a cheap apartment and a friend of mine made me an offer to carve in her shop for a small percentage of what I would sell on my nightly excursions to the bars.

Before we knew it, we had become city slickers for the winter of 1978-1979. At that time, Anchorage had about 220,000 inhabitants and it was still a fairly comfortable place as far as cities go. Alice had some relatives living nearby and a school for our daughter was just down the road from where we now lived. At any case, my wife was happy to be able to spend that winter in town instead of in Ruby. I, on the other hand, just hoped to make enough money to cover our bills. On most days, I would carve at my friend's shop and half of the nights, I would spend in bars and related establishments to sell my wares. This might sound simple, but it also is an unstable and risky way to make a living, especially for a family. But somehow, we always seemed to make ends meet and to me it was almost an adventure, not adventures in the sense I always been dreaming about, but an adventure nevertheless. Stress was never far away, like the time when I had a repair bill for John's van and not enough money on hand to pay for it. Unexpectedly, I had been able to sell a couple of bigger carvings to a homeward bound pipeline worker, and thereby saved us from bigger problems.

Then, the novelty to have me as a coworker in her shop started to wear thin for my friend and I moved out of her shop in order to avoid a potentially destructive situation to our relationship. In a much smaller way, I kept on carving in an extra room at our apartment, but the lack of adequate ventilation, plus some partially rotten ivory I had been working on, led to an infection of my heart and lung lining and I had to stop carving altogether for the time being. By then, spring wasn't that far away anymore, and I still had carvings to sell. The one good thing that came out of my health problem was that I was not able to smoke during my recuperation time, which in turn caused me to give up smoking permanently.

When spring had sprung, even Alice was more than ready to retreat to our village life in Ruby. The oil pipeline and the people who worked for it certainly had helped me and my family to make it through that winter in town, but the impact of the pipeline construction in general, in my opinion, had a negative impact on the lifestyle of the bush communities.

Money didn't seem to be a problem for our state government and a lot of it was spent on the bush communities. New streets were built in Ruby and a generator building was erected to provide electricity to the whole town. A public Laundromat with showers was next, besides a big new school with a gymnasium. All it took was writing grants for this or that and the people in our village had temporary construction jobs.

To get all that funding money, the village of Ruby became a second class city. But money for all kinds of far-fetched ideas was handed out and, like animals in a feeding frenzy, everything new and modern was enthusiastically and blindly embraced by the people in the bush villages. Apparently, nobody ever thought of looking farther ahead, or had heard of the phrase, "There is no such thing as a free lunch!

Not that all the changes in our community were bad. Who could argue against a decent school for the kids? And the electricity certainly was convenient, especially for my carving, since I didn't have to run my own little generator for that purpose anymore.

But considering that we had moved out into the bush to live a simpler life, we fought a losing battle. Civilization was catching up with us and so was the rising cost of living. It was not only the electric bill and eventually the phone bill, food prices climbed, along with the ever increasing shipping and transport cost. Flying from and to town was getting constantly more expensive, but the biggest threat was the growing reliance and dependency of the people in the villages on all the modern contraptions that were so vigorously promoted. To me, it looked very much a progressive enslavement of the people in the bush to the trappings of civilization without their awareness about it.

To visit your neighbor in the evenings and talk about the last hunting or trapping season by the light of a kerosene lamp was becoming a thing of the past and the stories of the elders were getting lost along with it. The televisions and the Nintendo games became popular so quickly that they replaced many other activities. People didn't even notice anymore when their neighbors were gone for a few days.

Motor vehicles of all makes and sizes arrived by barge in Ruby during the following years, while dog teams were on their way out. In other words, the twentieth century had arrived in the bush and change was coming no matter if we liked it or not. In order to survive, we were forced to go with the flow.

In spite of the drastic change in our lifestyle, Ruby still was not connected to any road system, and miles of wilderness separated us from other settlements. Therefore, we could and did spend as much time away from the village as possible, by going on boat rides during the warmer months of the year, on picnics, or on fishing, and camping trips.

On the way to check the trap line 1980

On our first fishing trip for that year, we certainly were reminded that we were still living close to wilderness. Grayling Creek, about eight miles up the Melozitna River from Ruby, is a popular destination for the people of our village to go angling for grayling and trout, and we went there with several other people to do just that. Alice, holding our son, Logan, was standing next to the mouth of the Grayling Creek, where it enters the Melozitna River. She was content watching the rest of us trying to catch some fish. From time to time, I would turn around to see that my family was all right and got the surprise of my life. No more than six yards away from my wife and child, on the other side of that small creek, a big multi-colored grizzly stepped out of the willows. It was a magnificent animal and I could not help but admire it. The bear apparently had not seen my wife and child and probably had not even noticed the rest of us either. But at that moment, one of the natives had become aware of the bear and ran toward his boat to get his rifle. To avoid a possible ugly scene, I waved my arms at the animal and called out to it to draw its attention. The bear looked at me with a surprised expression for a second or so, and then he turned to hurry back into the bushes.

I knew that I hadn't made any points with the Native for my action, but first of all, I didn't like the idea of taking a chance of having a wounded bear so close to my family, and secondly, I did not see any good reason to shoot that bear at all.

I also was real proud that my wife, with her inborn fear of bears, had kept her nerve and stood still and quiet during the whole incident. Naturally, she was a little shaken, but even she had to admit that she admired the beauty of that animal and was glad that we didn't have to shoot it.

Enjoying nature and angling, however, didn't pay our bills, and I had to carve now and then and make a couple of trips to town to generate some cash so I could buy our winter supplies. Then, the hunting season was upon us, and winter followed quickly. This time, we did not flee to Mexico or to live in the city. Fully aware of what to expect, I had confidence in my improvements on the house and believed to be more or less prepared for it. The winter of 1980-1981 greeted us with a cold spell down to 60 degrees minus and it lasted for about two weeks. When it finally went back up to minus twenty, it almost felt like a heat wave and I could go across the river again to catch a few martens to supplement the income from my arts and crafts sale. I rather would have liked to go on making my money by carving fossil bones and ivory during the winter months as well, but that would have required a separate, heated workshop, which I could not afford. When I wasn't out on my trapline, I joined my family in games or jigsaw puzzles to keep the boredom and the stress of the darker months to a minimum until spring finally returned. And with the return of springtime, all the pains of winter were soon forgotten. But the warmer weather also brought our village back in action, and brought a new spurt of modernization along with it. Next to a city building, a community freezer with butchering facilities was to be constructed, and just about every home had a telephone now. Like the year before, the hustle and bustle in our community caused us to get out on the river whenever we could. Trying to combine our outings with the search for carving material, we took a longer trip up the Nowitna River and promptly encountered another adventure which seemed to be Mother Nature's way of teasing my wife about her fears of bears.

We had pitched our tent for the night, and dinner was over and done with. Our daughter was playing near the tent, and Alice was busy with our son, Logan. Not quite ready yet to call it a day, I slowly walked the shoreline along the river in search of signs of fossils. I had walked quite a ways before I turned to check on my family, when I saw a large black bear walking straight toward our tent.

The outhouse at -45° F

Alice, too, had noticed the bear, but was still holding Logan in her arms, who pointed at the bear. Diana, at her mother's request, had gone into the tent to get the Winchester. I had no gun or rifle with me and that bear was a lot closer to the tent than I was, but I did not like the idea of my scared wife taking a shot at the bear and possibly wounding it. So I waved my arms while hollering at the animal, in the same manner I had scared off that grizzly the year earlier. The bear stopped, looked at me for a few seconds, but then decided that I wasn't scary enough to keep him from getting to the tent and he kept on going in that direction. I didn't like being ignored by that bear, picked up some rocks, ran full speed toward the bear while cussing at it and I chucked rocks at him, careful enough not to hit the animal. The bear stopped as he had done the first time, glanced at me for a moment as if he was considering the pros and cons of the situation and then, lucky for me, he must have decided that I was crazy enough to be of danger to him and he ran away.

"What would you have done if the bear wouldn't have run away?" asked Alice.

"I would have kicked his butt!" I stated, while acting cocky. Naturally, we both knew that I was kidding, but in my philosophy, one has to convince oneself in order to make a bluff work. Then Alice told me that Logan had enjoyed seeing the bear and had called it "Big puppy!" while he pointed at it. We laughed about it and I thought to myself, *There is a kid with the right attitude to make a good woodsman someday.*

Returning from this vacation, Alice took a part-time job as a Ruby City administrator. It sounds like quite a mouthful for a village of about hundred-fifty to hundred-eighty people, but after all, Ruby was now an incorporated second class city. Alice's idea about taking the job was probably more or less to assure herself the traveling money for her next trip to Nome, because the way she saw it, it still was me who was responsible for the living expense of our family.

At about that time, we also enjoyed a visit from my old friend, Horst Stumpf, from California. Horst always had a hard time believing what I had written about our life in Alaska, and now he wanted see it firsthand for himself. Horst actually enjoyed every minute of his visit and the time he spent with us, but he also had to admit that he would not be able to live our way anymore at his stage of life, not even mentioning his wife, Arlene, who would never have moved to Alaska, much less into the bush. It was a shame that Horst didn't have the time to stay a little longer and experience an actual moose hunt. The moose hunting season started right after Horst flew back home, but what was called moose hunting in Ruby at that time would certainly have been an experience for my friend. We have about forty miles of unpaved road into the back country, which leads to some still active gold mines. With the increase of private vehicles in Ruby, these forty miles turned into a well-traveled road for our resident subsistence hunters and some visitors alike. At opening day of the season, truckloads of armed hunters could be seen with their rifles ready to shoot anything that moved, and by the trail of whiskey bottles and beer cans, one could often estimate the size of such an invasion force on Mother Nature. It would stand to reason that not only the moose were in danger under such conditions, but only God knows why nobody ever got shot during those days.

Not that it was impossible to bag a moose by driving out the road, but a person would have to carefully choose the time and stay away from the partying hunters. Luckily for everybody, this kind of hunting was soon restricted by occasional law enforcement officers. The first time I tried hunting along the road, I had to borrow a pickup truck, because I didn't have any personal transportation yet. Normally, I would hunt by motor-boat and drive up the Melozitna River to get my moose. But because of the bad weather we had and I just wanted to try something new, I had decided to join the Ruby Road Hunters. Dusk was setting in when I returned from my drive out the road without having seen a single moose. Close to Ruby, I met a native, who told me that a big black bear was sitting by the city dump. At that time, the city dump was only one quarter of a mile away from town and as I approached it slowly, sure enough I could see that bear sitting there as if he was waiting for somebody to come along. Since it was all downhill for me, I turned off the engine and rolled closer, but the animal got up and went across the road into a small gravel pit. My heart wasn't really into shooting that animal, but if that bear kept on hanging around the dump, he certainly would get shot at from everybody that went by there, and most likely would die a painful death somewhere in the woods after being wounded. It was getting dark already, but because of the size of that bear, I wanted to get another look at it. So I stopped the truck, took out my 45-70 Marlin, and walked after the bear into the gravel pit. But there was no bear to be seen and I assumed that he had run away. I was just about to put my Marlin back into the truck when I saw, out of the corner of my eye, that the bear was coming out of the brush next to the gravel pit in a steady trot toward me. By the time I had the bear in my sights, there were only about six or seven yards between us when I pulled the trigger. The animal veered to his right, slipped at the edge of the road, and stumbled down to the bottom of the dump. I put another shell in the chamber and heard the sound of the breaking branches in the brush below me. Then I checked the road for blood and found none. So I assumed that I had overshot my target because of the close range and considered the case closed. At any case, I certainly was not willing to follow a bear in the dark through the brush, wounded or not.

Considering the close range, the darkness and the hurry in which I had to shoot at the bear, I still had a hard time settling on the idea that I had missed, and the thought that I might have wounded the animal was even more unpleasant to me.

When I went to bed that night, I still was thinking about the incident and in the morning at the first sign of light, I was on my way and walked up the creek bed, which would lead me right below the city dump. When I found my bear lying in a bush with all four legs stretched to the sky, I was not surprised. My bullet had entered the animal right below the jaw and had traveled the full length of its body. From the way the innards of the animal looked, the bear must have been dead while he still was running. According to his teeth, he certainly was not the youngest animal anymore, but it was one of the biggest black bears I had ever seen around Ruby. His hide, which is still hanging on the wall in my cabin, measured six foot and two inches.

This certainly had not been one of my most romantic hunting experiences, but I somehow felt good about it, since I believe, just as my friend Frank would have done, that this bear was waiting to be shot by me in order to avoid a more painful or troublesome death. Why else would the animal have made it so easy for me to kill him?

Chapter 28
Scenery and the Memories Is What Remains

W hile I continued to carve and produce some arts and crafts, the big sales trips to town eventually became a thing of the past, as the oil pipeline of Alaska became old news. The workforce at the pipeline had stabilized and my income from my sales trips did not keep up with the general higher living cost, as well as shipping and traveling expenses. Our senators told us Alaskans to tighten our belts, while they gave themselves a 25,000.00 dollar raise at the same time. Many people in the bush, who had switched from woodstoves to burning oil, had to have their heating cost subsidized by the government, since the oil that was supposed to make all the Alaskans affluent, already was too expensive for the ordinary people in our state.

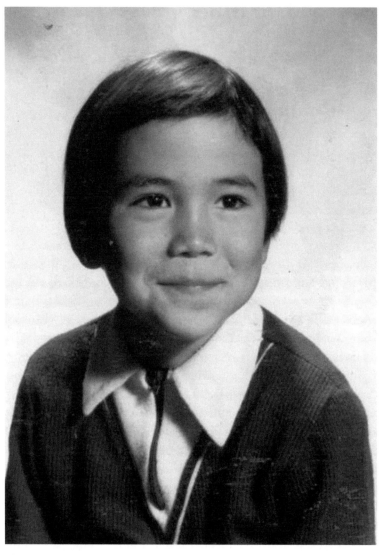

Logan 1985

I had foreseen this development and had stuck to burning wood, so I wouldn't become dependent on another modern entrapment. My wife, in the meantime, was now a full time employee of the city of Ruby, which left me with less time for my artwork, because my daily priorities had changed to housework and watching after our children. True to my predictions, the modernized lifestyle had brought tension into my marriage and the so-called progress once again caused nothing but problems and dissatisfaction. But before I get too far out of the chronological order, I should give an account of another fact in our lives during this period.

Since our friends Pat and Leonard Veerhusen had passed away during the seventies, the eighties were no improvement along that line. First, both of my parents back in Germany died only a few months apart in 1983. And if that wasn't enough, I lost several good friends and acquaintances during that decade. My friend, Frank Titus, died in October 1985 in his sleep, in a senior home in Fairbanks, followed by his life partner, Josephine Corning, almost to the day three years later. But in springtime of 1987, I got an invitation from the University of Alaska to attend an official retirement party for my friend, John Bradbury. Since we were strapped for money and I always visited John on my yearly shopping trips to Fairbanks, I had to seriously think about making that extra trip to town. It was my wife who urged me to go, and my appearance at the party was a success. When John brought me back to the airport, he did not just drop me off and leave, as he usually had done, but insisted on staying till my plane left and we shook hands for a long time at my departure. A couple of months later or so, I got a call and was informed that John had died from the after effects of a prostate operation.

My wife had been dissatisfied with her life in Ruby for quite a while, but the death of her father in Nome during a house fire in 1989 most likely contributed to Alice's decision to finally move to Nome. I was not ready to leave my home in Ruby, and we decided on a separation. By that time, Diana had already left home and was living in Fairbanks. It was our twelve-year-old son, Logan, who probably was most affected by the situation. We also left it up to him to decide if he wanted to stay with me or go with his mother. Not an easy decision for a boy that age, but Logan decided to stay with me. About that time, my old time friend, Horst Stumpf, from California, called me up just to say hello and tell me that he always thought of me more like a brother than just as a friend. Two or three weeks later, Horst's wife called to let me know that Horst had died in the hospital after a liver exploratory operation.

Wolf 1994

I probably could mention a few more unpleasant happenings, but enough of
the bitter side of life. After my wife's departure from Ruby, I took Logan out of
school and taught him at home. This was not alone for my lack of confidence

in the Ruby school system at the time, but also because I had planned to take Logan on a trip through the lower states that winter in order to make it easier for him to get over his parents' separation, and get to see life outside of Alaska. Eventually, Alice and I later finalized our separation by filing for dissolution, but when Logan became of high school age, I sent him to his mother in Nome to enter the high school there. Suddenly, living all by myself certainly took some getting used to, and it made me aware how quickly time had passed.

Government funding for all the modern conveniences was slowing down and so was the growth spurt of our community. The local employment opportunities vanished, and without the proper upkeep, some facilities, such as the public freezer building, fell in disrepair and eventually had to be rebuilt without the addition of the public butcher shop.

But life went on. Vacationers paddling down the Yukon had become a fairly common occurrence in the meantime. Few of them were Americans; most of them were Swiss, Germans, and Austrians who spent their vacations paddling down the rivers of the last frontier. When these travelers stopped in Ruby, they often had already heard about a German living in that village, and therefore stopped by at my place for a visit, as they still do nowadays. Over time, I have made some very good friends that way and some of them have returned to Ruby repeatedly. Many of these drifters and travelers on the Yukon come to fulfill a lifetime dream, or to see the nature and its wildlife in a still relatively pristine state while experiencing a little adventure and getting a chance to get away from their everyday, hectic world .

When my visitors step back into their boats to continue their trip, I'm always reminded of my first trip down the Yukon and get the sudden urge to go with them. But I only know too well that reliving the old days is only a pipe dream. Sure, the scenery would be generally the same as in the years before, but the general atmosphere of those years when only a few of us undertook such a venture and I still could live like Daniel Boone in the old village of Kokrines could not be recreated. It is hard to pinpoint all the details that have changed, and my getting older probably is part of it. But besides that, modern times have brought all kinds of new laws and regulations, which have changed the attitude of the people along the river as well. Frank and Josephine and other people like them are gone and not even one building standing anymore in what used to be Kokrines. Kokrines is now just a name for an old village site with little meaning for most people. Personally, I will always hold this place in reverence; it is inseparable from my Alaska experience and from the best years of my life. It belongs to a time when we could set a net in the river at any time we needed fish, when we shot a moose because our meat supply ran low, and when motor noises were so rare that they usually meant to us that a visitor was arriving.

Nowadays, besides the required licenses, there are specified times when the net can be in the river and when it has to be taken out. Other regulations specify the mesh-size of the netting and there are now Fish and Game officers to enforce these regulations. I don't even remember ever having seen any kind of law enforcement personal in the earlier days. Hunting, fishing, and trapping is now also strongly regulated and controlled by officials in boats and planes with floats or on skis. The general traffic on the rivers especially during the hunting season is now manifold of what it used to be. Modern, heavy-motorized boats or planes are a constant, irritating intrusion on the old way of the life in the bush.

For this situation, not only the outside hunters are to blame; the general modernization, which allows also the more affluent natives of the villages along the rivers to acquire the more expensive equipment, are also to blame for it, because along with the bigger and faster transportation, their attitude changed as well.

While living in Kokrines, we had time to put on the coffee pot when we discovered somebody in his wooden boat with a 35 or 45 hp motor coming upriver. Now, the big modern aluminum boats, with God knows what size motor, would be upon us before we could get back to the cabin. The big waves that some of these modern boats create sometimes even endanger the canoeists or swamp small boats parked at the shore. Not everybody might be bothered by these noisy contraptions or by the reckless pilot, but they bother me just as much as the camouflaged, heavily armed so-called sports hunters who arrive during the moose hunting season. These people, armed to the teeth and dressed as if they were ready to go to war, often stop at our village to refill the tanks of their gas-guzzling vehicles. Many of them probably have destroyed enough environment and natural habitat while earning their money as industrial or land developers, so that they were able to buy their fancy equipment. The worst part is that they also assume to have the right to invade our backyard to play and kill for fun. In other words, they are using the space which is occupied by people of a different lifestyle as their amusement park. The money those hunters spent for fuel alone would probably be enough for them to buy themselves a butchered cow or two.

Why our supposedly enlightened, modern society still classifies "Hunting" as a sport is something else that is hard to understand. To me, hunting is merely a necessary activity for a subsistence lifestyle and, in rare cases, a method to controlling the overpopulation of a species, but where is the sport in killing animals for fun with our modern weaponry?

Spruce Grouse

When people talk about progress, I always wonder, "Progress toward what?" The people along the Yukon were fairly happy when I first arrived there. We visited each other in the evenings, sat by the crackling fire telling old stories, or talked about our hunting and trapping experiences. Then, suddenly, they were told that they were not happy, unless they live like everybody else, enslaved by modern contraptions like electric lights, TVs, phones, and all kinds of other gadgets to make their life easier. In reality, these gadgets made them more dependent on the government and turned them into slaves of our modern economy.

Now, we have officials visiting the bush communities, to teach the people how to behave and survive in an environment they have lived in for thousands of years. It seems to me that modern society always wants to improve the lifestyle of other people because their old way of living is not beneficial enough to the economy. Therefore, it has to be changed, so the business corporations and our self-serving politicians can benefit from it.

Before I get carried away too far in all the pros and cons of our society, let's step back into what is left of life along the Yukon. One kind of visitors we get during the summer month are those people we call drifters. By drifters, I mean people who are not hunters or vacationers from foreign countries, but in most cases they are late comers who are merely trying to escape modern society, looking for the same things I had been looking for some years earlier. But a few rarer species of these travelers are downright social outcasts. One of those I had described earlier, when my wife and I returned to Kokrines in a rubber raft. Another somewhat more recent case of obviously slightly deranged members of the human race drifted into Ruby in an empty canoe without even a paddle. With his uncombed, dirty, blond hair and dirty clothes, he walked around in our community for a while without talking to anybody. When he finally climbed back into his canoe, he passed a steaming drum of freshly boiled dog food. With his bare hands, he fished a couple of salmon heads out of that hot soup and ate them. Using only his hands again, he then paddled his canoe back into the main current of the river and drifted on, leaving me to wonder what could drive a man to such a low level of existence.

Bull moose

A further example of a different sort actually consisted of visitors from Europe. It happened when my whole family was still living in Ruby, as a group of inexperienced and misinformed adventurers arrived at our home. At the time, my whole family was still living in Ruby and a few of my childhood friends from Germany had been visiting us. At that time, I, too, had owned a truck already, and I had taken my friends on a trip out the forty miles of mining road from Ruby. Returning from this outing and stepping out of the truck, we heard guitar music coming from my house. Inside my house, we found four more Germans, belonging to some Christian Youth Group. My wife had invited them in to wait for our return. These four young minnesingers had come down the Yukon on a homemade raft and planned to march out from Ruby on foot.

"From here on we walk!" stated the leader of the group as he pointed to the indicated winter trail on his outdated map. The old overgrown winter trail, which, extending from the end of our mining road farther south, had not been used in ages and certainly was not useable during the summer, because of many swampy areas. Our eager adventurers, however, believed that they could just march through the Alaskan wilderness, back to the road system, and then hitchhike to Fairbanks or Anchorage from there. Even after I acquainted them with the realities and gave them an idea about the conditions along the way, I was not able to dissuade them from their plan.

The Yukon from my property

"God and song will get us through!" they stated, full of confidence. How could I argue with people who had assurances from God? So, I drove them to the end of our forty miles of unpaved road and let God take care of them from there. Not that their idea of their undertaking would be a total impossibility for an experienced woodman armed with the right equipment and knowledge. But those young, inexperienced men in their short pants and without any other gear outside of a guitar and a pennon, would need a little more than singsong and God's help.

A couple of days after I had sent them on their way, I received a phone call from a state trooper in Galena, asking me if I could pick the boys up again from the end of our road. An old gold miner had persuaded the quartet in unwavering manner to retrace their steps and head back to Ruby. Their singing apparently had ended at the first hip-deep swamp, and their prayers were not much help against the mosquitoes and the rain.

As it turned out, the quartet now was drenched, muddy, and one experience richer, but also totally broke. They had no money to fly out from Ruby and I certainly could not house or feed them for an unspecified time.

The funny part was that these adventurers actually and literally received help from above. A traveling preacher with his private plane had made a short stop in Ruby and took our uninvited guests back to civilization. I have no idea if that traveling preacher ever got so much as a Christmas card from the adventurous quartet; my help apparently was not worth such an effort.

Today, I still live in my cabin in Ruby, considering it more or less my permanent home, even though the place is slowly falling into decay. The idea of the bigger permanent residence never materialized for various reasons, but with all the members of what used to be my family gone and living in different parts of Alaska, I only reside in Ruby during the summer month, while visiting my children and grandchildren in the winter.

But during these warmer months of the year, I'm still visited by first time river travelers and old friends alike. In between those visits, I enjoy my solitude, carve or paint a little, dabble in writing, and take walks with my latest dog, Thorak.

I also might take short river trips in my motorized canoe or accompany my friend and neighbor, Tim Gervais, when he goes upriver for one reason or another, but otherwise, I'm just enjoying my peace and quiet away from city noise and hectic living.

Change being the only thing constant, the settlement of Ruby has changed as well since my arrival. There are many newer and more modern houses now, plus a fancy, up to date Laundromat in our second-class city. Most of the so-called old timers I was lucky enough to have met just about died out, and only a few of the younger people are staying home after graduation. More and more of the young people are looking for employment in the bigger towns or are even moving to the lower forty-eight states. The gold mining has all but vanished from the Ruby area in spite of rising gold prices. The constant rise in the cost of heating oil and gasoline prices might eventually cause many of the smaller settlements to vanish entirely. There seems to be neither growth nor decline in our community at the moment and some people might never leave, no matter what, but one thing is clear: when the government won't subsidize the fuel cost anymore, those people will have to revert from their oil stoves to burning wood again and they might have to dig up their old kerosene lamps for the dark winter months when our community can't afford to run the generators anymore either.

Logan with dogs and a trophy

In spite of it all, I can't think of a better place to spend the last years of my life than in the Alaskan bush, where a potential true adventure might be only a mere boat ride away from my home, and I'm able to visit the many places that hold my dearest memories. While getting older might make things a little harder, nothing would be harder for me than being forced to live a hectic life in a noisy town. I rather accompany my neighbor on a moose hunt or do some small game hunting near the village on my own. My meat consumption has decreased with age to the point where I certainly don't need a whole moose anymore to keep me supplied, and the memories of my hunting trips in the past will never fade, be it my last moose hunt with my son, or the last time I hunted alone and wished I had my camera instead of my rifle. It was on a sunny day and the golden fall foliage shone like gold along the banks of the Melozitna River. I stood on an island of that river enjoying the scenery and looking for a moose. A cow moose, followed by a younger bull, eventually came out of the brush across on the other side of the river channel. But instead of coming upstream toward me, the animals turned downstream. My imitation of a moose call didn't seem to make an impression on the cow or the bull, and they kept on walking out of my range. When I stepped back into the willow brush holding my rifle over my head and started beating the willows like I had antlers, the situation changed quickly. While the young bull still was not in the mood for fighting a rival, the cow must have thought that I was a stronger, more worthy bull to mate with and turned around to walk toward me. The young bull had no choice but to follow the cow and when the animals stopped directly across the channel from me, a bald eagle flew about ten yards above them. The whole setting certainly would have been a Kodak moment!

Right after the eagle had passed, the cow must have gotten my scent and decided to walk back into the brush. The young bull hesitated just long enough for me to take my shot.

As the animal fell, I could not help but remember Frank's word: "The game will give itself to the deserving hunter!" And as long as moose, bears, and wolves will leave their tracks along the riverbanks in Alaska, Frank's words and wisdom will stay alive for me.

Such experiences and my general knowledge I passed on to my children, and sometimes I tell my stories to my visitors in Ruby over a glass of Cognac and a good cigar, and will continue to as long as it will be granted me to do so.

The Pendulum of Life

Good and evil, dark and light,
Hot and cold or black and white.
The pendulum swings from side to side,
On its way from left to right.

Then it swings to where it was before,
Just to do the same once more.
In constant search for middle ground,
By its own action never found.

Its path will always stay the same,
Because the whole thing is a game.
It keeps crossing its goal between the lines,
Until its driving spring unwinds.

So it might stop at its point of thrive,
And thereby giving up its life.
Unless we keep it wound-up like before,
We won't hear that tick-tock anymore.

Wolf Hebel